潍坊

Weifang

历史文化图鉴大系

History and Culture Series

潍坊历史文化图鉴大系

Weifang History and Culture Series

乐道沧桑

The Courtyard of the Happy Way — Over One Hundred Years of History

吉树春 主编

文物出版社

图书在版编目（CIP）数据

乐道沧桑 / 吉树春主编. — 北京：文物出版社，2022. 2
ISBN 978-7-5010-5609-5

Ⅰ. ①乐… Ⅱ. ①吉… Ⅲ. ①教堂—历史—潍坊 Ⅳ. ①B977.252.3

中国版本图书馆 CIP 数据核字 (2021) 第 176909 号

乐道沧桑

主　　编：吉树春
责任编辑：李子裔
排版设计：刘　霞
责任印制：张道奇
出版发行：文物出版社
社　　址：北京市东城区东直门内北小街 2 号楼
邮　　编：100007
网　　址：http://www.wenwu.com
经　　销：新华书店
制版印刷：潍坊鑫意达印业有限公司
开　　本：889mm × 1194mm　1/16
印　　张：21
版　　次：2022 年 2 月第 1 版
印　　次：2022 年 2 月第 1 次印刷
书　　号：ISBN 978-7-5010-5609-5
定　　价：368.00 元

《潍坊历史文化图鉴大系》
Weifang History and Culture Series

总策划：
Planning Directors：
惠新安　田庆盈
Hui Xin'an, Tian Qingying

编纂委员会主任：
Directors of the Compilation Committee：
初宝杰　张永国　马清民
Chu Baojie, Zhang Yongguo, Ma Qingmin

编纂委员会副主任：
Deputy Directors of the Compilation Committee：
刘玉祥　田素英　权文松　吉树春
Liu Yuxiang, Tian Suying, Quan Wensong, Ji Shuchun

《乐道沧桑》
The Courtyard of the Happy Way — Over One Hundred Years of History

编纂委员会委员（以姓名笔画为序）
马道远　王　冰　王建新　吉树春　吕俊峰　孙敬明　李茂松　李跃进
赵守祥　郑树平　钟耕民　夏宝枢　崔书田　宿立军　崔永胜　梁玉华

Members of the Compilation Committee：
Ma Daoyuan, Wang Bing, Wang Jianxin, Ji Shuchun, Lü Junfeng, Sun Jingming, Li Maosong, Li Yuejin, Zhao Shouxiang, Zheng Shuping, Zhong Gengmin, Xia Baoshu, Cui Shutian, Su Lijun, Cui Yongsheng, Liang Yuhua

主编：吉树春
Chief Editor: Ji Shuchun

副主编：李师庆　巩世勇　孙　丽
Managing Editors: Li Shiqing, Gong Shiyong, Sun Li

编辑：
王晓璇　王培栋　王曦泽　田　彬　闫　冰　孙　聪　李宜龙　吴宗俊
武夫强　陈金城　韩　娜　郭俊琦　梁静瑶　郭　慧　魏茜茜
Copy Editors：Wang Xiaoxuan, Wang Peidong, Wang Xize, Tian Bin, Yan Bing, Sun Cong, Li Yilong, Wu Zongjun, Wu Fuqiang, Chen Jincheng, Han Na, Guo Junqi, Liang Jingyao, Guo Hui, Wei Qianqian

翻译：张　辛　许　叶
Translators: Zhang Xin, Xu Ye

总序

潍坊，地处山东半岛西部，雄踞海岱之间，是齐鲁大地上一颗璀璨的明珠，历史文化源远流长。早在8000年前，此地就有人类繁衍生息，后李文化、东夷文明孕育而生。夏商周三代，潍坊大地上古国林立；秦汉以降，经济文化渐趋繁荣，名人巨匠辈出，历久弥新，潍坊地区形成的独特文化成为齐鲁文化的重要组成部分，也是华夏文明的重要贡献者。

习近平总书记要求，“要讲清楚中华优秀传统文化的历史渊源、发展脉络、基本走向，讲清楚中华文化的独特创造、价值理念、鲜明特色，增强文化自信和价值观自信。”他同时指出，“历史文化是城市的灵魂，要像爱惜自己的生命一样保护好城市历史文化遗产。”

为了充分展现潍坊灿烂的历史人文、民俗风情及风景名胜，特别是我市独特的自然文化、农耕文化和海洋文化，晚清近代以来西学东渐形成的多元文化和红色革命文化，我市决定组织力量编纂出版《潍坊历史文化图鉴大系》系列丛书，旨在对潍坊历史文化进行全面、系统的整理研究，翔实记述潍坊的历史渊源、文化底蕴、文化特色和历史影响，深入研究潍坊历史文化形成、发展的规律，系统总结历史文化保护、传承和开发的成功经验。该丛书上起远古，下迄当代，全面梳理展示潍坊历史文化成就，图文并茂，具可读性，以荟萃历史，资治当今，启迪后人。

该丛书承担着传承历史、弘扬文化、存史教化的任务，必须坚持质量第一的原则，坚持历史唯物主义的观点，纵向立足潍坊大地的文明历程，横向涵盖政治、经济、军事、文化、社会各个层面，全景式展现潍坊波澜壮阔的发展历程，力求做到观点正确、体例严谨、内容全面、文风端正、表述准确、特色鲜明、资料翔实、图版精美，力争打造出一部经世致用的大系佳作，使之成为集中展示潍坊深厚历史文化底蕴的靓丽城市名片。

当前，世界正面临百年未有之大变局，中国人民正在中华民族伟大复兴的道路上阔步向前，潍坊正在聚焦建设“生态、开放、活力、精致”的现代化高品质城市。习近平总书记指出，“文化自信，是更基础、更广泛、更深厚的自信，是更基本、更深沉、更持久的力量。”我们梳理潍坊几千年来的历史文化，就是要让广大人民群众了解潍坊的古圣先贤和人民大众创造的灿烂文化，增强大家建设现代化潍坊的文化自信；就是要在现代化高品质城市的建设征程上，吸收借鉴潍坊历史发展过程中的经验，在发展上体现潍坊特色。

展望未来，具有深厚历史文化底蕴的潍坊，一定会为实现“两个一百年”奋斗目标和中华民族伟大复兴的中国梦做出更大贡献。潍坊的明天一定会更好。

中共潍坊市委常委　宣传部部长　初宝杰

Preface

Weifang, located in the west of Shandong Peninsula, and lying between the ocean and mountains, is the shining pearl on the land of Shandong Province with a long and rich history and culture. The first light of the civilization shed here as early as eight thousand years ago. The Houli, the ancient Eastern Yi tribes, and the dynasties of Xia, Shang and Zhou and their princedoms were amongst the first peoples who settled in the Weifang region. Since the days of Qin and Han dynasties, the economy and culture has been blooming as shown by the emergence of great historical figures and art masters. Weifang has always been an essential component of Shandong culture and a significant contributor to the Chinese rich civilization.

President Xi Jinping has emphasized the importance of preserving China's traditions and values. The President maintains that knowing our history and culture will help us build a sense of belonging and pride. History and culture of a city like the soul of human, so it is crucial to protect our historic and cultural relics.

The purpose of publishing Weifang History and Culture Series is to introduce the rich and long history, natural resources, customs and rituals of Weifang, which is particularly reflected in its unique agricultural and marine traditions, a diversified culture influenced by western civilizations since the late Qing Dynasty, and the revolutionary movements in the history; it also aims to explore Weifang's history and culture in depth and preserve them. We hope we have succeeded in providing a thorough and comprehensive portrait of Weifang's history from ancient times to the present day.

The books, employing historical materialism principles, discover political, economic, military, cultural and societal aspects of Weifang's history. The aim of this series is to provide a close, broad and profound look at the historical events and cultural features of the city.

Today, in a world full of turbulent changes never seen in a long time, the Chinese people are progressing on a road of national renaissance. Weifang is fully focused on building a modern city which values ecology, openness, vitality and elegance. A nation's strength, as President Xi has repeatedly stated, is determined by its cultural confidence, which is the most elemental, comprehensive, and sustainable factor. We are revisiting Weifang and its several thousand years of history and culture so as both local people as well as people from the rest of China and around the world learn about the ancient sages and paragons and the culture created by the ancient people. It also demonstrates that in order to build a modern cosmopolitan city, we need to revisit history and learn from our local historical events and traditions.

Looking into the future, Weifang, with its rich and profound history and culture, will make greater contributions to the accomplishment of the "Two Centenary Goals" and realization of the dream of Chinese renaissance. Weifang will enjoy a better future.

Chu Baojie
Member of CPC Weifang Municipal Standing Committee
Director of Weifang Publicity Department

目录

第二编　成为西方侨民集中营的乐道院

第三编　乐道院的红色记忆

第四编　新时代的乐道院

Contents

Chapter 2 It Becomes A Concentration Camp for Western Residents

Chapter 3 The Courtyard of the Happy Way at the Time of Revolutionary Movements

Chapter 4 The Courtyard of the Happy Way in the New Era

乐道院·西方侨民集中营旧址的前世今生(序)

在潍坊市奎文区虞河路和鸢飞路之间的虞河南岸，坐落着几座欧式建筑，这就是二战期间关押西方侨民的潍县乐道院暨西方侨民集中营旧址。乐道院集中营的故事，只有少数史料记载，很少被人提及。历史可以沉寂，但无法被遗忘。本书将打开尘封的记忆，寻根溯源，将这段历史重新展现在世人的面前。

百年乐道，肃穆庄重

1882年，美国基督教北长老会牧师狄乐播创建了潍县第一个基督教新教传播基地——潍县乐道院，集传教、施医、办学为一体。1900年，义和团运动期间，乐道院教堂等主要建筑化为灰烬。1902年，美国北长老会主要利用清政府的“庚子赔款”和美国教会的捐款开始在原地重建乐道院，至1904年基本完工。同年，登州的文会馆和青州的广德书院大学部合并为广文大学，迁往乐道院。潍县乐道院重建以后，一度成为当地教会、教育和医疗中心。1937年，七七事变爆发后，乐道院学校停办，乐道院成为当地百姓的避难所。1942年，乐道院被日军改造成外侨集中营。抗战胜利后，乐道院各项事业得以恢复。潍县解放前夕，乐道院美籍人员撤离。1948年潍县解放后，乐道院的医院、学校先后被人民政府接管。乐道院现存七座旧址建筑，经过了岁月沧桑的洗礼，这座百年建筑群依然巍然屹立，依然肃穆庄重。它是二战期间中国人民与西方侨民并肩反抗日本法西斯的历史见证，是中西文化交流的见证，是潍坊文化博大包容的见证。

大爱无疆，开放包容

乐道院集中营关押在华欧美侨民最多时达到1500多人，一度成为中国境内最大的平民集中营。总共有2000余名外国侨民被关押于此，其中包括327名儿童。被关押的侨民中有一批国际知名人士，如华北神学院院长赫士，齐鲁大学教务长德位思，原辅仁大学附中教师、后任美国驻华大使的恒安石等，还有曾获奥运会400米冠军的世界著名运动员英国人李爱锐。集中营侨民曾经得到了潍坊抗日军民的同情与帮助，可以说，集中营具有独特的国际主义、人道主义、和平主义内涵。乐道院是日本侵华历史和日本军国主义暴行的重要见证，也是国际主义合作的典范，对促进中西文化融合交流发挥了重要作用，是潍坊对外开放、走向世界的证明。

时序变迁，历久弥新

2019年5月潍坊市委做出决定，“理顺乐道院产权体制，乐道院所属建筑划归市博物馆统一管理”，并提出争创“全国爱国主义教育示范基地”的总目标。在市委主要领导高度重视下，经过市委宣传部多次协调调度、市文化和旅游局的大力支持和市博物馆的贯彻实施下，2019年9月16日，潍县乐道院暨西方侨民集中营旧址被中宣部表彰为全国爱国主义教育示范基地，成为山东省2019年度唯一一处获批的全国爱国主义教育示范基地；2019年10月16日被国家文物局公布为第八批国家重点文物保护单位。30天荣获两项国家殊荣，这座历经百年沧桑的建筑正在以全新的面貌聚焦人们的视线。

未来几年，潍坊市博物馆将积极推动乐道院·潍县集中营博物馆加入“国际二战博物馆协会”和“国际古迹遗址理事会城防与军事遗产委员会”，并以潍县乐道院暨西方侨民集中营旧址为基点，联合发掘坊茨小镇、1532大英烟厂等潍坊特色历史文化资源，向国际和平城市协会提出申请，争创国内第二家、山东首家“国际和平城市”。乐道院·潍县集中营展览还将走出国门，分别在美国、以色列、波兰、新西兰、日本等国家进行巡展，有效发挥文化旅游、国际交流和宣传教育作用，努力构建富有历史底蕴、反映时代精神的优秀传统文化传承创新区，为弘扬爱国主义、国际主义精神，培育和树立社会主义核心价值观，助推中外文明交流互鉴，为人类命运共同体建设做出积极贡献。这座历经百年的建筑正在以全新的面貌迎接未来。

潍坊市博物馆馆长　研究员　吉树春

Past and Present of the Courtyard of the Happy Way –Former Site of Weihsien Concentration Camp

In Kuiwen District of Weifang, by the south bank of Yuhe River lying between the Yuhe Road and Yuanfei Road, there are several European style buildings. These buildings were what once was the Courtyard of the Happy Way (hereinafter referred to as the Courtyard), which was during the Second World War turned into the Weihsien Concentration Camp, where some people from different Western nationalities were imprisoned. Due to the lack of historical documentation, people are not aware of the stories about the Courtyard and what happened inside the concentration camp. The stories must be told so the past will not be forgotten. The aim of this book is to retell these touching memories, revisit the past and share this history with the whole world.

Over A Hundred Years of History

In 1882, Robert M. Mateer, a missionary serving with the Presbyterian Church in the United States of America (PCUS), founded the Courtyard of the Happy Way. It was the first protestant missionary center in Weihsien. It served as a church, a hospital and schools. In 1900 during the Boxer Rebellion, the Courtyard was set on fire. The main buildings, including the church, were totally destroyed. In 1902, the PCUS started to rebuild the Courtyard at the original site with funds of Boxer Indemnity provided by the Qing government and donations from churches in the US. The new buildings were largely completed by 1904. In the same year, Tengchow College and Guangde Academy merged into Shantung Protestant University, which was relocated to the Courtyard. Upon the completion, the Courtyard of the Happy Way became the center of religious service, educational endeavor and medical care in Weihsien. In 1937, after the Lugou Bridge Incident, the Courtyard's schools were closed down and turned into a sort of refuge camp for the local people. In 1942 during the WWII, the Courtyard was transformed into a concentration camp for the

Western residents by the Japanese army. After the war, everything gradually went back to normal in the Courtyard. Before the liberation of Weihsien, the Americans who lived in the Courtyard, were evacuated. In 1948 shortly after the liberation, the new Chinese government took control of the Courtyard's hospital and schools. Today, after over one hundred years, passing through time and witnessing a lot of historical events, the Courtyard's seven buildings still stand tall on the site. The buildings has borne witness to a long history of international cultural exchanges. They, therefore, represent the inclusive, embracing and welcoming culture of the city of Weifang.

Boundless Love and Inclusiveness

At some point during the WWII, there were over one thousand and five hundred Western residents imprisoned in Weihsien Concentration Camp, making it the largest concentration camp in China. In total, more than two thousand Western residents, including three hundred and twenty seven children, were imprisoned in Weihsien Camp during the war. Among them were some internationally famous people such as Watson Mcmillen Hayes, president of North China Theological Seminary, Dr. L. J. Davies, academic dean of Shantung Christian University, Arthur William Hummel Jr, lecturer at the Affiliated Boys School of Fu Jen Catholic University, and later U.S. Ambassador to China, and Eric Liddell, an accomplished and famous British runner and the Olympic champion in 400 meters. The sympathy shown to the Western internees in the concentration camp by the local people as well as the Chinese forces demonstrated their spirit of internationalism, humanitarianism and pacifism. The Courtyard witnessed not only the Japanese invasion and militarism but also the importance of international compassion and cooperation. In fact, the Courtyard both enhanced and promoted the cultural exchange between China and the West and strengthened the connection between the city of Weifang and the rest of the world.

Renovation of the Museum and A New Look

In May of 2019, the Weifang Municipal Party Committee made the decision to reorganize the property rights of the Courtyard, transferring the responsibility of preserving the buildings to Weifang Museum. The Committee also proposed a broader goal, which was to establish "a national demonstration base of patriotic education". On September 16, 2019, the Courtyard of the Happy Way – the former site of the Weihsien Concentration Camp Museum – was designated a National Demonstration Base of Patriotic Education by the Publicity Department of the Central Committee of the CPC. It was the only site in Shandong which was awarded this remarkable title in 2019. On October 16, 2019, the Courtyard was also recognized as a State Protected Cultural Heritage Site by the National Cultural Heritage Administration. These two important national honors drew the people's attention to the Courtyard and a history of over one hundred years.

In the coming years, the Weifang Museum will rigorously work for the Courtyard Museum to join the International WWII Museum Association and ICOFORT. Alongside the Courtyard, other cultural historic sites in Weifang, such as Fangtze Eurotown and 1532 Cigarette Factory, should be also preserved and curated. Through applying to the Association of International Cities for Peace, Weifang is striving to become the first "International City of Peace" in Shandong, and only the second one in China. The Courtyard Museum will also have a world exhibition tour in the US, Israel, Poland, New Zealand and Japan. More work will be needed to establish a historical and cultural bridge between China and the rest of the world. In order to establish a dialogue between different countries and civilizations, we need to promote cultural tourism, international communication and education. This century-old building is heading toward the future with a new look.

Ji Shuchun   The Curator of Weifang Museum, Researcher

第一编 Chapter 1

1942年之前的乐道院

The Courtyard of the Happy Way before 1942

乐道院建筑群始建于1882年，重建于1902年，位于老潍县城东关李家庄西北、虞河南岸，占地13万余平方米，迄今已经有着130多年的历史。乐道院是美国基督教北长老会在潍县创办的一所集教会、学校、医院于一身的综合性场所，它的建立和发展推动了西方医学、科技、教育在中国的传播，对促进中西文化交流发挥了重要作用。在这里，曾经的广文大学，因教材、学制等仿效哈佛大学，常被称为“中国哈佛”。“文明因交流而多彩，文明因互鉴而丰富”。乐道院对东西方文明的发展、互鉴起到了桥梁和纽带的作用。

The historical building group of the Courtyard of the Happy Way was founded in 1882 and rebuilt in 1902. Located in the east of Weihsien, to the northwest of Lijiazhuang Village and by the south bank of Yuhe River, the Courtyard covers an area of over 130,000 square meters, and it has a history of more than 130 years. Set up by the Presbyterian Church in the United States of America, the Courtyard combined the functions of a religious site, an educational institute, and a medical center, which helped promote the spread of Western medicine, technologies and education in China. The Courtyard has played a significant role in the cultural exchanges between China and the West. The former Shantung Protestant University located in the Courtyard became known as the “Harvard University of China”, because of its imitation of the Harvard University educational system. “Exchanges and mutual learning are what make civilizations flourish.” The Courtyard of the Happy Way acted as a bridge linking the Eastern and Western civilizations in development and exchanges.

第一章　乐道院产生的历史背景

1 Historical Background of the Courtyard of the Happy Way

山东潍县，一个历史悠久的古城。在 19 世纪末那个风雨飘摇的大时代里，首次迎来了几位洋人，他们在城郊买下土地，建起了布道站，并将之称为“乐道院”。至于西方传教士为何选中潍县作为他们传教布道之所，还应从清代末期的社会形态，以及潍县所处的地理位置、社会经济和文化等方面进行考察和溯源。正是因为 1840 年鸦片战争后，中国社会形态剧烈变化，教禁渐驰，潍县地处山东半岛通往内陆的重要枢纽位置，工商业发达，文化繁荣，才使得西方传教士“瞄准”这里，也才有了后来乐道院的故事。

Weihsien (now Weifang), Shandong Province, is an ancient city with a long history. For the first time at the end of the 19th century, several foreigners bought land on the outskirts of the city and built a sermon station, called the Courtyard of the Happy Way. As for why the Western missionaries chose Weihsien as their preaching place, we should investigate and trace the social structure of the late Qing Dynasty, as well as the geographical location, social economy and culture of Weihsien. It was because of the drastic changes in Chinese society after the Opium War in 1840 and the gradual relaxation of religious activities. In addition, Weihsien was an industrial, commercial and cultural hub in Shandong Peninsula, leading to the inland. Only then did the story of the Courtyard of the Happy Way come out.

第一节　晚清中国的社会形态

1.1 Chinese Society in the Late Qing Dynasty

19 世纪中叶，东西方文明发生了剧烈的碰撞。依托着工业革命带来的近代化，西方列强用坚船利炮打开了中国紧锁的大门。越来越多的西方人开始踏足这个古老的国度，教会势力也不甘落后，他们试图以传播宗教的方式，来影响这片土地。

In the middle of the 19th century, there was a violent collision between East and West, tradition and modernity. The Western countries, which had embraced the Industrial Revolution and gained unprecedented power, forced China to open its doors. Therefore, more and more Westerners, including missionaries, began to come to China. They tried to affect the local people’s customs, traditions, and cultural values through inviting them to join their religious faith.

1840 年，鸦片战争的炮声震动了紫禁城。面对这“三千年未有之大变局”，闭关锁国已久的中国措手不及。与西方列强的坚船利炮和不平等条约一起到来的，还有十字架。在“用十字架征服中国”的口号中，一批批西方传教士乘船而来，涌入中国沿海与内陆。

In 1840, the sound of artillery shook the imperial palace in Beijing. China, which had closed its boarders to the rest of the world for more than three thousand years, was caught off guard. Along with large ships and powerful cannons of Western aggressors and unequal treaties came the Cross. A larger number of Western missionaries came by boat and poured into China's mainland.

图 1 第一次鸦片战争
Picture 1 First Opium War

图 2 签订《中英南京条约》
Picture 2 Signing the Nanking Treaty

在清代中前期的对外贸易中，依托着丝绸、茶叶、瓷器等商品，中国始终处于优势地位。巨大的贸易逆差，让以英国为首的西方国家，开始以倾销鸦片的方式打破不利局面。林则徐“虎门销烟”后，第一次鸦片战争就此拉开了序幕。面对坚船利炮，清朝统治者失去信心，与英国人签订了丧权辱国的《南京条约》，紧闭数百年的大门就这样被打开。

By the middle of the Qing Dynasty, China, relying on silk, tea, porcelain and other commodities, was a dominant and powerful figure in foreign trade. The huge trade deficit impelled the Western countries, led by Britain, began to dump opium onto China so as to tackle this disadvantage. The First Opium War began soon after Lin Zexu (a Chinese official) destroyed all the opium in Humen, Guangdong Province. In the face of the formidable power of the Western militarily force, the rulers of the Qing Dynasty retreated and signed the Treaty of Nanking with the British, thus opening the country's door that had been closed for hundreds of years.

鸦片战争后，西方列强掀起了瓜分中国的狂潮。在政治上，列强设立“租借地”，划分“势力范围”；在经济上，用大量输出资本和产品为手段，打垮中国原有经济模式，使中国沦为列强的倾销市场。与此同时，列强还展开了文化侵略，大批西方传教士深入城市、乡村，兴建教堂，进行宗教传播，充当“压制殖民地的工具”。于是，大大小小的教堂如同雨后春笋，在中国大地接连出现。它们中的许多至今依然保存完好。

After the Opium Wars, the Western powers started to divide China between themselves. In another word, by setting up “leased territories”, each Western country took a part of China. They exported a large number of products to China which destroyed the China’s economy, and China was reduced to the dumping market of its invaders. At the same time, the Western countries also carried out cultural aggression. A large number of Western missionaries went deep into cities and villages and built churches to spread religions, acting as a kind of “a hidden tool of colonial oppressors”. As a result, large and small churches, like mushrooms, appeared everywhere in China. Many of them are still well preserved.

图 3 北京西什库教堂
Picture 3 Xishiku Church (The North Church), Beijing

图 4 哈尔滨圣·索菲亚教堂
Picture 4 San Sofia Cathedral, Harbin

图 5　青岛圣·弥厄尔教堂
Picture 5 St. Michael's Cathedral, Qingdao

图 6　西方漫画里的传教士指引中国
Picture 6 Missionaries guided China (a Western comic)

图 7　西方传教士在中国
Picture 7 Western missionaries in China

第二节　晚清民国时期的潍县

1.2 Weihsien in the Late Qing Dynasty and the Early Republic of China

一、潍县概况

1.2.1 General Situation of Weihsien

潍县，是中华人民共和国成立前对现在潍坊城区的称谓，自古为北海名城、东莱首邑。这里地扼山东内陆腹地通往半岛地区的咽喉，交通便利，故而文化经济繁荣。乾隆年间，郑板桥曾有“潍州原是小苏州”的说法。史书记载，民国时期，潍县以“二百支红炉、三千砸铜匠、九千绣花女、十万织布机”名扬天下。

Weihsien, the old name of Weifang before the founding of the People's Republic of China, was a famous, prosperous, ancient city. It was a vital place to link the inland and the peninsula of Shandong. The convenient transportation promoted the cultural and economic prosperity. During the reign of Emperor Qianlong, there was a saying, “Suzhou in South and Weihsien in North”, which was used to describe their prosperity. During the period of the Republic of China, Weihsien was famous for its advanced copper, embroidery and textile industries.

图 8　潍县地图

Picture 8　Map of Weihsien

潍县人提及古城，一般是指潍县县城，也称主城或西城。城有四门，其中有 3 个城门均建有“瓮城”。出了东门，越过护城河，便是东关坞。元代时，商人临河而居，墟市交易，渐渐发展起来，逐步扩成东城。由于东城的坞墙沿河而筑，蜿蜒曲折，状如盘蛇，与主城相对，遂使潍县呈现一县双城的格局。

When talking about the ancient city, the Weihsien people generally refer to the main city or the west Weihsien. Of the four gates in the ancient Weihsien, three were built with a barbican entrance. If you exit through the east gate and cross the moat, you would see the Dongguan dock. In Yuan Dynasty, the businessmen lived by the river; as the local markets developed, the east part of Weihsien was gradually built. Walls in a zigzag pattern were built along the river in the east, which was different from the main city. That is how the structure of twin cities were formed in Weihsien.

隋代时，潍县有了城，但有记载的大规模修建是在明代。崇祯十二年（1639），大明王朝内忧外患，为了增强防御力，当时的县令邢国玺下令，将城池砌为石城。此后历经清代两次大修、数次小修，最终形成布局严谨，轴线对称的县城。鼎盛时的潍县，城内有街道 48 条，以县治前街为中心，附近有武衙门、察院、城隍庙、关帝庙、书院、考院、文庙等。城内还有诸多名胜古迹、坛庙寺院、园林和牌坊。

The City of Weihsien came into being in the Sui Dynasty. The recorded large-scale construction of city happened during the Ming Dynasty. Throughout 1639, the Ming Dynasty was beset by domestic problems and foreign invasion. To enhance the defensive measures, Xing Guoxi, the magistrate of Weihsien, ordered the mud walls be replaced by stony ones. After two major repairs and several minor repairs during the Qing Dynasty, an orderly and symmetrical city was built. At its peak, there were forty eight streets in Weihsien, and the local government building was on a street in the center of the town. The city center was surrounded by a military barrack, a supervision bureau, temples, academies, and an examination center. There were also interesting places such as scenic spots, monasteries, gardens and memorial archways.

图 9 中华人民共和国成立前的潍县县政府大门
Picture 9 Weihsien Government before the founding of the People's Republic of China

图 10 建于朝阳门城楼（现亚星桥西头）上的标准钟
Picture 10 Standard clock built on Chaoyang Gate tower (now the west end of Yaxing Bridge)

二、深厚的文化底蕴

1.2.2 Profound Cultural Heritage

潍县位于先秦时期齐国腹地，为北海名城，受儒家思想熏陶影响颇深，因而潍县人一向崇尚教育，这里自古人才荟萃、英杰辈出。在先贤们的影响下，潍县文风日益昌盛。有清一代，山东共出了 6 名状元，其中潍县就有 2 人。此外，据不完全统计，潍县曾出进士 78 人，举人达 296 名。据《潍县志稿》记载，潍县“明末清初人才彬蔚，嘉道后则户尽弦歌，里为冠盖。科目之盛，弁冕齐鲁。”进入民国后，潍县更是“教育之盛，为全省冠”（语出 1915 年出版的《山东通志》）。正是依靠着强大的人才储备，潍县才得以在晚清民国的时代洪流中，扮演着重要历史角色。

Weihsien is a famous ancient city by the Beihai Sea, which belonged to the territory of Qi State in ancient times. The Weihsien people, deeply influenced by Confucianism, have always valued education. Since ancient times, a great number of prominent people came from this region. Under the influence of scholars of the past, more and more people became interested in studying literature. In the Qing Dynasty, Shandong trained a total of six Zhuangyuan (Number One Scholar), two of whom were from Weihsien. According to some unofficial statistics, Weihsien had trained seventy eight candidates who successfully passed the highest imperial examinations, and two hundred ninety six candidates who excelled at the provincial level. Since the founding of the Republic of China, Weihsien has always been a pioneer in terms of educational achievements in Shandong Province. Because it continuously introduced new talents, Weihsien played a crucial historical role in the late Qing Dynasty and the Republic of China

潍县历史悠久，英杰辈出：五代南唐因《夜宴图》而广为人知的韩熙载，金末起义抗金的李全、李璮父子，清代在程符山麓台书院讲学的韩梦周，弃官不仕、毕生致力于金石研究的陈介祺，曾任陕西巡抚、主持打出中国陆上首口油井的曹鸿勋……都出自这片热土。此外周亮工、郑板桥等历史名人，都曾在潍县为官，政事之余，积极推动当地文化教育发展。

Throughout the long history of Weihsien, there have always been outstanding celebrities: Han Xizai, who was widely known for the painting “Han Xizai Evening Banquet” in the Southern Tang Dynasty; Li Quan and his son Li Tan, who fought against the government in the late Jin Dynasty; Han Mengzhou, who lectured at Lutai Academy in Chengfu Mountain in the Qing Dynasty; Chen Jieqi, who abandoned his official position and devoted his life to the study of inscription on ancient bronze tools and stone tablets; and Cao Hongxun, a former governor of Shaanxi Province who was in charge of the drilling of the first inshore oil well in China. In addition, Zhou Lianggong (a distinguished littérateur and calligrapher) and Zheng Banqiao (a painter, calligrapher and littérateur) served as the magistrate of Weihsien and made significant contributions to the education system in Weihsien.

图 11 《韩熙载夜宴图》局部
Picture 11 Part of the painting Han Xizai Evening Banquet

图 12 清代状元、曾任陕西巡抚的曹鸿勋
Picture 12 Cao Hongxun, Number One Scholar and Governor of Shaanxi Province in Qing Dynasty

三、繁荣的工商业

1.2.3 Prosperous Industry and Commerce

早在先秦时期，潍坊地区就有商业活动。先民勤劳肯干，充分利用优越的地理位置发展经济。在一代代人的努力下，潍县逐渐成为鲁东商业枢纽，至清代呈现出“东自登莱达济西”“若论五都兼百货，自然潍县甲青齐”的繁荣局面。这些，为后来潍县近代化打下了坚实的物质基础。

The earliest commercial activities in Weihsien appeared in Pre-Qin Dynasty. The local people were diligent and hardworking, taking full advantage of its favorable geographical location for developing and expanding the economical activities. Through the relentless efforts of one generation after another generation, Weihsien had gradually become the commercial hub of the east Shandong which helped to laid a solid foundation for its later modernization.

清末海禁开放后，潍县成为“自开商埠”之一。开埠之后，潍县的机器制造、染织、颜料化工、铁加工等行业发展迅速，涌现出了一大批在全省乃至全国都有知名度的商号。另一方面，1904 年胶济铁路开通，使得山东半岛的经济格局大有改变。凭借火车的运输力，沿着“胶济铁路”线，诸多城镇的贸易经济更趋繁荣。本就是重要商品集散地的潍县也因为这条铁路而获得了新的发展机遇，成为鲁东地区重要的商埠。大批进出口货物在这里云集，或是运往山东腹地，或者前往青岛，远洋出海。

After the ban of maritime trade was finally abolished in the late Qing Dynasty, Weihsien became one of the autonomous commercial ports. Since then, on one hand, its industrial machine manufacturing, fabric dyeing and weaving, pigment chemical industry, iron processing and other industries rapidly began to develop and a large number of business enterprises emerged in the region, which were not only known in Shandong Province but also in the rest of China. On the other hand, the Jiaozhou-Ji'nan Railway began its operation in 1904, which totally revolutionized the economic map of Shandong Peninsula. The railway line became a new line of merchandise flow, which greatly facilitated the circulation of commodities and strengthened the surrounding townships of contact. Due to the building of the aforementioned railway line, Weihsien, which was already an important distribution hub for commercial cargo, gained new development opportunities which made into an important commercial port in east Shandong. So, all sort of goods, both imports and exports, were first collected there, which would be subsequently transported to the hinterland of Shandong or to Qingdao to be shipped out overseas.

晚清以降，外国资本纷纷涌入，他们在潍县设厂，从而推动了潍县的工业化发展。许多民族工业者也在这时抱以“实业救国”的精神，加入到潍县的工业化发展中。他们将学自西方的先进技术、经营管理理念加以运用，建立起潍县第一批近代企业，使潍县进入到了“工业化初级阶段”，当地的机器制造业与青岛、天津、北平等大城市几乎不相上下。

Since the late Qing Dynasty, Weihsien attracted foreign investors who came and built factories, promoting the industrial development of the city in the process. Furthermore, following the motto of “saving the nation by engaging in industry”, a number of Chinese industrialists played a fundamental role in the industrial and financial development of the city. Using the Western advanced technological tools and management methods, they set up the first examples of modern enterprises in Weihsien. The city had entered the “primary stages of industrialization”, and its machine manufacturing industry retained a close alliance with those of Qingdao, Tianjin, Beiping (now Beijing) and other major cities.

图 13 胶济铁路潍县段

Picture 13 The section of Jiaozhou-Ji’nan Railway in Weihsien

图 14 潍县火车站老照片

（【德】弗里德里希·贝麦摄于 1903 年）

Picture 14 Weihsien Railway Station in 1903

图 15 清末潍县的布市

Picture 15 Cloth market in Weihsien

全国各地客户云集潍县，进行布匹交易。“自开商埠”后的潍县，工商业得到了迅速发展，并形成了以“七东”“八丰”“八祥”为代表的商号格局。这些诞生于具有迫切救国之心的工商界有识之士之手的商号，对当时潍县经济发展起到了极为重要的作用，也为潍县近代工商业发展做出了贡献。

Customers from all over the country gathered in Weihsien to trade fabrics and clothes. Since Weihsien set up its commercial port, industry and commerce were rapidly developing, and some prestigious firms were founded. Established by passionate patriots who wanted to help facilitate the country's path to progress and flourish, they played a fundamental role in the economic development of Weihsien; more importantly, they laid the foundation for creating a modern industrial and commercial city.

图 16 华丰机器厂生产的发动机

Picture 16 Engine manufactured by Huafeng Machine Factory

图 17 同盛铁厂大门

Picture 17 The gate of Tongsheng Ironworks

图 18 惠丰火柴厂运货出厂

Picture 18 Delivering goods from the factory of Huifeng Match Company

第二章　乐道院的建立

2 Establishment of the Courtyard of the Happy Way

1881 年底，潍县来了几位西方人，他们在这里停下脚步，买下城东大片土地。1883 年，写有“乐道院”的牌匾悬挂了起来。它就像是在传统的潍县社会中硬生生楔入了一个近代小社会，引发了轩然大波。潍县人纷纷传说，这乐道院为洋人所办，有教堂、新式学堂、医疗诊所。尽管在庚子年剧烈的东西方文化冲突中，乐道院并没有能够幸免，但当一切平息后，它又得到了重建，并从此根植在潍县的土地上。

At the end of 1881, a few Westerners came to Weihsien and bought large tracts of land in the east of the city. In 1883, the Courtyard of the Happy Way (also known as “Le Dao Yuan” in Chinese) was built. It seemed like wedging a little modern community into a traditional society. The Courtyard, which was run by foreign academics, missionaries and medics, comprised of a church, schools, and a medical clinic. It did not survive the severe cultural conflict between China and the Western countries in 1900. It was, however, rebuilt again and restored its original position in the city.

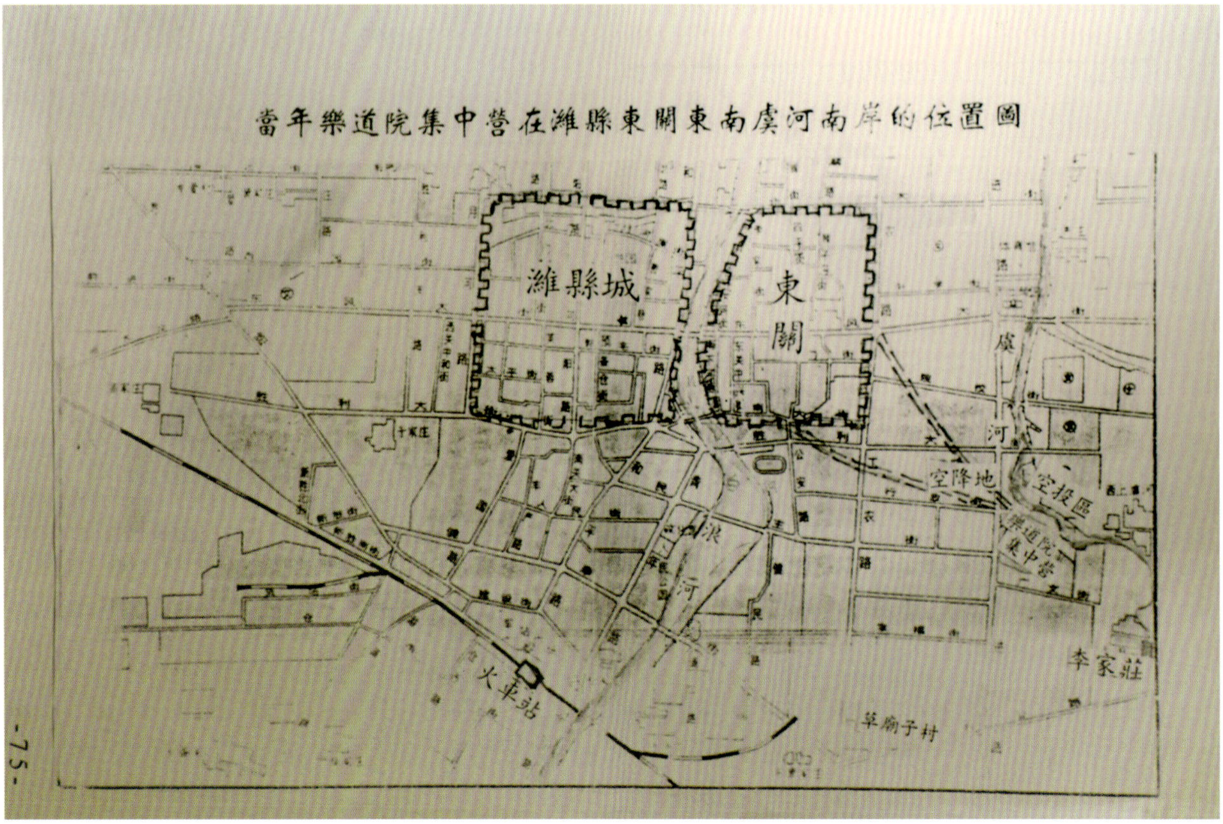

图 1　乐道院在潍县的位置

Picture 1 Courtyard’ location in Weihsien

不可否认，乐道院被强行楔入到潍县的土地，与中国传统文化发生碰撞时的确破坏了中国独立的一面，但它同样推动了潍县的发展。受到西方文化影响的潍县人，开始积极走向世界，并在中国近代化的浪潮中奋勇拼搏。

It is undeniable that the building of the Courtyard of the Happy Way instigated a kind of cultural exchange and at times cultural collision with that of the local residents, but, overall it promoted the development of Weihsien. Due to the close contact with the Western culture, Weihsien people began to assume an outward-looking approach to the world, promoting the demanding but at the same time rewarding process of modernization.

早在 1865 年，来中国已有 3 年的美国传教士狄考文与同伴郭显德自登州前往济南，路过潍县时，放眼望去，满是繁华喧闹。狄考文决心要在此处兴建教堂。数年后，狄考文又一次来到潍县，当地人李始元（潍县人，当时在烟台经商）协助他对潍县进行考察。但不知何故，狄考文的想法并没付诸实施。

As early as 1865, Calvin Wilson Mateer, an American missionary who had been in China for three years, and his companion Hunter Corbett traveled from Tengchow (now Penglai) to Ji'nan. As they were passing Weihsien, they noticed that it was a prosperous city. Calvin, who was determined to build a church in the city and preach there, traveled to Weihsien again a few years later. Li Shiyuan (a Weihsien native, who was in Yantai on business at the time) provided him a great deal of information about Weihsien. However, his idea was not eventually put into practice.

图 2 狄考文（1836 ~ 1908），美国宾夕法尼亚人，美国北长老会传教士，近代教育家、翻译家、慈善家

Picture 2 Calvin Wilson Mateer (1836-1908), born in Pennsylvania, USA, was a missionary of Presbyterian Church in the USA, educator, translator and philanthropist

图 3 狄乐播（1853～1921），狄考文之弟，乐道院的创建者。1881 年毕业于普林斯顿大学神学院
Picture 3 Robert M. Mateer (1853-1921) was Calvin Wilson Mateer's younger brother. He graduated from the Seminary at Princeton University in 1881

直到 1881 年，狄考文的弟弟狄乐播抵达登州，这位年轻人刚从美国普林斯顿大学神学院毕业，便漂洋过海来到中国。在兄长的关照下，他学习了几天汉语，了解了一些中国文化，便与夫人出发前往潍县。同行者还有良约翰牧师、Horace R. Smith 医生等人。刚到潍县时，狄乐播等人暂住在李始元家。某日，在前往城东南李家庄，拜访从登州文会馆肄业的李芳桂时，狄乐播见当地风景秀丽，于是在李芳桂的弟弟李芳龄（后为乐道院基督教长老会长老）协助下，购地建起乐道院。

In 1881, Robert M. Mateer, Calvin's younger brother, arrived in Tengchow. Before sailing across the sea to China, this young man had just graduated from the Seminary at Princeton University in the United States. Under the care of his brother, he studied Chinese and learned about the Chinese culture, before setting out for Weihsien with his wife. Along with him were minister John Hood Laughlin, Dr. Horace R. Smith,, to name a few. Upon arriving in Weihsien, they temporarily resided in Li Shiyuan's house. One day, when he went to Lijiazhuang in the southeast of the city to visit Li Fanggui, who had graduated from Tengchow College, Robert saw the beautiful scenery of the area and decided to settle down there. So with the help of Li Fangling, Li Fanggui's younger brother, who later became an elder in the Courtyard's church, Robert bought the land and built the Courtyard of the Happy Way.

狄乐播在潍县城东南部李家庄西北、虞河南岸买下土地 16.5 市亩，历经一年的时间，初步建成了以平房为主，占地面积 1.1 万平方米的潍县乐道院。以功能划分，整个建筑区域分三大部分：学校、诊所、教会。乐道院建成之初时，狄乐播夫妇亲自掌管具体事务，以传教布道为主。

Robert M. Mateer bought about one hectare of land in the southeast of Weihsien, lying towards northwest of Lijiazhuang Village and by the south bank of Yuhe River. One year later, the Courtyard of the Happy Way had been partially built. Most of the buildings were bungalows at the time. The whole building area covered eleven thousand square meters, which could be divided into three parts: a school, a clinic and a church. At the beginning, Robert M. Mateer and his wife managed the Courtyard by themselves, mainly preaching.

图 4 乐道院正门（拍摄于 1887 年）
Picture 4 Main gate of the Courtyard in 1887

乐道院刚建起来的那段时间里，门可罗雀，信众不多。附近也没有太多的住户，就连最近的李家庄距离也有 500 多米，加之道路崎岖不平，很少有中国人会来到这个位于偏僻处的“洋寺庙”。不得已，狄乐播等传教士只能改变布道途径，通过学校、医院等世俗事业，扩大教会的影响。于是，传道、教育、医疗三位一体的格局正式形成，并延续下来。

When the Courtyard was first built, not many people believers attended it. There were few households around, and even the nearest place, namely the Lijiazhuang Village, was more than one li away (one li equals half a kilometer) and the roads were rough. So few Chinese would go to this “Western temple” ran by foreigners. Robert and other missionaries had to change their preaching methods, expanding the influence of the church through secular undertakings, namely schools and a hospital. As a result, the combined functions of religion, education and medical care of the Courtyard were established and continued.

图5 乐道院男子学校——文华馆。1883年，狄乐播在创建乐道院之初即设立了学校——文华馆，当时只招收男生，学生全部是教徒子女，人数不多。学生除学习文化课外，还有宗教学科和读经、祷告时间

Picture 5 Boys' School in the Courtyard — Wenhua Academy. In 1883, right after the Courtyard was founded by Robert M. Mateer, its school, Wenhua Academy, was also built. At the time, only male students were enrolled. The school did not have many students as it only admitted the children of Christian families, who obviously constituted a very small community. In addition to learning the academic subjects, students also studied the religious subjects, read the scriptures, and attended the religious services

图6 乐道院文美书院（摘自1933年《山东潍县广文中学五十周年纪念特刊》，以下简称《纪念特刊》）。1895年建立女校——文美书院，仿照男校设置课程，是当时山东最早的一所女子中学，为潍县妇女逐步得到受教育的权利开了风气之先

Picture 6 Wenmei Academy in the Courtyard. Wenmei Academy, the girls' school, was built in 1895, offering the same courses that the boys studied. It was the first girls' middle school in Shandong, pioneering the women's right to equal education in Weihsien

图 7　早期的乐道院医院。早期的医院相对简陋，1887 年才有了正式医师，1889 年医院正式收治男女病人，并开始有正规药房

Picture 7　The early Courtyard hospital. At the beginning, it was a very simple clinic, without professional doctors. It was only in 1887 that a few professional medical practitioners arrived. In 1889, the hospital officially admitted male and female patients and opened its own pharmacy.

图 8　乐道院男子诊所

Picture 8　Men's clinic in the Courtyard

图 9　乐道院女子诊所

Picture 9　Women's clinic in the Courtyard

图 10 教士住宅（1900 年被焚毁后的照片）
Picture 10 The house where missionaries lived in (the picture was taken after it was burned down in 1900)

图 11 早期乐道院内的公告牌
Picture 11 Information board in the early Courtyard

第三章　乐道院的重建

3 Reconstruction of the Courtyard of the Happy Way

1900 年 6 月，义和团“反洋教”风潮波及潍县，民众围攻并焚毁乐道院。运动结束后，传教士们又多方筹措资金，在乐道院原址的基础上，又征用周边土地，重建扩建乐道院。20 世纪 20 年代中叶，乐道院又新建医院大楼。至此，乐道院的建筑格局基本完成。

In June 1900, the “anti-foreign religions” movement of the Boxer Rebellion spread to Weihsien. The local people besieged and burned the Courtyard. After the movement was suppressed, the missionaries raised funds through various sources. They expropriated the surrounding land to rebuild a new and much larger site. In mid 1920s, a new and bigger hospital was built in the Courtyard. At this point, the architectural pattern of the Courtyard was mainly completed.

第一节　焚　毁

3.1 Destroyed by Fire

Gate Where the Mob Entered Wei Hsien Mission, June 25th, 1900

图 1　早期乐道院南门
1900 年 6 月 25 日，潍县习武者从这个门进入，纵火焚毁潍县乐道院。摘自 1913 年出版的《旧中国的新震动》一书，作者贺乐德

Picture 1　South gate where the Boxers entered the Courtyard
On 25 June, 1900, the Boxers in Weihsien entered the Courtyard through this gate. From the book New Thrills in Old China published in 1913 by Charlotte E. Hawes

1900 年，义和团运动席卷华北大地，这场“反洋教”的浪潮波及潍县。包括狄乐播在内的外国人全部逃往烟台。当年 6 月 25 日（农历五月二十九日）晚，潍县习武者陈锡庆（又名陈双辰）、于江飞等 7 人冲入乐道院，在教堂内纵火，教堂、学校、医院全部被焚毁。据民国时期《潍县志稿・通纪二》记载，“二十六年庚

子夏五月二十九日晚，匪焚李家庄乐道院。焚死教民朱东光、刘作哲二人，楼房四十二间、瓦房一百三十六间”。另据当时传教士统计，乐道院总损失为 64421 两白银。

In 1900, the Boxer Movement swept across Weihsien and the rest of North China. All foreign residents, including Robert M. Mateer, fled to Yantai. In the evening of June 25, 1900, Chen Xiqing, Yu Jiangfei and five other local boxers entered the Courtyard and set fire to the church. The church, the schools and the hospital were all completely destroyed. According to the Weihsien Annals in the Republic of China, two Christians, Zhu Dongguang and Liu Zuozhe, died; 42 rooms in the storied buildings and 136 rooms in the tile-roofed houses were burned down. In addition, according to the statistics released by the missionaries at the time, the total damage to the Courtyard was estimated to be around 64,421 taels of silver.

Reverend F. H. Chalfant, D.D., Hero of June 25th, 1900 Wei Hsien, China

图 2　美国基督教传教士方法敛，美国基督教北长老会教士，甲骨学家。1887 年来华，在山东潍县传教，逝于山东

本图摘自贺乐德著《旧中国的新震动》。图注为“传教士方法敛，1900 年 6 月 25 日的英雄，中国潍县”。根据其他史料记载，方法敛，这位后来的甲骨文研究者，在 1900 年 6 月 25 日这一天，用左轮手枪对冲击乐道院的中国人开枪射击，并至少杀死一人。当愤怒的中国民众冲进来后，方法敛与宝安美等人利用梯子翻越围墙，在夜色和高粱地的掩护下，逃往坊子镇，寻求在那里的德国人的庇护

Picture 2　American Christian missionary F. H. Chalfant, a priest of Presbyterian Church in the USA and expert of oracle bones, went to China in 1887, preached in Weihsien, Shandong Province, and died there

This picture is excerpted from New Thrills in Old China by Charlotte E. Hawes, annotated as “Reverend F. H. Chalfant, D.D., Hero of June 25, 1900, Wei Hsien, China”. According to other historical records, F.H. Chalfant, the later oracle researcher, used a revolver to shoot at the local residents who attacked the Courtyard of the Happy Way, killing at least one person on June 25, 1900. After the angry local people invaded the Courtyard, Chalfant, F. Baughtov and their fellow members climbed over the wall and fled to Fangtze Town, seeking refuge from the Germans there

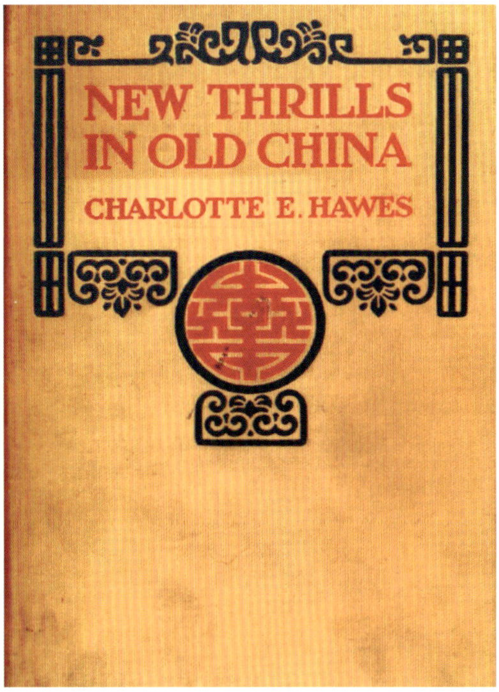

图 3 出版于 1913 年的《旧中国的新震动》一书封面。作者为贺乐德，是美国基督教北长老会传教士，她曾长期生活在潍县。1900 年，贺乐德亲历了义和团运动

Picture 3 Front cover of the book New Thrills in Old China. The book was published in 1913. The author, Charlotte E. Hawes, was a missionary of Presbyterian Church in the USA who lived in Weihsien for a long time. In 1900, she bore witness to the Boxer Rebellion

图 4 贺乐德教士在潍县的家中

Picture 4 Charlotte E. Hawes at home, Weihsien, China

第二节 重 建

3.2 Reconstruction

1902 年，教会利用清政府赔款，加上美国从所得“庚子赔款”中划拨的部分，以及美国教会捐赠的部分资金，又征地 160 亩，重建、扩建乐道院。1904 年，扩建的乐道院基本完工，面积扩大为 200 余市亩（正式征地为 176.5 亩，此数字为加上乐道院周边占地的总占地亩数），南至李家庄通东关南门的大路，北至虞河南岸。

In 1902, with the help of reparations by the Qing government, donations by the U.S. government acquired from the Boxer Indemnity, and donations made by the American church, another additional piece of land, approximately 10.6 hectares, was purchased for rebuilding and expanding the Courtyard. In 1904, the rebuilding process was mainly completed and the site was expanded to more than thirteen hectares (including the land around the Courtyard), stretching to Lijiazhuang Village in the south and Yuhe river in the north.

乐道院被焚毁后，在教会控告下，清政府逮捕了陈锡庆等人。经交涉，清政府赔款白银 4.5 万两用于乐道院重建。离开潍县前往烟台避难的狄乐播返回后，决定重建乐道院，并将诊所扩建成医院。整个扩建工程的耗银，除清政府赔款外，一部分来自美国所得的“庚子赔款”（投入乐道院白银 14773 两），另一部分主要来自美国教会的捐款（约合白银 3 万两）。

After the Courtyard was burned, the Qing government, at the request of the church, arrested Chen Xiqing and others. After some negotiations, the Qing government paid 45,000 taels of silver for the reconstruction of the Courtyard. When Robert M. Mateer returned from Yantai where he sought refuge, he decided to expand and reconstruct the Courtyard, including the clinic which turned into a hospital. The whole expansion project cost, Except for government compensation, part of the funds (14,773 taels of silver) came from the Boxer Indemnity given to the United States, and the rest (30,000 taels of silver) mainly came from the donation raised by the American church.

义和团运动结束后，狄乐播与夫人率领费习礼、方法敛等 16 人，从烟台乘船抵达小清河口寿光县羊角沟。时任山东巡抚的袁世凯早就派了军队在那里迎接，并护送一行人返回潍县。乐道院已经被烧成瓦砾，狄乐播等人无处安身，当地官员便将他们暂时安置在旅馆里。袁世凯还特意从济南打来电话慰问，命令当地官员代他送上礼物（图中即为袁世凯给传教士们送的肥羊），设宴为狄乐播等人接风洗尘。但关于乐道院被烧毁处置事宜，潍县知县一直不敢擅自做主，经请示袁世凯后，才开始与狄乐播等人商议重建。

By the end of the Boxer Movement, Robert M. Mateer and his wife, F. H. Chalfant and thirteen other people went from Yantai to Yangjiaogou, Shouguang County by boat. Yuan Shin-kai had sent troops to welcome and escort them back to Weihsien. Since the Courtyard was burned down to ashes, they had nowhere to reside in. Therefore, the local officials arranged for them to temporarily stay in a hotel. Yuan also made a special call from Ji'nan, ordering the local officials to send a present to the Western delegate on his behalf (the big sheep in the picture), and set up a banquet to welcome them. The magistrate of Weihsien did not dare to make any decisions in regards to the destroyed Courtyard without authorization; after receiving the official approval from Yuan Shin-kai, he consulted with Robert and his fellow members, and ordered the rebuilding of the Courtyard.

A FAT SHEEP PRESENTED TO THE MISSIONARIES BY YUAN SHIH K'AI AS A GOOD-WILL OFFERING

图5 狄乐播等人返回潍县。狄乐播等人从烟台返回潍县后，时任山东巡抚的袁世凯让当地官员为传教士代送肥羊作为礼物。本图摘自贺乐德著《旧中国的新震动》

Picture 5 Robert M. Mateer and other missionaries returned to Weihsien. After Robert M. Mateer and other missionaries returned to Weihsien from Yantai, Yuan Shin-kai, then governor of Shandong Province, ordered the local officials to send a big sheep to the missionaries as a good-will offering. This picture is excerpted from New Thrills in Old China by Charlotte E. Hawes.

第三节　重建后的乐道院建筑
3.3 Reconstructed Buildings

重建后的乐道院，面积扩大到200市亩，规模宏大，建筑类型丰富。经此一劫，狄乐播等人意识到士绅阶层对推动传教事业的重要性，他们开始主动接触当地士绅。1916年，反袁战事波及潍县，乐道院便成为潍县城内大户人家的避难所。战事结束后，士绅对乐道院的救助很是感激，曾特意送上匾额一方，上书“仁里德邻”四个大字。

After reconstruction, the Courtyard expanded its area to about thirteen hectares with larger and new style buildings. Robert M. Mateer and his fellow members, who had realized the importance of the upper class in promoting the missionary cause, began to woo them. In 1916, when the Anti-Yuan Shin-kai War spread to Weihsien, the Courtyard became a refuge for the wealthy families. After the war, these wealthy families were very grateful for their assistance. In order to show their gratitude, they made a special plaque with four Chinese characters on it, which read “Loving people, Caring neighbors”.

图 6　重建后上挂“仁里德邻”匾的乐道院正门
Picture 6　Courtyard front gate decorated by the plague reading “Loving people, Caring Neighbors”, which was installed on the gate after the reconstruction

图 7 重建后的乐道院正门（内景）
Picture 7 Courtyard front gate after reconstruction (from the inside of the Courtyard)

图 8　重建后的乐道院教堂（即礼拜堂），【美】霍勒斯·钱德勒拍摄于 1908 年。该建筑圆棱形，白墙红瓦，圆形琉璃窗子，八角尖顶。可容纳 1000 余人

Picture 8 Reconstructed Courtyard church (taken by Horace Chandler, an American, in 1908). The building was round and prismatic with white walls, red tiles, round glass windows and octagonal spire. It could hold more than one thousand people.

图 9　乐道院主教学楼（钟楼）

Picture 9 The main teaching building (Bell Tower) in the Courtyard

图 10 现存的文华楼
Picture 10 Today's Wenhua Building

图 11 现存的文美楼
Picture 11 Today's Wenmei Building

图 12 现存的乐道院女子圣经学校楼
Picture 12 Today's Girls' Bible Academy Building in the Courtyard

图 13 集中营时期侨民绘制的乐道院女子圣经学校楼，1942 年起日军用来集体关押单身男性侨民

Picture 13 The Girls' Bible Academy Building drawn by a concentration camp internee, where Japanese army imprisoned Western single male residents from 1942.

图 14 潍县乐道院教士住宅区。【美】霍勒斯·钱德勒拍摄于 1908 年

Picture 14 Missionaries' residential area in the Courtyard, taken by Horace Chandler in 1908

图 15 乐道院学校的科学馆
Picture 15 Science Museum in the Courtyard's school

图 16 重建后的乐道院内通往外籍教授办公住宅区的月亮门及花墙
Picture 16 Moon gate and lattice wall leading to the foreign professors' offices and residential area in the reconstructed Courtyard

图 17 乐道院内学校区的建筑
Picture 17 Courtyard school buildings

图 18 乐道院自南向北鸟瞰，远方的尖顶建筑为教堂。【美】霍勒斯·钱德勒拍摄于 1908 年
Picture 18 Aerial view of the Courtyard from south to north. The spired building is the church. Taken by Horace Chandler in 1908

图 19 乐道院的教职员工住宅区
Picture 19 Residential area for faculty and staff

图 20 乐道院鸟瞰（局部）
Picture 20 Aerial view of the Courtyard

图 21 1933 年拍摄的乐道院全景图（摘自《纪念特刊》）
Picture 21 A panorama of the Courtyard taken in 1933

第四节　乐道院医院大楼——“十字楼”落成
3.4 The Hospital — Completion of the Cross Building

庚子事变后，乐道院重建，尽管医院获得了很大发展，但医院条件依然很差。乐道院当时的住院病房普遍房屋低矮，光线不足，通风不良，而且只有病床 40 张；病人多时，虽然能够加至 70 张，但每间病房设两张病床后，就显得十分拥挤。

Although it had made great progress through reconstruction after the Siege of the International Legations, the hospital was still in a very poor condition. At that time, the inpatient wards were generally ordinary houses with insufficient lighting and poor ventilation, with only forty beds available. Although the number of available beds could be increased to around seventy in peak hours, which means each ward had two beds, it was still very crowded and inconvenient for the patients.

为适应病患要求，乐道院决定扩大医院规模。1923 年，梅仁德医生专程返回美国，为医院筹集扩建资金。据美国匹兹堡市（Pittsburgh）长老会 Shadyside 教区档案（教区档案号：REF BX 8951.A3）记载，当时美国匹兹堡市长老会 Shadyside 教区牧师柯尔（Hugh Thompson Kerr，1897–1951）在 1922–1923 年间主持了这个教区捐赠给潍县长老会医院一所医院楼事宜，除了在乐道院内扩建外，其规模大小、设计式样、各项配备完全和位于匹兹堡市内的 Shadyside 医院一样。柯尔牧师要求全部建筑材料也由募捐人在美国购买后运往潍县，建成后在长老会内部就称 Shadyside 医院，并在这一建筑墙基部位立碑以纪念。该大楼 1924 年动工，各项建筑材料、门窗、地板等均在美国制成后运到潍县，由中国人张同信（张执符）主持建造事务，该楼于 1925 年建成，加上附属建筑物，共耗资白银 9 万余两。医院楼房基石也在美国雕刻，石板雕刻为“Shadyside Hospital 1924”（见本章图 27）。这栋大楼共有 4 层，建筑面积 2461 平方米。因楼呈“十字”形，故而人称“十字楼”。

The Courtyard, therefore, decided to enlarge the hospital. In 1923, Dr. E.E. Murray went back to the United States of America to raise funds for the expansion project. According to the Parish Archives of Shadyside Presbyterian Church in Pittsburgh, U.S. (file No.: REF BX 8951. A3), the Pastor Hugh Thompson Kerr (1897-1951) from the Shadyside Presbyterian Church was in charge of collecting the donations made for the Weihsien Presbyterian Hospital in the period between 1922 to 1923. The size, design, and equipment of the Weihsien Presbyterian Hospital were exactly the same as the Shadyside Hospital in Pittsburgh. Pastor Hugh required that all construction materials should be purchased in the United States and shipped to Weihsien by the fund raisers. Upon the completion of the expanding process, the hospital was also called the Shadyside Hospital by the Presbyterian church and a monument was erected on the foundation of the building. In 1924, the construction of the hospital building began, with Zhang Tongxin, a Chinese doctor, in charge of the construction operations. All the construction materials, doors, windows and floors were made in the United States and shipped to Weihsien. The building was completed in 1925, together with ancillary buildings. They cost a total of 90000 taels of silver. The cornerstone of the hospital building was also carved in the United States, reading “Shadyside Hospital 1924” (see picture 27 in this chapter). The hospital building had four floors, covering an area of 2,461 square meters. Because the building looked like a cross, it was called the “Cross Building”.

图 22 1925 年十字楼建成启用时的纪念合影
Picture 22 The Cross Building was completed and opened to public in 1925

图 23 乐道院基督教医院美籍院长梅仁德（E. E. Murray）
Picture 23 E. E. Murray, the American Director of the Courtyard Christian Hospital

图 24 张同信，又名执符，名医，潍县人。1914 年毕业于齐鲁大学医学院，同年进潍县教会乐道院医院任医师，后升任主治医师、院长。抗战胜利后，被聘为青岛信义会医院董事会董事兼名誉院长。中华人民共和国成立后，信义会医院改为青岛医院，仍任院长
Picture 24 Zhang Tongxin, a Weihsien native, was a famous medical doctor. He graduated from the Medical College of Shantung Christian University in 1914. In the same year, he was admitted to the Courtyard Hospital as a physician, later promoted to the position of the attending physician and the director. After the the War of Resistance against Japanese Aggression, he was appointed as the Honorary President and Director of the Board of Directors of the Qingdao Lutheran Church Hospital. Following the founding of the People's Republic of China, the Lutheran Church Hospital was renamed the Qingdao Hospital and he still served there as director

图 25 1925 年落成的十字楼
Picture 25 Cross Building completed in 1925

图 26 1925 年落成的十字楼（局部）
Picture 26 Cross Building completed in 1925

第五节 乐道院建筑大事记
3.5 History of the Buildings

1882 年 狄乐播在潍县城东南部李家庄西北、虞河南岸买下土地 16.5 市亩，次年初步建成了以平房为主，占地面积 1.1 万平方米的潍县乐道院。

In 1882, Robert M. Mateer bought about one hectare of land in the southeast of Weihsien, lying towards northwest of Lijiazhuang Village and by the south bank of Yuhe River. One year later, the Courtyard of the Happy Way had been partially built. Most of the buildings were bungalows. The whole building area covered eleven thousand square meters.

1900 年 6 月 25 日 潍县习武者陈锡庆（又名陈双辰）、于江飞等人焚毁乐道院。

On June 25, 1900, the Boxers Chen Xiqing, Yu Jiangfei and others burned the Courtyard of the Happy Way.

1902 年 利用清政府赔银，加上美国所得“庚子赔款”中划拨的部分，以及美国教会捐赠的部分资金，教会又征地 160 亩，重建、扩建乐道院。

In 1902, with reparations from the Qing government, donation of U.S. government from Boxer Indemnity and donation from American church, another about 10.6 hectares of land were purchased to rebuild and expand the Courtyard.

1904 年 重建的乐道院基本完工，面积扩大为 200 余市亩，南至李家庄通东关南门的大路，北至虞河南岸。院门改在北面，大门上仍悬挂“乐道院”大字匾额。

In 1904, the rebuilding process was basically completed and the area was expanded to more than 13 hectares, stretching to Li Jiazhuang in the south and Yuhe river in the north. Its main gate was in the north, while the plaque of the Courtyard of the Happy Way (Chinese: 乐道院) was still hung over the gate.

1916 年 反袁战事波及潍县，乐道院便成为潍县城内大户人家的避难所。战事结束后，城里的士绅对乐道院的救助很是感谢，曾特制匾额一方，上书“仁里德邻”四个大字，并备厚礼一起送去。乐道院则将北大门上原有的“乐道院”旧匾摘下，挂到大门内侧，而将“仁里德邻”匾挂在大门的外部。

In 1916, when the Anti-Yuan Shin-kai War spread to Weihsien, the Courtyard became a refuge for the wealthy families. After the war, these wealthy families were very grateful for their assistance. In order to show their gratitude, they sent them gifts and made a special plaque for the Courtyard with four Chinese characters on it, which read “Loving people, Caring neighbors”. Then, the Courtyard took off the old plaque and hanged it on the inside of the gate, while putting the new plaque on the outside of the gate.

1925 年 乐道院的鼎盛时期。病房大楼建成，病房大楼平面与立体布局呈“十”字型，人称“十字楼”，4 层，2400 余平方米。乐道院医院成为综合性医院，名称也改为“潍县基督教医院”。

1925 was the heyday of the Courtyard of the Happy Way. The ward building was completed and took the shape of a cross, known as the “Cross Building”. It was a four-storied building with an area of 2,400 square meters. The hospital in the Courtyard of the Happy Way became a general hospital, and its name was changed to “Weihsien Christian Hospital”.

20 世纪 40 年代 根据 1936 年出生于乐道院的潘理达回忆，20 世纪 40 年代的乐道院建筑大致是这样——

The 1940s. According to Pan Lida, who was born in the Courtyard in 1936, the construction layout in the 1940s was roughly like this—

"乐道院"地处虞河南沿，周围设有高大的围墙。有两个大门，正门（北大门）和医院北门。正门是个黑漆大门，门两旁各有一座半米多高的青石墩。

The Courtyard of the Happy Way was located in the south bank of Yuhe River, surrounded by tall walls. There were two gates, the main gate (the north gate) and the north gate of the hospital. The main gate was a black lacquer gate, with a blue stone pier more than half a meter high on each side of the gate.

路西石坝上面，靠院墙是一座圆棱形大教堂，白墙红瓦，圆形琉璃窗子，八角尖顶。教堂东南方向有狄乐播纪念碑，坐落在铁栅栏护围内。

Above the stone dam in the west of the road was a round and prismatic church building which stood against the wall. It had white walls, red tiles, round glass windows and octagonal spire. To the southeast of the church was the Robert M. Mateer Monument, surrounded by iron fences.

教堂西面是广文中学的篮球场，球场西北角围墙内有一个圆形的"观星台"，可登高眺望。再往南是"圣经学院"和"灵修院"，这里是一片红瓦平房。

In Kwangwen Middle School, there was a basketball court which located to the west of the church. There was a round "star-viewing platform" in the northwest corner of court, from which you could look into the distance. In the south, there was the "Bible College", a "monastery", and a row of bungalows with red tiles.

教堂南面是广文中学，进入开放式的东校门后，可见西面与北面各有一排西洋式建筑风格的二层教学楼。教学楼顶上建有高耸的方形钟楼。

Kwangwen Middle School was situated in the south of the church there. Walking through the school's east gate, a row of Western style two-story buildings could be seen on both sides, that was, the west side and the north side. A square-shaped bell tower was on the top of the teaching building.

教室后面有一片平房，是学生宿舍区和教师宿舍区。教室南面是环境幽雅的"南外国院子"，这里有数座青砖红瓦小洋楼。院子的南端，可见不少外国人的卧式墓碑。

Behind the teaching building, the students' dormitory and the faculty's apartments were located. To the south of the building, there was the beautiful "south foreign yard", where several small Western-style buildings with green bricks and red tiles were located. At the southern end of the yard, you could see many tombstones of foreigners.

"乐道院"医院北门是铁栅栏样，左边是医院病房大楼，呈"十"字型，故而得名"十字楼"。大门两边各有一排小平房，是医院职工居住的地方。西面平房前有一个黄色厅房，是医院的门诊部。再往前走，上去台阶是数座西洋式小楼房，名为"专家楼"。

The north gate of the Courtyard Hospital was a Prague-style wrought iron gate; on the left, the hospital ward building was situated. Since it resembled the shape of a cross, it was named the "Cross Building". There was a row of one-floor houses on each side of the gate, where the hospital staff lived. On the west flank, across from the houses, there was a yellow building which used as the outpatient department of the hospital. Moving forward and walking up the steps, one could see several small Western-style buildings, called the Experts' Buildings.

“乐道院”外还有南、北乐道村，村里有不少人在医院工作。

Outside the Courtyard, there were two villages, one to the south, another to the north. Many people from these two villages worked in the hospital.

第六节 “十字楼”建筑的秘密
3.6 Secrets of the Cross Building

从 1882 年美国传教士狄乐播在潍县建造乐道院的第一所房子至今，百余年间，这里出现过许多不同类型的建筑。与当时南京、上海等气势恢宏的西洋建筑比，乐道院的建筑规模要小得多，但却具备自己独特的个性。诸如保存至今的乐道院“十字楼”，其“十字形”建筑结构尤为独特。又如乐道院曾经的教堂，看起来像是一座复杂而精巧的中式亭子。尽管这些近代建筑的诞生，源于外国教会势力的传入，但从客观上为老潍县的城市面貌增添了独特的一笔，更是潍县近代社会发展变迁的见证者。

Since 1882, when the American missionary Robert M. Mateer built the first house for the Courtyard of the Happy Way, there had been a variety of buildings, structures, and architecture designs. Compared with that of Nanjing and Shanghai at that time, the Courtyard is much smaller, but it has a unique, outstanding architecture and appearance. For example, the Cross Building, which has been preserved until today, is particularly unique in its cross-shaped design and structure. And the former church of the Courtyard looks like a complex and exquisite Chinese pavilion. Although the construction of these modern structures was part of the Western powers' missionary plans, it has greatly changed the bearing of the city, witnessing its social development in modern times.

如今的“十字楼”，是当时乐道院医院的病房大楼，该楼地上有 3 层，地下 1 层，规模庞大，功能合理，是近代医院的代表性建筑。从建筑风格上看，有专家认为，“十字楼”具备典型的巴洛克风格。比如，它的建筑立面是有层次的，中间突出，两侧渐渐后移。又如，其两侧窗户的间距也并非等距，而呈现递减的规律。但“十字楼”的装饰细节又呈现出中西合璧的风格。

The Cross Building was in fact the Courtyard Hospital's ward. It has three floors above the ground and one floor underground. Considering its large scale and functionality, it is a good example of a modern hospital structure. Many experts believe that the Cross Building features a typical Baroque architectural style. For example, the facade is stratified, with the central part protruding and both sides denting. Also, the pitch of the windows on both sides is not equidistant, but declining gradually. In addition, there seems to be a combination of Chinese and Western style in the decoration of the Cross Building.

奠基石 Cornerstone

图 27 这块奠基石显示了“十字楼”建造的年代和功能：1924，医院

Picture 27 The cornerstone shows the age and function of the Cross Building: 1924, hospital

十字户型 Cross type

图 28 欧洲建筑的结构通常都有范式，诸如“L”形、“H”形可能是宫殿或者住宅。“十字楼”的“十字形”十分罕见

Picture 28 There is usually a paradigm in the structure of European architecture, such as “L” shape and “H” shape, which may be commonly seen in palaces or houses. While the shape of the Cross Building is very rare and unique

提拉窗 Vertical sliding window

图 29 提拉窗是美式建筑的特点，有密闭性好、不易掉落等特点，窗户框上有特殊的构造，使得窗扇能停留在不同的位置

Picture 29 Vertical sliding windows are a typical characteristic of the American architecture, which are known for their good sealing features and safety. There is a special structure on the window frame, so that the window sash can stay in different positions

老虎窗 Dormer Window

图 30 坡屋顶上开的天窗，像伸出屋顶的老虎头，故得名，是西洋建筑的典型特征
Picture 30 The skylights on the slope roof, like tigers stretching their heads out of the roof, is a typical feature of the Western architecture

清水砖 Ganged brick

图 31 “十字楼”的外墙，是灰色清水砖墙
Picture 31 The outer wall of the Cross Building is made of gray ganged bricks

第四章　乐道院的教育

4 Education in the Courtyard of the Happy Way

地处齐鲁腹地的潍县，自古文风昌盛，读孔孟、考科举，是每一个潍县人心中的正道所在。当西方人远道而来，在深受儒家道德熏陶的潍县停下脚步时，他们发现，教育是这片土地的根本所在。若将外来思想植入潍县人的生活中，布道传教是行不通的。于是，新式学堂办了起来，先是只招男生，后来女子学堂也有了。

Weihsien, located in the inland of Qi and Lu states, had created a prolific academic environment since the ancient times. Weihsien people had always showed a lot of enthusiasm for reading Confucius's and Mencius's texts and taking the imperial examination. Therefore when the Westerners first arrived in Weihsien, they noticed that education was much valued by the locals. They had to open new schools rather than just inviting the local people to their faith and preaching in churches, if they wanted to spread the Western ideas. The first school they opened only admitted boys; later, a second school was built for girls.

数学、物理、化学、博物……于近代中国人而言，洋人学堂里开设的这些教学内容甚是陌生。以至于最初时，入学者寥寥无几。历史的进程终究是在前进，科学带来的冲击影响巨大。诸多潍县人因为接触、学习、吸收先进知识，而得以开眼看世界，他们将为一个近代化的中国，贡献自己的力量。

At the time, the Chinese students were not familiar with the subjects taught in Western schools, such as mathematics, physics, chemistry, natural science and others. So, at first, there were not many students. However, history was moving forward, and science had an enormous impact of everybody's life. Being in close contact with and acquiring the advanced modern knowledge opened the eyes and minds of the Weihsien people, enabling them to see the new, modern world. Using their new knowledge and strength, they began to contribute to building a modern China.

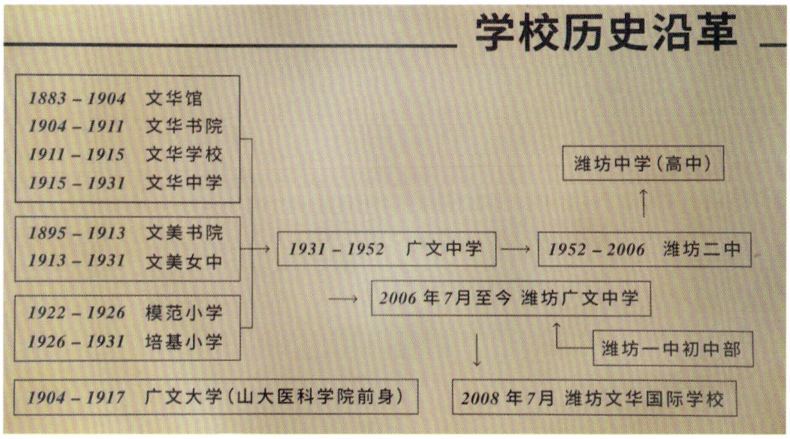

图 1 乐道院学校沿革图表

Picture 1 History chart of the Courtyard schools

第一节　1900 年之前的乐道院学校
4.1 Schools Before 1900

1883 年，狄乐播在乐道院建院之初就设立了男子学校，即文华馆；1895 年又设立女子学校，即文美书院。当时，学生全部是教徒子女，学生数量不多。除学习文化课外，还增加了宗教学科和读经、祷告时间。1900 年乐道院被焚毁，学校停办。文华馆的第一任校长为美国人狄乐播，文美书院第一任校长为宝安美。

In 1883, the boys' school, namely, Wenhua Academy was set up, shortly after the founding of the Courtyard by Robert M. Mateer; in 1895, the girls' school, namely, Wenmei Academy was built and began to register pupils. In the beginning, there were not many students because the children only came from the Christian families. In addition to learning academic subjects, the students also studied religious subjects, read the scriptures, and participated in religious ceremonies and activities. In 1900, the schools were closed after the Courtyard was burned down. Mr. Robert M. Mateer and Miss Emma F. Baughton were the first headmasters of Wenhua Academy and Wenmei Academy, respectively.

图 2 文美书院校长宝安美教士（任期为 1895 年至 1900 年），本章第一至第三节图片均摘自《纪念特刊》
Picture 2 Miss Emma F. Baughton, Headmaster of Wenmei Academy (term of office: 1895-1900)

图 3 1898 年文华馆师生合影
Picture 3 Teachers and students in Wenhua Academy in 1898

图 4 1898 年，文美书院第一届毕业女生，大部分还缠着小脚
Picture 4 First female graduates from Wenmei Academy in 1898, most of whom still were foot-binding

图 5 文美书院第一班的毕业女生田心慈及长子，她给长子取了一个英文名字叫约翰
Picture 5 The graduating student from Class One of Wenmei Academy Tian Xinci and her eldest son. She gave him an English name John

第二节　1900 年—1930 年的乐道院中小学校
4.2 Primary and Middle Schools from 1900 to 1930

1900 年，乐道院遭焚，学校停办。后乐道院重建，学校也相继恢复。1904 年，文华馆恢复，改称文华书院，1911 年改称文华学校，1915 年改称文华中学；女校文美书院 1913 年改称文美女子中学。与男校不同的是，文美女子中学为了使女学生在毕业后，拥有胜任小学教师的能力和资格，便将女中三年制改为四年制，在中学最后一年增设了师范训练内容。

In 1900, the schools were closed after the Courtyard was destroyed in the fire. After the reconstruction, they reopened again and resumed their activities. Wenhua Academy, which reopened in 1904, was renamed Wenhua School in 1911, whereas Wenhua Middle School resumed its classes in 1915; Wenmei Academy was given a new name, Wenmei Girls' Middle School, in 1913. Different from boys' school, Wenmei Girls' Middle School changed the duration of the program, from three years to four years, so as to make the students acquire the required skills and qualifications to become primary school teachers after graduation. It also added a hand-on-job training in the last year.

另外，乐道院还适应形势发展需要，开办小学。李恩惠在任文美女中校长期间，同美国人阮芝仪创办了模范小学，位置在乐道院中学女生部偏北。1922 年，乐道院模范小学开班，1926 年模范小学改称培基小学。此外，乐道院内还开办过妇女道学院、幼稚园及圣经学校。妇女道学院，程度略同于小学，以宗教课程为主。

Besides meeting the needs of the local community, the Courtyard of the Happy Way also opened a primary school. During her tenure as the headmaster of Wenmei Girls' Middle School, Miss Grace M. Rowby and Marjorie Rankin (an American lady whose Chinese name was Ruan Zhiyi) founded a sort of model primary school, which was located in the north flank of the girls' middle school. The model primary school was opened in 1922, which later, in 1926, was renamed Peiji Primary School. Furthermore, there was a women's school, a kindergarten and a school of biblical studies. In terms of its standards, the women's school was very similar to the primary school, mainly focusing on religious courses.

图 6　文华馆（书院、学校、中学）校长卫礼士（1903 ~ 1925 在任）
Picture 6　Dr. R. C. Wells (1903-1925), Principal of Wenhua Academy

图 7 文华中学校长尹焕斋（1926 ~ 1931 在任）
Picture 7　Yin Huanzhai, Principal of Wenhua Middle School (1926-1931)

图 8　文美书院校长方振义（1903 ~ 1908 在任）
Picture 8　Jenia Chalphant, Principal of Wenmei Academy (1903-1908)

图 9　文美书院校长狄珍珠（1908 ~ 1913 在任）
Picture 9　Madge D. Mateer, Principal of Wenmei Academy (1908-1913)

图 10 文美女中校长李恩惠（1913 ~ 1927 在任）
Picture 10　Grace M. Rowby, Principal of Wenmei Girls' Middle School (1913-1927)

图 11　文美女中校长徐焕滋（1928 ~ 1930 在任）
Picture 11　Xu Huanzi, Principal of Wenmei Girls' Middle School (1928-1930)

图 12 1910 年文华书院的男生合影，可以看到学生们的装束还是长袍、辫子发型，依然传统
Picture 12 Schoolboys, Wenhua Academy, 1910, still wearing traditional long gowns and with braided hairstyle

图 13 1913 年文华学校师生合影，男生们都穿上了军装。两年前，辛亥革命爆发
Picture 13 Teachers and students, Wenhua Academy, 1913. The schoolboys are wearing military uniforms. Two years earlier, the 1911 Revolution broke out

图 14 1919 年文华中学的这张毕业照上，写着：挥手自兹去，千载难逢齐
Picture 14 Graduates of Wenhua Middle School, 1919

图 15 1921 年文华中学毕业照，十足的民国风
Picture 15 Graduates of Wenhua Middle School, 1921

图 16 1925 年文华中学毕业生
Picture 16 Graduates of Wenhua Middle School, 1925

图 17 1925 年文华中学教职工及家属合影
Picture 17 Faculty and their families, Wenhua Middle School, 1925.

图 18 1926 年文华中学毕业生
Picture 18 Wenhua Middle School's graduates, 1926

图 19 1930 年文华中学毕业生
Picture 19 Wenhua Middle School's graduates, 1930

图 20 1905 年的文美书院毕业生，依然是旧式着装
Picture 20 Wenmei Academy's graduates, 1905, still wearing traditional costumes

图 21 1910 年文美书院全体女生合影
Picture 21 Schoolgirls, Wenmei Academy, 1910

图 22　1913 年，文美书院举行毕业典礼。虽然学生穿着打扮依然传统，但典礼现代气息已经浓厚

Picture 22　Wenmei Academy's graduation ceremony, 1913. There was a stark contrast between the students' traditional costumes and the Western-style formalities

图 23　1913 年文美书院毕业生，女生们的服饰有了很大变化

Picture 23　Wenmei Academy's graduates, 1913. One can notice the significant change of their dresses and hairstyle alike

图 24 1914 年文美女中毕业生
Picture 24 Graduates of Wenmei Girls' Middle School, 1914

图 25 1919 年文美女中毕业生，新思想也影响了文美中学的女生，许多人都开始留短发
Picture 25 Graduates of Wenmei Girls' Middle School, 1914, who were deeply influenced by new ideas and began to cut their hair short

图 26　1924 年文美女中的毕业生
Picture 26　Graduates of Wenmei Girls' Middle School, 1924

图 27　1927 年文美女中的毕业生，毕业的女生们已然是一副新女性的形象了
Picture 27　Graduates of Wenmei Girls' Middle School, 1927, whose appearance and costumes have changed a lot

图 28　1930 年文美女中的初中毕业生
Picture 28　Graduates of Wenmei Girls' Junior Middle School, 1930

第三节　1931—1937 年的乐道院学校
4.3 Schools from 1931 to 1937

1931 年，文华中学、文美女中与同属乐道院教会的培基小学合并，并向国民政府“山东省教育厅”正式立案。1932 年 9 月，经“山东省教育厅”批准立案，鉴于校舍大部分是广文大学旧址，而“文华、文美以联合而文益广”，所以正式定名为“山东省潍县私立广文中学”。次年，学校举办了“广文中学五十周年”校庆，出版了《广文中学五十周年纪念特刊》。齐鲁大学校长朱经农、齐鲁大学代校长林济青等均写有贺词，潍县地方著名士绅亲临祝贺者甚多。

In 1931, both Wenhua Middle School and Wenmei Girls' Middle School were merged with Peiji Primary School, and were officially registered in the Shandong Education Department. In September 1932, with the approval of the Education Department, the school was officially named “Kwangwen Private Middle School of Weihsien Shandong”. The 50th Anniversary of Kwangwen Middle School was held in the next year, and the Journal of 50th Anniversary of Kwangwen Middle School was published. Zhu Jingnong, president of Shantung Christian University, and Lin Jiqing, Acting president of Shantung Christian University, sent congratulatory letters. A lot of government officials and significant citizens from Weihsien attended the anniversary ceremony.

图 29　1931 年广文中学成立时的名誉校长张达忱，当时的张达忱为济南基督教青年会总干事

Picture 29 Zhang Dachen, the honorary headmaster of Kwangwen Middle School, 1931, when it was first established. He was also the director-general of Ji'nan Young Men's Christian Association (YMCA) at the time

图 30　1932 年任广文中学校长的崔德润先生

Picture 30 Cui Derun, Principal of Kwangwen Middle School in 1932

图 31 1931 年合并后的广文中学毕业生合影，背景为女子圣经学校楼
Picture 31 Kwangwen Middle School's graduates, after the big merger in 1931. In the background, the Girls' Bible School building is seen

图 32 1932 年广文中学毕业生合影
Picture 32 Kwangwen Middle School's graduates, 1932

图 33 1933 年，广文中学的高中毕业男生，其身后的建筑为学校阅览室，牌匾上写着：唤起民众
Picture 33 Kwangwen Senior Middle School's graduates, 1933, with the plague behind them saying "Wake up the public"

图 34 1933 年广文中学的初中毕业女生
Picture 34 Kwangwen Junior Middle School's female graduates, 1933

图 35 1933 年，乐道院幼稚园毕业生，大部分都是乐道院内各单位职工的幼儿，多为基督教徒的孩子。保育员均为教徒，向幼儿教唱宗教诗歌，讲圣经故事等
Picture 35 The kids in the Courtyard kindergarten, 1933. Most of them were the children of the Courtyard staff, who were mostly Christians. The staff were all Christian, too. They taught religious songs and Bible stories to the children

图 36 1932 年，潍县乐道院学校校友会合影
Picture 36 Members of Alumni Association of the Courtyard of the Happy Way in 1932

第四节　1937 年之后的乐道院学校

4.4 Schools after 1937

七七事变后，广文中学一度照常开学，学生约 800 人。但随着战事的发展，在日军侵占潍县前，广文中学停办了。1938 年 1 月，日寇侵占潍县。由于太平洋战争爆发前，美国在中日两国之间保持中立，乐道院也因此成为一个小小的安全区，是许多人躲避日寇的避难所。但人多事杂，秩序大乱，乐道院内的许多少年儿童失学。在这种情况下，自广饶培德中学返回潍县的黄乐德建议整顿乐道院，他借《圣经》的名义办起了“圣经学院”，最先成立的是小学部，共设 6 个年级。当年 9 月 1 日，中学部也开学，分男生部和女生部，黄乐德为院长。这种情况一直持续到太平洋战争爆发，乐道院成为日军的“敌国人集团生活所（即集中营）”，“圣经学院”方才停办。日本投降后，广文中学重新开办，黄乐德任校长。1952 年 11 月，潍坊市政府正式接管广文中学，改名为“山东省潍坊第二中学”。

After the July 7 Incident of 1937, Kwangwen Middle School opened as usual with about eight hundred students in campus. However, with the development of the war, it was closed before the Japanese army occupied Weihsien. In January 1938, the Japanese invaders occupied Weihsien. Before the outbreak of the Pacific War, the United States remained neutral between China and Japan, which made the Courtyard of the Happy Way a small security area and a refuge for many people who flee from the Japanese soldiers. However, since there was a large number of people as well as a series of complicated affairs that the Courtyard's staff had to deal with, nothing was in its own place. Many children were out of school in the Courtyard. Under such circumstances, Huang Lede, returning to Weihsien from Guangrao Peide Middle School, proposed to rectify the Courtyard of the Happy Way. He established the Bible Academy in the name of Bible. The first to be set up was the primary school with 6 grades. Subsequently, on 1 September 1938, the the boys' and the girls' middle schools were opened, with Huang Lede as the dean. This continued until after the outbreak of the Pacific War, when the Courtyard was transformed into the "Civil Assembly Center (i.e. concentration camp)" by the Japanese army. The Bible Academy was closed. After the surrender of Japan, Kwangwen Middle School resumed its classes and Huang Lede served as the headmaster. In November 1952, Weifang Municipal Government officially took over Kwangwen Middle School and renamed it Weifang No.2 Middle School of Shandong Province.

图 37　1940 年广文中学师生合影
Picture 37 Faculty and students of Kwangwen Middle School in 1940

图 38 黄乐德

抗日战争胜利后，1946 年秋广文中学重新开办。1948 年 4 月潍县解放后，学校很快开学。1949 年秋，黄乐德校长辞职，教工推选范其春为代理校长。图为黄乐德牧师

Picture 38 Huang Lede

After the victory against the Japanese aggression in the War of Resistance, Kwangwen Middle School began to resume its classes in the autumn of 1946. Soon after the liberation of Weihsien in April 1948, the school was reopened. In the autumn of 1949, Headmaster Huang Lede resigned and the faculty elected Fan Qichun as the acting headmaster. The picture shows Pastor Huang Lede

图 39 抗战胜利后，广文中学复学时全体师生合影

Picture 39 Faculty and students of Kwangwen Middle School when it was reopened after the victory of the war of against Japanese

第五节 中学的课程与学校生活
4.5 Curriculum and School Life in Middle Schools

早期的文华馆，以及文华中学、文美女中，除学习中西文化课程外，还增加了宗教学科和读经、祷告时间。广文中学建立后，在办学上，选聘齐鲁大学及其他名牌大学优秀毕业生和有经验、有能力的知名教师来校任教，狠抓教学质量，注重学生公共道德修养，确立了德、智、体、群四育并举及学用结合的办学宗旨，为学校制定了“互助、服务、牺牲”的校训，富有时代特色。20 世纪 30 年代，针对华北局势紧张的情况，为了增强学生体魄，广文中学还增加了军训课程，主要是对高中生进行军事训练。

In addition to the Chinese and Western academic courses, the students also studied religious subjects, read scriptures, and attended the religious services in the early years of Wenhua Academy, Wenhua Middle School and Wenmei Girls' Middle School. Kwangwen Middle School selected and recruited outstanding graduates from Shantung Christian University and other famous universities, as well as experienced, competent and reknown teachers who tried to foster a positive, supportive yet challenging classroom environment. Since the school took great pains to cultivate the public moral, it established the principles of moral, intellectual, physical and collective education. It also strove to teach the students turn the theoretical learning into everyday, practical actions. The school motto, thus, was formulated as "mutual assistance, service and sacrifice". In view of the tense situation in North China, Kwangwen Middle School also added some military training courses to strengthen students' physical health and fitness.

图 40 化学实验课
Picture 40 Chemistry experimental class

图 41 物理实验室
Picture 41 Physics laboratory

图 42 1933 年的全体教职员合影
Picture 42 Faculty in 1933

下列图片为 1933 年广文中学部分教职员照片，摘自 1933 年的《纪念特刊》。从广文中学的教员中，可以了解到学生们学的课程，包括：国文、历史、地理、生物学、算术、物理学、化学、卫生学、社会学、英文、艺术等，另外还有音乐、体育、图画等，从他们所学科目可以看出，办学中西合璧。

The following picture shows a number of teachers at Kwangwen Middle School in 1933, extracted from the Special Issue for the 50th Anniversary of Kwangwen Middle School in Weihsien, Shandong in 1933. The courses included Chinese, history, geography, biology, arithmetic, physics, chemistry, hygiene, sociology, English, art, music, sports, drawing and painting, to name a few. From the subjects offered, it can be seen that the school taught both Chinese and Western topics.

图 43 广文中学教职员（1）
Picture 43 Faculty of Kwangwen Middle School (1)

走近圣贤丛书

走近韩非子

丛书总主编 舒大刚

黄也平 著

◎ 在先秦诸子之中，韩非无疑是一个思想和精神的“另类”。作为法家的代表人物，他集前人的“法、术、势”政治思想之大成，为后世的帝王统治术做出了重大贡献。其犀利的思想，来源于他对人性的深刻洞察。他由“人性恶”出发，搭建起了自己的法家思想大厦，对我们今人认识现代社会和理解复杂的社会关系，又颇多启迪。

山东城市出版传媒集团·济南出版社

山东城市出版传媒集团·济南出版社

ISBN 978-7-5488-4082-4

9 787548 840824 >

定价：37.00元

图 44 广文中学教职员（2）
Picture 44 Faculty of Kwangwen Middle School (2)

图 45 广文中学教职员（3）
Picture 45 Faculty of Kwangwen Middle School (3)

图 46 广文中学教职员（4）
Picture 46 Faculty of Kwangwen Middle School (4)

图 47 广文中学教职员（5）
Picture 47 Faculty of Kwangwen Middle School (5)

英文教員
林惠卿

社會學教員
姚慈惠

圖畫教員
丁東齋

化學教員
余瑞徵

數理教員
段紹先

理化教員
林文幹

图 48 广文中学教职员（6）
Picture 48 Faculty of Kwangwen Middle School (6)

图 49 广文中学教职员（7）
Picture 49 Faculty of Kwangwen Middle School (7)

除了学习文化课，乐道院中学的学校生活也丰富多彩。下面一组照片，摘自 1933 年的《纪念特刊》，从留存的图片中可以看出，中学的学校生活有劳动、各种体育活动、趣味体育赛事、自行车赛、各种球队、运动会、演讲比赛、下乡布道等等。

The following photos are excerpted from the Special Issue for the 50th Anniversary of Kwangwen Middle School in Weihsien, Shandong in 1933. One can see that they had a vibrant, exciting school life, which included labor work (for example working on a farm to get some kind of hands-on-job experience), sports, speech competitions, and preaching the gospel in the countryside.

图 50 广文中学的课外生活（1）
Picture 50 After school life (1)

視工作如游戲

工罷歸來

國慶路賽車

图 51 广文中学的课外生活（2）
Picture 51 After school life (2)

試　路

紀念路慶成典禮

图 52 广文中学的课外生活（3）
Picture 52 After school life (3)

農　　　事

收　　　穫

種　　　植

图 53　广文中学的课外生活（4）
Picture 53 After school life (4)

图 54 广文中学的课外生活（5）
Picture 54 After school life (5)

足球

排球 ↓

↑ 籃球

图 55 广文中学的课外生活（6）

Picture 55 After school life (6)

網　　球　　隊

籃　　球　　隊

图 56　广文中学的课外生活（7）
Picture 56 After school life (7)

民國二十二年春全校演講會各組優勝紀念留影

民國二十二年春濰縣全縣小學聯合運動會本校附小優勝紀念

图 57 广文中学的课外生活（8）
Picture 57 After school life (8)

第六节　乐道院的高等教育——广文大学

4.6 Higher Education—Shantung Protestant University

伴随着20世纪初义和团运动席卷华北大地，包括乐道院在内的许多西方教会建筑设施被焚毁。运动结束后，传教士们对教会学校的性质、作用、地位等问题进行了思考。他们决定整合教会教育资源，提高高等教育水平，以期进一步促进宗教的传播和发展。

As the Boxer Rebellion swept across the northern regions of China in the early years of 20th century, many Western-style buildings, including the church in Courtyard of the Happy Way, were burned down. At the end of the war, the Western missionaries rethought and reevaluated the function and role of church schools. They maintained that in order to spread religion in China, it was necessary to establish higher education institutions.

1902年6月，青岛已开辟为商港，两年后胶济铁路也建成通车。潍县位于胶济铁路中段，很有发展前景。1904年，美国传教士狄考文在登州（治所在今烟台蓬莱市）创办的文会馆迁至潍县乐道院，与英国浸礼会在青州创办的广德书院大学部合并，取两所学校校名首字，建立了联合的高等教育学府——广文学堂（后改称广文大学，英文名称为“山东基督教共合大学”）。广文大学建制等同于美国哈佛大学，并沿用哈佛大学办学宗旨、教材和管理模式，其师资和设备在当时都是全国一流的，有文、理、工、化各科，仪器齐全、并有试验工厂，加之师生都是一时精英，为中国培养出了不少一流人才。所以美国人称其为“中国的哈佛”和“现代教育的温床”。1917年，广文大学在济南千佛山下购地600余亩，建立校舍，潍县广文大学、青州神道学院和济南共和医道学堂合并，成立齐鲁大学。1952年9月，齐鲁大学撤销，依据专业分别并入山东大学等相关大学。

In June 1902, Qingdao was established as a commercial port and the construction of the Jiaozhou-Ji'nan railway was completed two years later. Weihsien was right in the middle of this railway, which significantly facilitated its route to development. As a result, the Presbyterian Church in the USA and the English Baptist Missionary Society came to a crucial decision: They merged Tengchow College and Qingzhou Guangde Academy, moving their respective departments to the Courtyard of the Happy Way, which was eventually named "Shantung Protestant University". It was, in fact, an imitated version of Harvard University in its educational system as well as mission, textbooks and managerial method. At that time, it boasted the best teachers and highest quality equipment in the whole country. It offered a wide range of subjects, including literature, science, industry, and chemistry, to name a few. The university also possessed experimental factories. Its graduates were amongst the best in China. Accordingly, the Americans called it the "Harvard University of China" and the "hotbed of modern education". In 1917, Shantung Protestant University purchased more than forty hectares of land at the foot of Qianfo Mountain in Ji'nan to build a university campus. Shantung Protestant University, Qingzhou Theological Seminary, and Ji'nan Union Medical College merged to create what was called Shantung Christian University. In September 1952, Shantung Christian University was merged into Shandong University and other universities.

图 58 广文学堂（广文大学）第一任校长博尔根博士

Picture 58 Dr. Bergen, the first President of Shantung Protestant University

图 59 曾任广文大学代理校长的方伟廉（方法敛之兄）

Picture 59 William P. Chalfant (brother of F. H. Chalfant), former Acting President of Shantung Protestant University

图 60 原广文大学校长德位思，后任齐鲁大学总教务长

Picture 60 Dr. L. J. Davies, former President of Shantung Protestant University, and then General Dean of Shantung Christian University

图 61 广文大学主教学楼
Picture 61 Main Teaching Building of Shantung Protestant University

图 62 广文大学康伟楼(科学馆)
Picture 62 Science Hall in Shantung Protestant University

大楼共有 4 层，其中一、二层为物理、化学及生物实验室、仪器室和预备室，可见对实验的重视程度。广文大学仪器制造所的设备齐全，制造技术先进，教学仪器和设备不但数量多，而且种类齐全，全班学生可以两三人一组同时进行实验。

The science hall was a four-story building. The physical chemistry and biology laboratories, instrument and preparation rooms were located on the first and second floors. This shows the importance of this experiment. The instrument manufacturing institute of Shantung Protestant University possessed a complete set of equipment and highly-advanced manufacturing technology. Teaching instruments and equipment were not only large in number, but also complete in variety. A whole class, with two or three students in each group, could do a certain experiment at the same time.

广文大学的教师除外籍者外，其余多为登州文会馆的毕业生。学校课程，有道学、中国经学、算学、理化、博物等。学校名义上文、理分开，但实际上文理界限并不明显。学制为四年，个别的六年，供个别突出的学生进一步研究学习。在建校初期，除增添英文为选修课外，其余课程基本上和文会馆时一样。校内当时已设立了理化实验室、博物馆、天文台等。

In addition to foreign teachers, most of the teachers in Shantung Protestant University were graduates from Tengchow College. The school curriculum included religion, Chinese classics, arithmetic, physics, chemistry, natural science and so on. The school seemed to separate literature and science but, in fact, there were no clear, obvious boundaries. The school curriculum was four years, sometimes six years, for the outstanding students who had an extended study. In the early days of school establishment, except for the addition of English as an elective course, the rest of the courses were basically the same as those in the Tengchow College. At that time, the school had set up physical and chemical laboratories, museum and observatory.

附六年级课程表如下：

类别 / 年级	道学	中国经学	一般科学（算数、理论、博物）
一	天道溯源	书经 诗经 论语 诗文 策论	代数备旨
二	天路历程	礼记 书经 孟子 读诗文 作诗文	形学备旨 圆锥曲线
三	救吉之妙	礼记 诗经（重读） 学庸 读诗文 作诗文	八线备旨 测绘学 格物 （水、气、热、磁）地质学
四	天道溯源	左传 礼记 书经 读作诗赋文	量地学 航海学 格物（声、光、电）
五	圣 经	左传 礼记 读作诗赋文	代形合参 物理测算 化学 动植物学
六	心灵学 （心理学） 是非学（逻辑）	经易 讲系辞 读文作文	微积学 化学 辩质 天文揭要

图 63 广文大学的课程表（图表来源：《山东潍坊二中校志》）
Picture 63 Class schedule in Shantung Protestant University (courses include religion, Chinese classics, science, etc.)

自1905年有首届毕业生到1917年迁到济南为止，12年间，广文大学的毕业生共有433名。这些毕业学生，多数从事教员职业，其余的有牧师、布道员、经商者等。

From 1905, when the first students graduated from Shantung Protestant University till 1917 when it was relocated to Ji'nan, there was a total number of four hundred and thirty three graduates. Most of these graduates would end up working in the education sector, and the rest would make a living as pastors, evangelists, business people, and so on.

图64 广文大学毕业证书
Picture 64 Shantung Protestant University Diploma

第七节　广文大学西迁济南——齐鲁大学诞生

4.7 Shantung Protestant University Relocated to Ji'nan — Birth of Shantung Christian University

20世纪初，山东境内已有诸多教会学校，其中较为有名的包括美国基督教北长老会狄考文创办的文会馆、英国浸礼会库寿龄创办的青州广德书院等。1902年6月13日，浸礼会和长老会在青州召开会议，组成联合校董会，整合资源，共同建立山东基督教共合大学。该大学共分三部分，包括潍县的广文大学（文理科）、青州广德书院的神学班和师范班，济南的共合医道学堂。1907年，共合医道学堂在济南南新街购地建设新址及医院。1911年学校落成。6年后的1917年，潍县广文大学迁来济南，新校址开学，同时启用"齐鲁大学"作为中文校名。

At the dawn of the 20th century, there were many church schools in the province of Shandong, including Tengchow College, which was set up by Dr. Calvin Wilson Mateer from the Presbyterian Church in the USA, and Qingzhou Guangde Academy, founded by Samuel Couling from the English Baptist Missionary Society. On 13 June 1902, the representatives of the Baptist Missionary Society and the Presbyterian Church had a meeting in Qingzhou; the aim of this meeting was to form a joint school board, integrate resources, and establish a Christian university which basically was the combination of Shantung Protestant University (arts and science), Guangde Academy (theology) and Ji'nan Union Medical College (medicine and religion). In 1907, Union Medical College bought more land to build a new campus and hospital in the Nanxin Street, Ji'nan. The new campus was completed in 1911. Six years later, Shantung Protestant University was relocated to the new campus in Ji'nan and was named "Shantung Christian University" (Chinese name Cheeloo University).

1917年9月，齐鲁大学正式开学，设文理科、医科、神科。按照学校规定，文理科为4年制、医科为7年制。齐鲁大学全盛时期，老舍、钱穆、顾颉刚、栾调甫、马彦祥、吴金鼎、胡厚宣等学术名家先后在此执教，号称"华北第一学府"，和燕京大学并称"南齐北燕"。学校以医学院实力最强，坊间有"北协和、南湘雅、东齐鲁、西华西"之称。

In September 1917, Shantung Christian University officially opened, offering courses in arts, science, medicine and mythology. According to its curriculum, the arts and the science programs were four years each, and the medicine program would take seven years to complete. In the heyday of Shantung Christian University, Lao She, Qian Mu, Gu Jiegang, Luan Tiaofu, Ma Yanxiang, Wu Jinding, Hu Houxuan and other celebrated scholars taught there and it was unanimously acclaimed as "the number one university in North China". The renown Medical School of Shantung Christian University was, in particular, highly esteemed. It was rated as one of the top four medical universities in China.

教会学校的性质决定了宗教课程在课程设置中不可缺少。大多数中国教会大学在设立之初，皆重在文、理和神学学科的教育，最多再设个医科，此外，就是中国文学、英语、数学，以及历史及哲学课程。

The religious activities occupied a necessary position in Christian schools. At the beginning of the establishment of most Chinese Chrisian universities, the emphasis was on teaching liberal arts, science, theology and medicine. In addition, they also offered courses in Chinese literature, English language and literature, mathematics, history and philosophy. As for other professional disciplines, they were rarely or never presented.

中华人民共和国成立后，人民政权决心办好自己的教育。于是在 1951 年 1 月，由华东军政委员会教育部接管齐鲁大学，解聘所有外籍人员，至此中国人彻底收回了这所山东著名大学的教育主权。而作为一所教会大学，齐鲁大学的历史也走向了终点。

After the founding of New China, the People's Government was determined to run its own educational methods and programs. In January 1951, therefore, the Ministry of Education of East China Military and Political Commission took over Shantung Christian University, dismissing all foreign staff. For the first time, the acclaimed university in Shandong had a fully Chinese faculty and staff. The Shantung Christian University's life as a church university had come to an end.

1864年	登州：文会馆
1866年	青州：广德书院
1903年	青州：广德书院神学班和师范班仍在青州开课
	潍县:广德书院大学部与登州文会馆合并，组成“山东基督教共合大学”的文理科，取两校名首字曰“广文学堂（后改名为广文大学）”。
	济南：济南聂会东、青州武成献、邹平巴德顺所办的医校合并为共和医道学院
1917年	济南：三科合并，迁校济南，启用“齐鲁大学”校名

图 65 齐鲁大学的沿革图
Picture 65 History Chart of Shantung Christian University

图 66 齐鲁大学校门
Picture 66 Gate of Shantung Christian University

图 67 齐鲁大学校内鸟瞰
Picture 67 Aerial view of Shantung Christian University

图 68 在教室中上课的齐鲁大学学生
Picture 68 Students of Shantung Christian University having class

图 69 齐鲁大学校徽
Picture 69 Badge of Shantung Christian University

第五章　乐道院的医院

5 The Hospital in the Courtyard of the Happy Way

无论东方还是西方，任何宗教，大都以救助他人为善。传教士们漂洋过海来到中国，也将西方逐步开始现代化的医学理念带到这个古老的国家。那时正是清朝晚期，时局动乱不安，洋医生们竭力地救治前来看病的中国人。在那白色的祥和之地，没有肤色、种族、宗教、民族之分，只有医与患。正是这种妙手仁心，化解了两种文明之间尖锐的矛盾。

Whether in the East or the West, helping others is a shared virtue of all religions. When the missionaries first arrived in China, they brought modern Western medicine to this ancient country as well. It was in the late Qing Dynasty. The society was turbulent at the time. The foreign doctors tried their best to treat the local patients. In hospitals, there was not any sort of racial, religious, or national origin discrimination. The caring and kindness shown by the Western doctors and staff greatly contributed to resolve the differences between the two divergent civilizations.

潍县的医学近代化，也恰是从乐道院肇始。最初的诊所，因为需求的增长而逐步扩建为山东境内少有的大医院。从那时起，手术、X 光、输液，这些在当时还属先进的外科、内科检查等诊疗手段，就在这个山东城市扎根下来，并随着潍县现代医学的进步延续至今。

Similarly, in Weihsien, the modernization of the medical practice and health system also initiated in the Courtyard of the Happy Way. The early simple and small clinic gradually was expanded into a large, equipped hospital which was a rarity in Shandong Province. Since then, performing surgical operations, taking X-rays, and doing injections, which, at the time, were regarded as parts of the modern diagnosis and treatment methods, began to be used in hospitals in Weihsien.

乐道院的医院大致可分为三个时期：庚子赔款前（1900）为建院初期。此时期医院人员少，设备简陋，其规模略同诊所。1900 年以后至 1924 年医院大楼落成前，为该院发展时期。此时期仍以门诊为主，同时逐渐附设简易病房，部分病号可以住院。这时期男、女诊所分开。1925 年病房大楼（十字楼）落成后，为乐道院医院发展的第三个时期，医疗设施配备齐全，成为当时胶东一带有规模、现代化水平很高的综合性医院。

The life of the Courtyard hospital can be divided into three periods: the time before the Boxer Indemnity (1900) when the hospital was first built and began to offer medial service. During this period, the hospital was nothing more than a small clinic, with a limited number of staff members and basic, outdated equipment. The period from 1900 to 1924 was the second stage when a number of wards were added, so the patients could be hospitalized; the men's and women's clinics were separated, though. The time after the completion of the ward building (the Cross Building) in 1925 was the third stage. Equipped with a complete set of medical facilities and state-of-art equipment, it turned into a large, modern hospital in the east of Shandong Province at the time.

第一节　早期的乐道院医院
5.1 The Hospital in the Early Years

医院是乐道院的重要组成部分。自狄乐播 1881 年来潍县至 1889 年，美国北长老会先后差派 Horance R. Smith 等 5 位医生来潍县从事行医传教工作。

The hospital was an essential part of the Courtyard of the Happy Way. Since Robert M. Mateer came to Weihsien in 1881 to 1889, the North Presbyterian Church in the United States successively sent five doctors including Horance R. Smith to Weixian to engage in medical and missionary work.

早期的乐道院医院，只有部分中国人可以从事护理工作，医生全部为外国人。1913 年，该院逐渐有了中国籍医生，如杨秀山、罗友清、张同信、张学俭、韩炳南等。不过由于宗教原因，无论医生，还是护理人员，均为教会人员。此外，医院的医疗水平也在日益提高。据记载，到 1918 年时，即能做白内障摘除术、全眼球摘除术、截肢术、碎胎术、胸骨切除术、乳腺癌切除术、食道狭窄扩张术、虹膜切除术、乳窦手术等。

In the early days of the hospital, only a small number of nurses were selected from the local people, whereas all the doctors were foreigners. Gradually some Chinese doctors began to work in the hospital in 1913, including Yang Xiushan, Luo Youqing, Zhang Tongxin, Zhang Xuejian, and Han Bingnan, to name but a few. Due to some religious reasons, all doctors and nurses were the church members. The hospital continually improved and expanded its medical services. Records show that by 1918 the following surgical operations could be performed: cataract extraction, total eyeball extirpation, amputation, fatal shredding, sternoctomy, breast cancer resection, esophageal stenosis dilatation, iridectomy, and breast sinus surgery.

民国初年，乐道院医院发展迅速，门诊量每年达 1 万余人次，与之对应的是，医院的护理力量极为不足，除露丝・A・布兰克护士外，无其他专职护理人员，大多由一些被称之为“苦力女”的勤杂人员担任。针对这一情况，乐道院医院于 1918 年春自办护士学校一所，专门培训护理人员。护士学校创办之初，男女生均收，半工半读，学制四年。任课教师多为本院大夫与护士长。学员毕业后即留院成为正式护士。

In the early years of the Republic of China, the hospital developed rapidly, with more than ten thousand outpatients per year. However, there was a shortage of trained nurses. Apart from Ruth A. Blank, there were no other professional nurses in the hospital. Many of the nurses were actually general workers. In view of this situation, the hospital opened its own nursing school in the spring of 1918. At the beginning, it offered a four-year, part-time program for both men and women. Most of the teachers were the doctors and the head nurses of the hospital. After graduation, the students would work as professional nurses in the hospital.

图 1 乐道院早期即将启用的外科病房
Picture 1 Early surgical wards of the hospital

图 2 医生检查女病人，外间女病人候诊
Picture 2 Female patients

图 3 乐道院护士楼

Picture 3 Nursing building of the hospital

图 4 乐道院医院化验室

Picture 4 Laboratory of the hospital

图 5 当时的护士学校教学楼（位于现在的潍坊人民医院西侧宿舍院内）

Picture 5 Teaching building of nursing school

第二节　1925 年“十字楼”落成后的乐道院医院

5.2 The Hospital after the Completion of the Cross Building in 1925

尽管在庚子事变后，乐道院重建时，医院获得了很大发展，但医院条件依然很差。乐道院当时的住院病房普遍房屋低矮，光线不足，通风不良，而且只有病床 40 张；病人多时，虽然能够加至 70 张，但每间病房设两张病床后，就显得十分拥挤。

Although it had made great progress through reconstruction after the Siege of the International Legations, the hospital was still in a very poor condition. At that time, the inpatient wards were generally ordinary houses with insufficient lighting and poor ventilation, with only forty beds available. Although the number of available beds could be increased to around seventy in peak hours, which means each ward had two beds, it was still very crowded and inconvenient for patients.

为满足日益增多的病患需求，美籍医生梅仁德决心扩大医院规模。1923 年，梅仁德医生专程返回美国，为医院筹集扩建资金。第二年，乐道院医院大楼开始动工，由中国人张同信（张执符）主持建造事务。这栋大楼共有四层，建筑面积 2461 平方米。因楼呈“十字架”形，故而人称“十字楼”。

In order to meet the needs of the rising number of the patients, E. E. Murray, an American doctor, decided to expand the the hospital. In 1923, he travelled to the United States to raise funds for his ambitious project. In the following year, under the supervision of Zhang Tongxin, the construction of a new building began. It was a four-storied building, with a total area of 2461 square meters. Since it looked like a “cross”, it was called the “Cross Building”.

1925 年，大楼建成，乐道院医院举办新大楼落成典礼，并正式改名为“潍县基督教医院”。社会名流百余人前来祝贺，并合影留念。病房大楼可容 120 张床位，设有暖气、X 光室、化验室、设备较齐的手术室，人员已超过 80 人。这时的乐道院医院已成为胶东一带规模大、档次高的医院，远近前来就诊者日增。

In 1925, upon the completion of building, it was renamed as Weihsien Christian Hospital. More than a hundred celebrities attended the opening ceremony. It had one hundred and twenty beds, a heating system, an X-ray room, a laboratory and a well-equipped operating room with over eighty personnel. It had turned into a large, advanced hospital in the east of Shandong. Therefore, the number of hospital patients, who came from far and near, increased day by day.

民国年间，“十字楼”总体布局是以二楼为内科、妇产科病房，三楼为小儿科、外科病房。另设有手术室、X 光室、化验室。依托较为先进的技术，乐道院医院已经能够实施复杂的腹部手术，如肾脏、肠穿孔、肠梗阻等手术。

In the period of the Republic of China, the internal medicine, obstetrics and gynaecology wards were on the second floor, and pediatrics and surgical wards on the third floor. There were also operating rooms, X-ray room, and clinical laboratory. Equipped with advanced technology, the hospital could carry out complex abdominal surgeries, such as operations for kidney, intestinal perforation, as well as intestinal obstruction.

由于“十字楼”落成后，病床不再短缺，故而不再实行男女分院，甚至当时病房还分特等、二等、三等，不同等级收费也不同，特等病房每天收住院费 5 块大洋、陪人费 2 块大洋。

As there were enough beds after the Cross Building was completed, the male and female patients were no longer needed to be separated. At the time, the wards were divided into three different classes, namely, special, second and third, so the admission fees were different. The admission fee of the special ward was five silver dollars per day, and the accompanying fee was two silver dollars.

潍县基督教医院鼎盛时期，有美籍外科医生梅仁德、内科医生章和鸣，护士长露斯・A・布兰克，护士梅马大，还有几位中国医生。然而，中外医生之间的不平等，使得医院内部矛盾重重，加上派系冲突，最终导致了 1929 年“风潮事件”爆发，直接导致医院停业半年之久。直到次年秋天，医院才恢复工作，美籍医生梅仁德出任院长。

In the heyday of Weihsien Christian Hospital, the following people worked there: E. E. Murray, an American surgeon, Zhang Heming, physician, Ruth A. Blank, head nurse, Martha Mei, nurse, and several Chinese doctors. However, the inequality between Chinese and foreign doctors caused a lot of problems. It, coupled with faction conflicts, eventually led to the outbreak of the 1929 “storm incident”, which led to the closure of the hospital for half a year. It was not until the following autumn that it resumed its services, with Doctor E. E. Murray as the president of the hospital.

图 6 1946 年潍县基督教医院全体职工合影
Picture 6 Staff of Weihsien Christian Hospital, 1946

第六章　乐道院的布道活动

6 Preaching Activities in the Courtyard of the Happy Way

1860年后，基督教新教开始大规模进入山东，美国北长老会和英国浸礼会等是第一批进入山东的新教差会。据20世纪20年代基督教会在全国进行的统计，山东有布道区1330个，位居全国第一。

As early as 1860, a large number of protestant missionaries began to enter Shandong Province. The first missionary societies in Shandong were the Presbyterian Church in the USA, and the English Baptist Missionary Society. According to the statistics released in the 1920s, there were around 1,330 Christian parishes in Shandong, which made it the first in the whole country.

从组织形式上看，山东的基督教新教差会，大都分大区教会、县区教会和布道所等几个层次。大区教会是新教差会在一个较大区域内进行各种传教活动的中心，也是该区域内传教活动的大本营，一般都设有直接开展布道活动的教堂，还有教会办的学校、医院、药房以及培养中国布道人员的机构。

In terms of the organization, most protestant missionary societies located in Shandong were divided into three levels: regional churches, county churches, and preaching houses. A regional church was the place for performing various preaching activities in a larger area, and also the missionary center of the area. A regional church generally included a church, a school, a hospital, a pharmacy and a specific organization for training Chinese preachers.

在山东势力最大的美国长老会，在全省设立了9个传教大区，分区传教。

The Presbyterian Church in the USA, which was the most influential in Shandong, had established nine regional churches around the province.

图 1　始建于 1909 年的青州基督教堂（又称“拜主圣堂”）
Picture 1 Qingzhou Christian Church founded in 1909

图 2　始建于 1922 年的潍城区基督教堂（又称“北宫教堂”）
Picture 2 Weicheng Christian Church (Beigong Church) founded in 1922

第一节 乐道院的宗教活动和布道方式
6.1 Religious Activities and Preaching

美国基督教北长老会在潍县创办乐道院，目的是传教。因此，乐道院在潍县的所有活动中，传播基督教的布道活动理所当然占有重要位置。狄乐播建起乐道院后，这里便成为了潍县当地的传教中心，以及西方教会最为重要的宗教活动基地之一。乐道院设有教堂，每星期日在乐道院的大教堂里，教徒即望道者们诵经、唱诗，听传教士布道。此外，每逢基督教的节日，教徒们也会齐聚教堂进行庆祝。但早期来教堂做礼拜的人很少，教徒多为乐道院学校的师生和医护人员。

In order to preach the Gospel and invite people to church, the Presbyterian Church in the United States of America established the Courtyard of the Happy Way in the city of Weihsien. Therefore, amongst all the activities these missionaries performed, preaching the Gospel was the most fundamental task and objective. After the establishment of the Courtyard, it turned into a kind of missionary center in Weihsien, and without any doubt one of the most important bases for Western missionaries in China. Every Sunday, the Christians gathered in a chapel in the Courtyard to read scriptures, sing palms and listen to sermons. On every Christian festival, they would gathered to celebrate and perform religious activities. But in the beginning, only few people went to the church, mostly teachers, students and medical staff of the Courtyard.

教堂布道是乐道院布道活动的中心内容。除此之外，还组织专门的乡村旅行布道。旅行布道是和教堂布道相辅相成的重要手段。早期的旅行布道吸引了一定数量的农民对基督教产生兴趣，造就了最初的问道者、望道者和教徒，为新教教会建立乡村教会奠定了基础。

Delivering sermons in the church was the essential part of the preaching activity in the Courtyard. In addition, the missionaries would travel to rural areas, preach the Gospel and invite the people to join their faith. Traveling preachers were critical element of the church's mission; they succeeded in drawing the attention of a number of farmers who would eventually convert to Christianity. This eventually led to the foundation of protestant churches in the rural areas.

乐道院推动布道活动的另一个重要途径就是通过乐道院学校、医院等世俗事务的开展来扩大教会的影响。

Another decisive scheme to spread religion was to increase the influence of church through developing such institutes as school and hospital.

图 3 乐道院内的教堂（礼拜堂）
Picture 3 Church (Chapel) in the Courtyard of the Happy Way

1904年，胶济铁路全线通车后，山东各城市之间的交通线更为密集、方便。乐道院也成为昌潍一带基督教的传播中心，它统辖潍县、昌乐、安丘、寿光、昌邑、广饶、博兴、诸城、平度、临朐、饮马镇等十多个教区，大多教区建有教堂，并配有专职牧师。

In 1904, the construction of the Jiaozhou - Ji'nan railway revolutionized the transportation system in the province of Shandong. It helped to transfer large number of people and goods in a much shorter amount of time. The Courtyard was the hub for spreading Christianity in Weihsien, ruling more than ten parishes, including Weihsien, Changle, Anqiu, Shouguang, Changyi, Guangrao, Bohsing, Zhucheng, Pingdu, Linqu, and Yinma Town. Most of the parishes had built churches and had full-time priests.

第二节　教会生活
6.2 Church Life

按照美国基督教长老会的规定，乐道院内所有人员必须“敬神”，过宗教生活。乐道院内对基督教的有关节日——圣诞节、复活节、感恩节等极为重视，教徒必须参加。另外，星期天上午要举行礼拜，每日早晨举行小礼拜，晚睡前默祷等。平时的宗教课由教会牧师主讲。举行宗教仪式时，也有牧师主持讲经、祈祷或唱赞美诗。每日三餐，院内人员须唱谢饭歌。

According to the regulations of the Presbyterian Church, all members of the Courtyard shall attend religious services. Christmas, Easter, thanksgiving and other Christian festivals were highly valued in the Courtyard and the believers were required to attend the religious rituals and activities. Every Sunday morning, they were expected to go to church to listen to the sermon; they were instructed to worship every morning after they got off the bed, and pray in silence every evening before going to bed. The religious classes were usually run by the priests. Similarly, during the religious ceremonies and rituals, these priests delivered lectures, led the service or sang hymns. The Courtyard's staff sang songs of gratitude to God before meals.

图 4　在乐道院教堂内做礼拜的中外基督徒
Picture 4 Chinese and foreign Christians worshiping together in the Courtyard church

第三节　多样化的传教方式

6.3 Various Missionary Methods

潍县乐道院重建以后对自身的传教政策也作了一些调整。开始注重培养和使用中国布道人员，1905 年广文大学毕业的学生中就有孙吉祥、葛维常在潍县长老会从事传教事业。在传教方式上，集中力量大力发展教育、医疗等世俗活动。

After the reconstruction, the Courtyard missionary made some changes in their strategic policy. They began to focus on training Chinese missionaries. Sun Jixiang and Ge Weichang, who graduated from Shantung Protestant University in 1905, were engaged in missionary work at the Presbyterian Church of Wenhsien. Their efforts were also concentrated on developing education and medicine.

在教育方面，增大西学课程在教学中的比例，扩大办学规模，通过传播西方文化知识，消除传教的文化障碍。

In schools, on the other hand, a larger number of Western courses were taught. The schools were expanded, and the Western culture was introduced to China, therefore the cultural barriers were eliminated.

在医疗方面，将诊所改为医院，扩大规模，增加设备等，将医疗作为推动传教事业的重要手段。乐道院的门诊、病房内都设有布道员，他们见缝插针，不失时机地向病人讲经传道，千方百计地争取病人及家属信教并成为教徒。乐道院的医院还利用节假日派护士“送教下乡”，以此拓展基督教的活动空间，扩大教会的影响力。

In order to enhance the medical service, the clinic was expanded into a much larger, better equipped hospital. This helped the medical care became an important means to spread Christianity and achieve the missionary objectives. The missionaries, thus, would be sent to the outpatient clinics and wards to preach the Gospel to the patients. On holidays, the Courtyard hospital also sent its nurses to the countryside to promote their missionary activities.

图 5　乐道院的学生布道团下乡布道。旅行布道是和教堂布道相辅相成的重要手段
Picture 5 Students preaching team went to the countryside

图 6 乐道院学校师生欢送伯特利布道团
Picture 6 Teachers and students of the Courtyard's school biding farewell to the Bethel preaching team

图 7 乐道院学校建立的基督徒少年服务团
Picture 7 Christian Youth Service Group of the Courtyard

第七章　从乐道院走出的杰出人才

7 Outstanding People from the Courtyard of the Happy Way

清朝同治年间，中国开始兴起洋务教育改革，这是社会各界在鸦片战争后，经过二十多年的争辩、探讨推动的一场洋务教育运动。它要求培养中学、西学兼通的人才，从而掌握“制器之法”，培养“制器之人”，在中国有了外语人才、工业技术人才和军事人才后，才具有竞争力。

In the period of Emperor Tongzhi (1862-1874), after more than twenty years of debate since the Opium War, China finally initiated a sort of reform of its education system. The objective was to train mechanical engineers with an excellent knowledge of Chinese and Western languages. The idea was that in order to compete with powerful Western countries, China needed skilled experts who possessed a good knowledge of foreign languages, industrial technology and military principles.

以乐道院为代表的西方传教士建立的机构，在传教的同时，也带来了西方现代的教育理念和教育内容，开创了潍坊现代学校教育、女子教育和大学教育的先河，客观上打开了学习西方科学技术的窗口，培养了大批掌握现代科学技术的新型人才。那些在乐道院学习和工作的中国人，开阔了视野，接受了新鲜事物，思想得到了解放，他们迅速地成长起来，并成为了潍县的中坚力量。可以说，他们是潍县近代知识分子队伍中的杰出代表，也是潍县改变自己的新驱动力。许多学生毕业后成为教育界、科学界和工商界等社会各界卓有建树的专家学者和实业家，成为推动社会和经济发展的重要力量，对近代中国社会的转型与发展产生了深远的影响。

The institutions established by the Western missionaries introduced modern Western educational methods and knowledge to China, pioneered modern education, women’s rights to education and higher education in Weifang; moreover, they paved the way by teaching modern science, training a considerably large number of professionals who acquired ample knowledge of modern practices and technologies. The Chinese students who graduated from the Courtyard’s schools or worked in the Courtyard learned new ideas and obtained an unprecedented view about life and the world. They, therefore, became an important driving force in the transition of Weihsien as a modern city. After graduation, many of the students became distinguished experts, scholars and industrialists in education, science and business sectors. As a key element in promoting social and economic reforms and sustainable development, they made great contribution to the transformation and modernization of China.

一、华丰机器厂创办人滕虎忱

7.1 Teng Huchen, Founder of Huafeng Machine Factory

滕虎忱 (1883 ~ 1958) 原名景云，字虎忱，安丘县滕家庄子人，著名民族企业家。1917 年任职于乐道院医院和文华中学开办的理化制造所，负责发电机、蒸汽机、水塔等设备的维修。1920 年开办华丰机器厂，经过多年发展，生产的柴油发动机、救火机、织布机、弹花机、轧花机、水车等产品行销全国。1948 年潍县解放后，在潍县原华丰机器厂二厂旧址重建厂房，添置设备，生产弹花机、轧花机、榨油机、12 马力柴油机等。1952 年 5 月华东军政委员会任命他为潍坊市人民政府委员。1954 年 8 月被选为第一届全国人民代表大会代表。1955 年 3 月被选为山东省人民委员会委员。同年，“华丰”实行公私合营，他继续担任经理。

Teng Huchen (1883-1958), a famous Chines entrepreneur, from the Teng Village in Anqiu County, Weihsien. In 1917, he worked in the Courtyard hospital and the physical as well as the chemical manufacturing office of Wenhua Middle School; he was in charge of the maintenance and repair department which dealt with generators, steam engines and water towers. In 1920, he established Huafeng Machinery Factory. It manufactured such products as diesel engines, fire extinguishers, weaving machines, stretching machines, ginning machines and waterwheel, which were sold all over the country. After the liberation of Weihsien in 1948, the factory was rebuilt at the former site of the second factory of Weihsien Huafeng Machinery Factory, adding the required machinery to manufacture stretching machines, ginning machines, oil-press machines, 12-horsepower diesel engines, an so on. In May 1952, East China Military and Political Commission appointed him as the committee member of Weifang Municipal People's Government. In August 1954, he was elected as the representative of the first National People's Congress. In March 1955, he was elected as the member of Shandong Provincial People's Committee. In the same year, after Huafeng implemented what was called the public-private partnership, he continued to serve as the manager of the factory.

图 1 滕虎忱

Picture 1 Teng Huchen

二、辛亥革命时期著名革命人士邓天乙

7.2 Deng Tianyi, Revolutionary during the 1911 Revolution

邓天乙 (1886 ~ 1930) 原名邓峻德，山东广饶县人，辛亥革命时期著名革命人士。14 岁入登州文会馆求学。按照《广文校谱》记载，邓天乙在文会馆被编入选学班，该班“招考汉文明通年庚老大者选学数门学科”，后随文会馆迁来潍县广文学堂（广文大学）学习，1904 年离开广文学堂到安丘德育学堂任教习。1907 年加入中国同盟会，积极投身于反帝爱国斗争。1912 年，邓天乙被选为中华民国第一届国会众议院候补议员、山东省议会议员。后追随孙中山先生，积极参与二次革命、护国运动和护法运动。孙中山逝世后，邓天乙对新军阀抛弃“三大政策”的行为十分鄙夷和不满，返济南闲居。1930 年，被国民党“山东省政府”主席韩复榘杀害于济南。

图 2 邓天乙

Picture 2 Deng Tianyi

Deng Tianyi (1886-1930) was born in Guangrao County, Shandong Province. He was a famous revolutionary during the 1911 Revolution. At the age of 14, he was registered in Tengchow College; he was transferred to Shantung Protestant University in Weihsien, and later he went to teach in Anqiu Deyu School. In 1907, he joined the Chinese League and actively participated in the anti-imperialist and patriotic movement. In 1912, Deng Tianyi was elected as the alternate member of the first House of Representatives of the Republic of China as well as the member of Shandong Provincial Assembly. Later, following Mr. Sun Yat-sen, he also actively participated in the Second Revolution, the Nation Protection Movement and the Law Protection Movement. After Sun Yat-sen's death, Deng returned to Ji'nan and lived in idleness because he did not agree with the new warlord's practices. In 1930, he was killed by Han Fuju, the chairman of the Kuomintang Government of Shandong Province, in Ji'nan.

三、著名实业家、教育家尹焕斋

7.3 Yin Huanzhai, Industrialist and Educator

尹焕斋（1882 ~ 1938），山东潍县人，毕业于广文大学。1925 年，文华中学原校长卫礼士博士调任上海，由他接任校长。1931 年文华中学、文美女子中学和培基小学合并建立广文中学，尹焕斋离职。尹焕斋是潍县当地著名的实业家，他创办的信丰染印公司是当时山东印染业之首，并与滕虎忱共同创办华丰机器厂。

Yin Huanzhai (1882-1938) , a Weihsien native, graduated from Shantung Protestant University. In 1925, Ralph C.Wells, the former president of Wenhua Middle School, was transferred to Shanghai and his position was given to Yin. In 1931, after Wenhua Middle School, Wenmei Girls' Middle School and Peiji Primary School merged to establish a new school called Kwangwen Middle School, he left his position. Yin Huanzhai was a famous industrialist in Weihsien. He founded Xinfeng Printing Company, which was rated as the best in Shandong printing and dyeing industry at the time; he and Teng Huchen were also the founders of Huafeng Machinery Factory.

图 3 尹焕斋
Picture 3 Yin Huanzhai

四、进步人士、教育家徐焕滋

7.4 Xu Huanzi, Progressive Educator

徐焕滋（1901 ~ 1991），曾就读于燕京大学，1927 年应邀前来潍县担任文美女子中学校长。她是文美女子中学的第三任校长，任期至 1930 年。在担任校长期间，她曾经资助部分进步青年寻找和加入中国共产党。

Xu Huanzi (1901-1991) , a Yenching University graduate, served as the principal of Wenmei Girls' Middle School in 1927. She was the third principal of the school and her office term ended in 1930. During her tenure as the principal, she funded some progressive youth to find and join the Communist Party of China.

图 4 徐焕滋
Picture 4 Xu Huanzi

五、教育家崔德润

7.5 Cui Derun, Educator

崔德润（1902 ~ 1994），名鸿泽，以字行。1902 年生，山东潍县人。1914 年小学毕业后考入潍县乐道院文华学校，1919 年考入济南齐鲁大学文理学院。毕业后留校成为助教。广文中学组建后，崔德润受校董事会推举，出任校长一职。

Cui Derun (1902-1994) , a Weihsien native, was born in 1902. After graduating from primary school in 1914, he was admitted to Wenhua School in the Courtyard of the Happy Way; in 1919 he enrolled in the School of Arts and Sciences in Shantung Christian University. After graduation, he worked in the same university as a teaching assistant. After the establishment of Kwangwen Middle School, Cui Derun was elected to serve as the principal by the school's board of directors.

图 5 崔德润（前排居中者），本图片为 1933 年春广文中学校执行委员会合影
Picture 5 Executive Committee of Kwangwen Middle School in the spring of 1933 (Cui Derun: front, middle)

六、名医张同信

7.6 Zhang Tongxin, Doctor

张同信（1894 ~ 1967），又名执符，名医，山东潍县人。1914年毕业于齐鲁大学医学院，同年进潍县教会乐道院医院任医师，后升任主治医师、院长。抗战胜利后，被聘为青岛信义会医院董事会董事兼名誉院长。中华人民共和国成立后，信义会医院改为青岛医院，仍任院长。

Zhang Tongxin (1894-1967) was a famous doctor from Weihsien. He graduated from the Medical College of Shantung Christian University in 1914. In the same year, he began to work as a physician in the Courtyard of the Happy Way Hospital, later, he was promoted to the position of attending physician and dean. After the WWII, he was appointed as the Honorary President and Director of the Board of Directors of Qingdao Lutheran Church Hospital. After the founding of the people's Republic of China, Lutheran Church Hospital was renamed Qingdao Hospital where he still served as the President.

图 6　张同信
Picture 6 Zhang Tongxin

七、教育家、全国政协委员张雪岩

7.7 Zhang Xueyan, Educator and Member of the CPPCC National Committee

张雪岩（1893 ~ 1950），山东潍县人，曾就读于乐道院文华中学，大革命时参加北伐，1934年创办《田家》半月刊。1938年留学加拿大，获法学博士学位。曾任齐鲁大学社会学系主任、教授，九三学社理事、常务理事，任燕京大学、北平师范大学教授。参加第一届全国政协会议，当选为全国政协委员，并成为《共同纲领草案》整理委员会委员。1949年10月1日，参加了开国大典。

Zhang Xueyan (1893-1950), a Weihsien native, studied at Wenhua Middle School. He participated in the Northern Expedition during the Great Revolution. He was the founder of the semi-monthly Farming Family Journal in 1934. He went to study in Canada in 1938, and obtained a doctoral degree in laws. He was also the director of and a professor in the Sociology Department of Shantung Christian University, the director and executive director of Jiusan Society, and a professor in Yenching University and Beiping Normal University. He participated in the first session of the National Committee of the Chinese People's Political Consultative Conference, was elected as a member of the Chinese People's Political Consultative Conference, and a member of the Common Program Draft edition committee. On October 1, 1949, he attended the Ceremony of Founding of the PRC.

图 7　张雪岩
Picture 7 Zhang Xueyan

八、著名考古学家吴金鼎

7.8 Wu Jinding, Archaeologist

吴金鼎（1901 ~ 1948），山东安丘人，著名考古学家。曾就读于文华中学和齐鲁大学。1930 年到当时的国民党政府的“中央研究院历史语言研究所”考古组任职。其间，参加了河南安阳殷墟、山东章丘城子崖、安阳后岗等著名遗址的发掘。1933 年赴英国留学，1937 年获博士学位。回国后，先后在云南、四川从事考古发掘和研究工作。抗日战争胜利后，任齐鲁大学训导长、文学院院长、国学研究所主任和图书馆主任等职。

Wu Jinding (1901-1948), from Anqiu, Weihsien, was a famous archaeologist. He studied at Wenhua Middle School and Shantung Christian University. In 1930, he worked in the archaeology group of the Institute of History and Language, Academia Sinica of the Kuomintang government. Meanwhile, he participated in the excavation of famous sites such as Yin Dynasty Ruins and Hougang relics in Anyang, Henan Province, and Chengziya relics in Zhangqiu District, Shandong Province. In 1933, he went to study in England and graduated with a doctoral degree in 1937. After returning to China, he was successively engaged in archaeological excavation and research in Yunnan and Sichuan. After the WWII, he served as the dean of students, dean of School of Arts, director of the Institute of Traditional Chinese Studies and director of the library in Shantung Christian University.

图 8 吴金鼎

Picture 8 Wu Jinding

九、著名胸外科专家张纪正

7.9 Zhang Jizheng, Thoracic Surgery Expert

张纪正（1905 ~ 1984），山东潍县人，曾就读于文华中学，著名胸外科专家。1928 年入北京协和医学院学医，获博士学位。1931 年至 1937 年在协和医学院担任院医师、副教授。曾在 1933 年长城喜峰口等地从事抗日救护工作。1940 年任协和医学院外科主任，著述颇多，在医学界德高望重。1941 年成功地进行了我国（也是亚洲）首例“左全肺切除术”，成为中国医学史上第一位切除左全肺获得成功的医生，被誉为“亚洲第一刀”。

Zhang Jizheng (1905-1984), from Weihsien, and a Wenhua Middle School graduate, was known for his expertise in performing thoracic surgery. He studied medicine in Peking Union Medical College in 1928 and graduated with a doctoral degree. From 1931 to 1937, he served as a physician and associate professor in the Union Medical College. In 1933, he was engaged in anti-Japanese activities in Xifengkou of the Great Wall and other places. In 1940, he served as the director of the Department of Surgery of Union Medical College. He wrote many books and was highly regarded in the medical field. In 1941, he successfully performed the first left pneumonectomy in China (and in Asia), becoming the first doctor in the history of Chinese medicine who successfully removed the left lung, known as “the First Knife in Asia”.

图 9 张纪正

Picture 9 Zhang Jizheng

十、杰出医疗专家魏一斋

7.10 Wei Yizhai, Medical Expert

魏一斋（1906 ~ 1975），山东寿光人，医疗行业杰出人物。1927 年入文华中学读书。1934 年毕业于齐鲁大学医学院，1936 年进北平协和医院深造，结业后留任妇产科医师。1938 年 9 月，经王梓木、钱之光介绍，他到西安八路军办事处。在办事处的协助下，于当月 16 日到达延安。在延安期间，历任中央卫生部直属卫生所医务主任，八路军医院医务主任，中央医院医务主任、院长，并一直兼任中央医科大学教师和中央主要领导人的保健大夫。1941 年 1 月加入中国共产党。他医学知识渊博，医术精湛，在卫生医学事业中做出卓越贡献，1940 年受到毛泽东、周恩来、朱德等中央领导人的题词勉励。中华人民共和国成立后，他先后任山东大学医学院院长兼青岛市卫生局局长、卫生部医学教育司副司长、中华医学会妇产科学会副主任委员等职。

Wei Yizhai (1906-1975), from Shouguang, Weifang, was an outstanding medical expert. In 1927, he enrolled in Wenhua middle school. He graduated from the Medical College of Shantung Christian University in 1934. In 1936, he went to Peking Union Medical College to continue his studies. After graduation, he worked as an obstetrician and gynaecologist. In September 1938, Wang Zimu and Qian Zhiguang recommended him to serve in the Xi'an Eighth Route Army Office. Later, he was transferred to Yan'an. During his time in Yan'an, he served as the medical director of the health center, which was directly supervised by the Ministry of Health. He later worked as the medical director of the Eighth Route Army Hospital, and the medical director and the dean of the Central Hospital; He had also been serving as a health care doctor for the teachers of Central Medical University and the central directors. In January 1941, he joined the CPC. In 1940, because of his outstanding contributions to medicine, he was commended by Mao Zedong, Zhou Enlai, Zhu De and other officials. After the founding of the People's Republic of China, he served as dean of Medical School of Shandong University, director of Qingdao Municipal Health Bureau, deputy director of the Medical Education Department of the Central Ministry of Health, and deputy director of the Obstetrics and Gynecology Association of Chinese Medical Association.

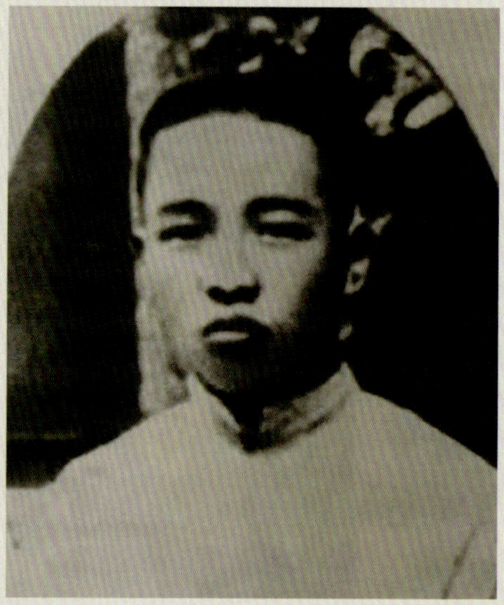

图 10　魏一斋
Picture 10 Wei Yizhai

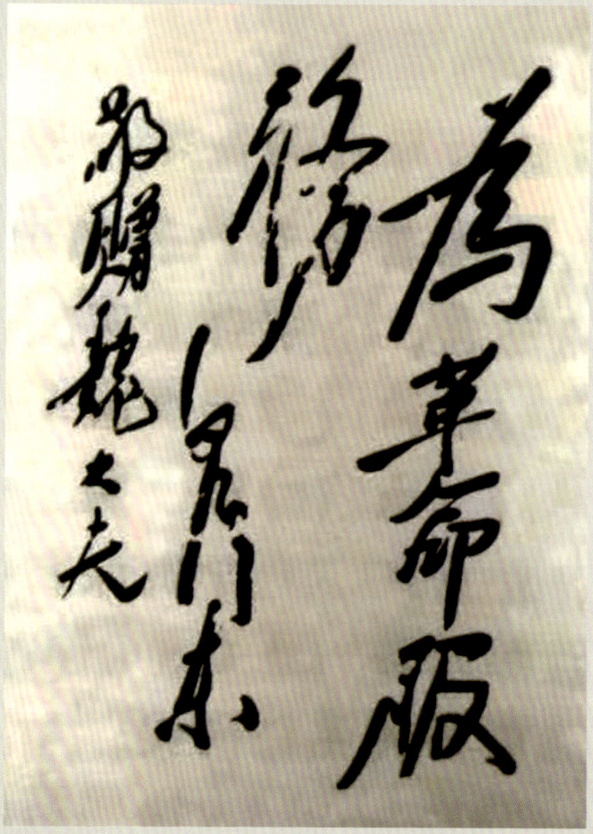

图 11　毛泽东同志为魏一斋的题词
Picture 11 Mao Zedong's inscription for Wei Yizhai

十一、教育家、科学家、山东省原副省长刘先志

7.11 Liu Xianzhi, Educator, Scientist and Former Vice Governor of Shandong Province

刘先志（1906 ~ 1990），山东高密人，我国杰出教育家、科学家，早年就读于文华中学，曾先后任山东工学院教授、教务长、副院长、山东省工业厅副厅长、山东省副省长、山东省政协副主席等职。刘先志长期从事力学教学、研究和教学组织工作。在固体力学、流体力学、一般力学、振动力学、传热学、应用数学和机械工程等许多领域中都进行过研究工作，并做出重要贡献。

Liu Xianzhi (1906-1990), from Gaomi, Weifang, was an outstanding educator and scientist in China. He studied in Wenhua Middle School, and served as a professor, academic dean, and deputy dean of Shandong Institute of Technology, deputy director of Shandong Provincial Department of Industry, vice governor of Shandong Province, and vice chairman of Shandong CPPCC. Liu Xianzhi was a great mechanics teacher and a studious researcher. He conducted research work and made great contribution to solid mechanics, fluid mechanics, general mechanics, vibration mechanics, heat transfer, applied mathematics and mechanical engineering.

图 12 刘先志
Picture 12 Liu Xianzhi

十二、著名艺术家于希宁

7.12 Yu Xi'ning, Artist

于希宁（1913 ~ 2007），山东潍县人，著名艺术家。曾就读于广文中学，1936 年毕业于上海新华美专，受业于黄宾虹、潘天寿、俞剑华等。毕业后从事艺术教育，曾在山东大学、山东师范学院、山东艺术学院任职，曾任美协山东分会副主席、主席、名誉主席，山东艺术学院名誉院长，山东省美术家协会名誉主席，山东省文联名誉主席，山东画院院长。

Yu Xi'ning (1913-2007), from Weihsien, was a famous artist. He went to Kwangwen Middle School and graduated from Shanghai Xinhua Arts College in 1936. He worked in Shandong University, Shandong Normal University, and Shandong Art College. He was the vice chairman, chairman, and honorary chairman in the Shandong Branch of Art Association, the honorary president of Shandong Art College, the honorary chairman of Shandong Artists Association, the honorary chairman of Shandong Federation of Literature and Art, and the president of Shandong Academy of Painting.

图 13 于希宁
Picture 13 Yu Xi'ning

除以上列举的几位杰出人才外，在乐道院学习和工作并走向全国的名人还有：

中国共产党早期革命家、曾担任过闽浙赣省苏维埃政府文化部长的张眺；

同盟会会员、曾任鲁东革命军支队司令的张同普；

潍县名医、曾任青岛公安医院院长的张众航；

中国共产党早期革命者、1949年后曾任潍坊市建设局代理局长的张同俊；

全国著名外科专家、医疗教育家张同和；

革命家、曾任全国总工会副主席的陈少敏；

曾任北京市民政局长、全国人大常委会机关党组成员的董汝勤；

著名画家、同志画社创始人丁启喆；

曾任山东省立医院院长的刘先身；

著名农学家、曾任山东农学院院长的张瑞泰；

曾任山东师范学院副院长、山东文联副主席的田仲济；

曾任北京理工大学教授的张纪昌；

中科院院士、地球物理学家秦欣菱；

原空军某部副司令员魏光修；

著名冶金专家徐宝升；

著名历史学家张维华；

中国工程院院士、著名眼科专家张士元；

著名数学家刘书琴。

In addition to the people listed above, other famous officials and professionals who studied or worked in the Courtyard of the Happy Way are as follows:

Zhang Tiao, an early revolutionary and a member of the Communist Party of China, the former minister of Culture Department of the Soviet Government of Fujian, Zhejiang and Jiangxi Provinces;

Zhang Tongpu, member of Chinese Revolutionary League and former commander of East Shandong revolutionary army detachment;

Zhang Zhonghang, a famous doctor in Wenhsien and former president of Qingdao Public Security Hospital;

Zhang Tongjun, an early revolutionary and a member of the Communist Party of China, and acting director of Construction Bureau of Weifang after the founding of the People's Republic of China;

Zhang Tonghe, famous surgeon and medical educator in China;

Chen Shaomin, revolutionary and former vice chairman of the National Federation of Trade Unions;

Dong Ruqin, former director of Beijing Municipal Civil Affairs and member of the Party Group of the Standing Committee of the National People's Congress;

Ding Qizhe, famous painter and founder of Comrade Painting Society;

Liu Xianshen, former president of Shandong Provincial Hospital;

Zhang Ruitai, famous agronomist and former president of Shandong Agricultural College;

Tian Zhongji, former vice president of Shandong Normal University and vice chairman of Shandong Federation of Literature and Art;

Zhang Jichang, former professor at Beijing Institute of Technology;

Qin Xinling, academician of Chinese Academy of Sciences and geophysicist.

Wei Guangxiu, former deputy commander of a certain Air Force;

Xu Baosheng, famous metallurgical expert;

Zhang Weihua, famous historian;

Zhang Shiyuan, academician in the Chinese Academy of Engineering and famous ophthalmologist;
Liu Shuqin, famous mathematician.

从乐道院学校走出的山东省内各大医院专家名医、各地邮电局局长、火车站站长、大专院校的专家教授更是不胜枚举。可以说乐道院开办的学校，为中国的近现代化培养了大批优秀人才。

There are more outstanding doctors, postmasters, stationmasters, and professors graduated from the schools of the Courtyard who have made important contributions to China’s development.

结　语

Conclusion

130 余年前，在潍县，西方传教士建起乐道院。这个集学校、医院、教堂于一身的建筑群，就这样生硬地兀自嵌入到传统中国的大地上，和远处蜿蜒环绕的城墙、高耸的谯楼共同见证着晚清民国激荡的风云变幻。

Over 130 years ago, the Courtyard of the Happy Way was built by the Western missionaries in Weihsien. It comprised of a number of spectacular buildings designed based on Western architecture, including schools, a hospital and a church; the Courtyard witnessed remarkable social, cultural, scientific and technological changes and social movements in the late Qing Dynasty and during the Republic of China.

楔入进来的乐道院曾引起潍县人的排斥，但他们很快秉承着“经世致用”之道，埋头“师夷长技”，在汲取了近代文明中的养分后，推动了近代中国的发展进程——就这样，十字架下的乐道院，以一种耐人寻味的方式，改变了潍县，并在一定程度上推动了中国的社会进步。

At the beginning, the Courtyard of the Happy Way was not welcomed by the people of Weihsien. But the Western residents of the Courtyard gradually won their trust, the local people began to send their children to their schools to learn modern science and technology, which would contribute to the establishment of a modern, developing China. Hence, the Courtyard of the Happy Way had a huge, lasting impact on the city of Weihsien and its residents, prompting progressive movements in the region and the rest of China.

第二编 Chapter 2

成为西方侨民集中营的乐道院

It Becomes A Concentration Camp for Western Residents

20世纪30年代，世界局势波诡云谲。在东方，1931年日本帝国主义发动侵华战争，并迅速占领中国东北。1937年日本进一步发动全面侵华战争。在欧洲，1939年德国悍然进攻波兰，第二次世界大战爆发。1938年初，日军占领了胶东半岛。

In 1930s, the world experienced great changes. In 1931, in the East, the Japanese imperialists launched a war against China and quickly occupied Northeast China. Later, in 1937, Japan attempted a full-scale invasion of China. In Europe, after Germany attacked Poland in 1939, the Second World War broke out. In early 1938, the Japanese army occupied Jiaodong Peninsula.

珍珠港事件之前，乐道院属于美国人管辖，日本人不加干涉，乐道院一时成为了战争避难所，容纳避难人数达4000多人。

Before Japan's attack on Pearl Harbor, the Americans ran the Courtyard of the Happy Way, and the Japanese forces respected their sovereignty over the Courtyard. For this reason, it was regarded as a kind of sanctuary for more than four thousand people.

太平洋战争爆发后，1941年12月8日，日军侵占乐道院。1942年3月，日本为报复美国限制日裔美籍人士在美国本土活动，将乐道院改造为西方侨民集中营，先后关押了2000余名外国侨民，他们分别来自美国、英国、加拿大、澳大利亚、新西兰、荷兰、比利时、伊朗、菲律宾、古巴、希腊、挪威、乌拉圭等国家，其中以欧美人士居多，儿童有327名。美国前驻华大使恒安石、华北神学院院长赫士博士、英国奥运会短跑冠军李爱锐等都曾被囚于此。

However, after the outbreak of the Pacific War, the Japanese army occupied the Courtyard of the Happy Way on December 8, 1941. In March 1942, they secretly set up a concentration camp in the Courtyard of the Happy Way. Its sole purpose was to retaliate against the restrictions imposed on the activities of Japanese Americans by the U.S. government in this country. There were about 2,000 foreign residents imprisoned in the Japanese camp, from the United States, the United Kingdom, Canada, Australia, New Zealand, the Netherlands, Belgium, Iran, the Philippines, Cuba, Greece, Norway, Uruguay and other countries. Most of the camp internees were Europeans and Americans, including 327 children. Arthur William Hummel Jr., former US ambassador to China, Dr. Watson McMillan Hayes, dean of the North China Theological Seminary, and Eric H. Liddell, a British Olympic sprint champion, were among the ordinary citizens imprisoned in the concentration camp.

集中营的人士曾经得到了当地农民和抗日部队的同情和帮助。当集中营内物资匮乏的时候，当地人民悄悄为他们运送食物，抗日组织为其发送信件，并帮助恒安石等人成功逃脱，及时把这一消息告知重庆的美国大使馆。当地人民还把美军空投的物资偷偷送进了集中营，帮助集中营的大多数人员幸运地度过了囚禁岁月，直到 1945 年 8 月 17 日被解放。

Local farmers and Chinese troops showed a lot of sympathy to the internees in the concentration camp and tried to help them in different ways. When, for example, there was a shortage of food in the camp, the local people secretly delivered food to them. The Anti-Japanese organizations and individuals helped them send messages, assisted Arthur William Hummel, among others, to escape from the camp, and promptly informed this news to the U.S. embassy in Chongqing, China. The local people secretly delivered the food and goods, airdropped by American army, to the camp residents, which helped them survive until they were finally liberated on August 17, 1945.

集中营解放后，被囚禁的人士大多回到了自己的国家，主要散居在欧美和澳洲，其中有的成为所在国政界、商界中的知名人士。对于集中营的幸存者而言，潍坊的特殊经历已成为他们永远的、挥之不去的回忆。他们相互联络、组织潍县集中营营友会、建立网站、撰写回忆录，并且拍摄了一部涉及此事的影片。潍县集中营给那些经历者和潍坊人民都留下了大量不可磨灭的记忆，成为一段弥足珍贵的往事。

After the liberation, most of the internees, in particular Europeans, Americans and Australians, returned to their own countries. Some of them entered the world of politics; some became successful business people and entrepreneurs. However, all the concentration camp survivors share the unique but painful experience of living through those years in Weifang. They kept in touch with each other, organized the Weihsien Concentration Camp Internees Association, set up websites, wrote books, and made videos and films inspired by their memories. Weihsien Concentration Camp had left a lot of indelible and precious memories for the former internees and Weifang people.

图 1　1938 年初，日军开始侵占山东半岛。图为 1938 年 2 月 1 日，日军攻占即墨县城

Picture 1　In early 1938, Japanese Army occupied Shandong Peninsula. The photo shows the Japanese army capturing Jimo County on February 1, 1938

图2　1938年1月8日，国民党山东省第八区专员兼游击司令厉文礼率部撤离潍县。10 日，伴随着凛冽的寒风，日寇铁蹄踏入潍县城，扫荡乡村、烧杀抢掠。图为日军侵占潍县后运送物资

Picture 2　On January 8, 1938, Li Wenli, the Eighth District Commissioner and guerrilla commander of the Kuomintang in Shandong Province, ordered his troops to retreat from Weihsien. Two days later, on January 10, the Japanese invaders entered Weihsien, mopped up the villages, burnt houses, killed people and looted everything. The picture shows the Japanese army transporting materials after occupying Weihsien

图 3 1939 年，德军发动了进攻波兰的战争，第二次世界大战爆发。图为德军占领波兰
Picture 3 In 1939, Hitler ordered the German army to attack Poland, which led to the breakout the World War II. The picture shows the German occupying Poland

图 4 1940 年 9 月 27 日，德、意、日三国在柏林签订《德意日三国同盟条约》，法西斯军事同盟建立。图为德军飞机
Picture 4 On September 27, 1940, Germany, Italy and Japan signed Tripartite Pact in Berlin, which declared the establishment of Fascist military alliance. The picture shows a German plane

图 5 1941 年 12 月 7 日，日军偷袭美国太平洋海军基地珍珠港，成为第二次世界大战太平洋战争爆发的导火索。图为被日军炸沉的美军主力战舰“亚利桑那”号

Picture 5 On December 7, 1941, the Japanese army attacked Pearl Harbor, the U.S. Pacific naval base, which triggered the outbreak of the Pacific War in the WWII. The picture shows “Arizona”, the main U.S. warship, sank after the attack by Japanese troops

图 6 太平洋战争爆发后，国际反法西斯统一战线形成。1942 年 1 月 1 日，中、美、英、苏等 26 国签署对德、意、日法西斯共同行动的《联合国家宣言》

Picture 6 After the outbreak of the Pacific War, the International United Front against Fascism was formed. On January 1, 1942, in order to carry out joint actions against Germany, Italy and Japan, 26 countries, including China, the U.S., the UK and the Soviet Union, signed the United Nations Declaration

第一章　日军将乐道院改建为西方侨民集中营

1 Transformation by Japanese Army

抗日战争期间，日军在中国一共建立了40余座集中营，其中潍县乐道院集中营是关押西方侨民最多的一座。下面一组图片是一些 1942 年至 1945 年日本在中国的集中营和非正式关押的数据。

During WWII, the Japanese army set up more than forty concentration camps in China, including the one in the Courtyard of the Happy Way in Weihsien, which imprisoned the largest number of Western residents. Here are some data about the concentration camps and informal detention centers set up by Japan in China from 1942 to 1945.

TABLE 3

INTERNEES GROUPED UNDER MEN, WOMEN & CHILDREN at 15 Aug. 1945

	Total	Men	Women	Children
China	9,174	4,464	3,216	1,494
Hong Kong	2,376	1,222	865	289
TOTAL	11,550	5,686	4,081	1,783
%	100	49	35	16

Source: "*The Japanese Internment Camps for Civilians during the 2nd World War*" by Dr. D. van Velden - with some adjustments

图 1　日军在中国设立的集中营被关押人员按照男人、女人、儿童情况分析表
Picture 1　Data on the internees grouped under men, women and children in concentration camps set up by Japanese troops in China

PRISONERS OF THE SAMURAI

THE RAID WHICH STARTED IT ALL

Table 4.

Statistics on Internment Camps & Informal Centres in China, 1942-1945& Informal Centres in China, 1942-1945

Name of Camp	Type of Building	Period of Internment	1942 Interned	1942 Repatriation 18/06/42	1942 Total 31/12	1943 Interned	1943 Repatriation 01/10/43	1943 Transfers	1943 Total 31/12	1944 Interned	1944 Total 31/12	1945 Transfers	1945 Deaths 42-45	Total 16/08/45
INFORMAL CENTRES														
Peking R.C	Mission Compounds	Aug 43-Aug 45						440	440		440			440
Other Centres (Harbin, Siping, Shenyang, Xiujiahui, Xiamen, Canton)	Schools & Hotels	Feb 43-Aug 45				298	-38		260		260			260
FENGTAI	Warehouse	Jun 45-Aug 45										307		307
CHEFOO, Temple Hill	Residences	Nov 42-Sep 43	450		450			-450	0		0			0
WEIXIAN	Mission Compound	Mar 43-Aug 45				2029	-390	450 / -440	1649	*87	1736		-34	1702
YANGZHOU A	Mission Compound	Mar 43-Oct 43				375		-375	0		0			0
YANGZHOU B	Mission Compound	Mar 43-Oct 43				300		-300	0		0			0
YANGZHOU C	Mission Compound	Mar 43-Aug 45				609			609	^38	647		-5	642
SHANGHAI														
- HAIFONG ROAD	Residence	Nov 42-Jun 45	360		360		-43		317		317	-307	-10	0
- YU YUEN ROAD	Schools	Feb 43-Apr 45				870	-167	200	903		903	-885	-18	0
- ASH CAMP	Army Huts	Feb 43-Aug 45				430		30	460		460		-10	450
- COLUMBIA C. CLUB	Sports Club	Feb 43-Apr 45				358			358		358	-350	-8	0
- ZHABEI	University	Feb 43-Aug 45				1425	-350		1075		1075		-25	1050
- PUDONG	Warehouses	Feb 43-Aug 45				1065	-150	-200 / 400	1115		1115		-12	1103
- LONGHUA	Schools	Mar 43-Aug 45				2000	-480	245	1765		1765		-40	1725
- LINCOLN AVE.	Residences	Jun 44-Aug 45								300	300		-40	260
- YANGSHUPU	Convent Hospital	Apr 45-Aug 45									0	1235		1235
HONG KONG														
- STANLEY	College & Residences	Jan 42-Aug 45	2787	-264	2523		-20		2503		2503	-173	-127	2203
- KOWLOON (Technicians)	Barracks	Aug 45-Aug 45										173		173
		TOTAL:	3597	-264	3333	9759	-1638	0	11454	300	11879	0	-329	11550

* Italians

^ Belgians

NOTES:

1. Some of this information comes from *The Japanese Internment Camps for Civilians during the 2nd World War* by Dr. D. van Velden. This has been supplemented by information from other sources.
2. The Repatriations included many non-internees - hence the low figures of internees having been repatriated.

Deaths have been treated statistically as all occuring in 1945, though they relate to the whole period. The figures for Stanley Camp include 7 executions by the Japanese in Oct. 1943 and 14 killed in an American air raid in Jan. 1945.

Total interned during the War:

1942	3,597
1943	9,759
1944	425
TOTAL	13,781

图 2 1942 年～1945 年日军在中国设立的集中营和非正式关押数据

Picture 2 Data on Japanese-run concentration camps and informal detention centers in China from 1942 to 1945

太平洋战争爆发后，1941 年 12 月 8 日，日军侵占乐道院。1942 年 3 月，日本为报复美国限制日裔美籍人士在美国本土活动，将乐道院改造为西方侨民集中营。

After the outbreak of the Pacific War, the Japanese army occupied the Courtyard of the Happy Way on December 8, 1941. In March 1942 they transformed the Courtyard into a concentration camp for Western residents. Its purpose was to retaliate against the restrictions that the U.S. government had imposed on the activities of Japanese Americans in the U.S.

图 3　日军占领乐道院后，开始对乐道院大肆改造，以适合作为关押之用。图为在乐道院建立的警戒塔和电网

Picture 3 After the Japanese army occupied the Courtyard, they built new structures, transforming it into a detention place. The picture shows the guard tower and electrified Fence set up in the Courtyard

图 4　全副武装的日本士兵

Picture 4 An armed Japanese soldier

第二章　西方侨民被押送到潍县集中营

2 Western Residents Transferred to Weihsien Concentration Camp

太平洋战争爆发后，乐道院就被日军强行占领，改为西方侨民集中营，日本人称为“敌国人集团生活所”，用于关押美国、英国、加拿大等多个国家的2000多名侨民。从1942年3月起，西方侨民从中国北方各处被陆续押送到乐道院。

After the outbreak of the Pacific War, the Japanese army occupied the Courtyard of the Happy Way. They converted the Courtyard into a concentration camp for the Western citizens, calling it “Civil Assembly Center”, which imprisoned over 2,000 residents from a number of countries, mainly form the United States and Canada, the United Kingdom and other Western countries. Since March 1942, the Japanese forces brought Western citizens from various parts of North China to this concentration camp.

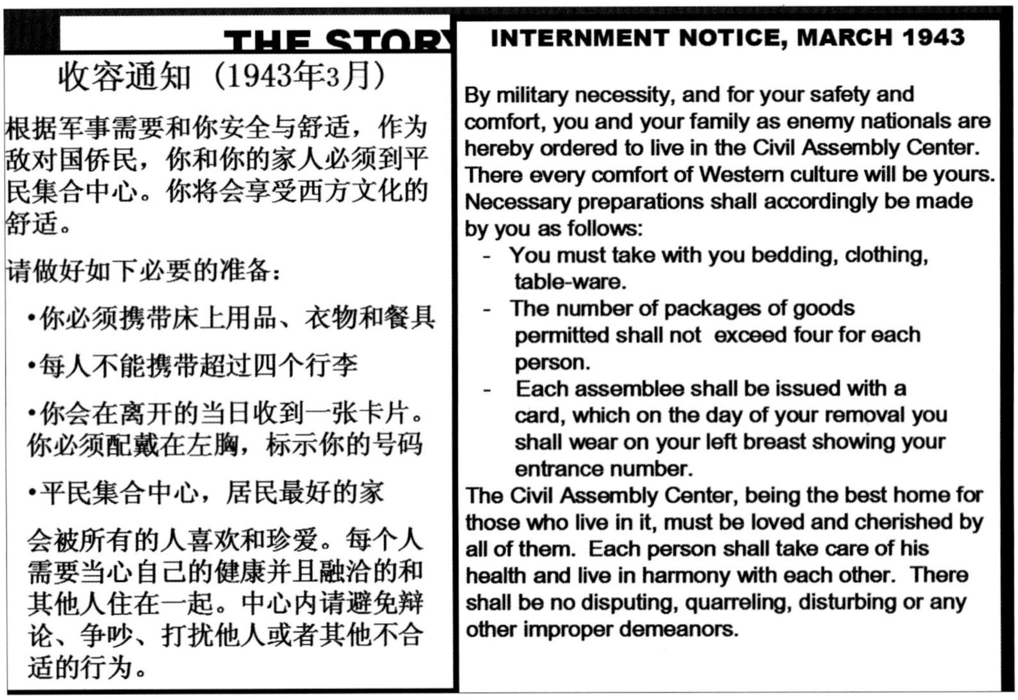
THE STORY

收容通知（1943年3月）

根据军事需要和你安全与舒适，作为敌对国侨民，你和你的家人必须到平民集合中心。你将会享受西方文化的舒适。

请做好如下必要的准备：

- 你必须携带床上用品、衣物和餐具
- 每人不能携带超过四个行李
- 你会在离开的当日收到一张卡片。你必须配戴在左胸，标示你的号码
- 平民集合中心，居民最好的家

会被所有的人喜欢和珍爱。每个人需要当心自己的健康并且融洽的和其他人住在一起。中心内请避免辩论、争吵、打扰他人或者其他不合适的行为。

INTERNMENT NOTICE, MARCH 1943

By military necessity, and for your safety and comfort, you and your family as enemy nationals are hereby ordered to live in the Civil Assembly Center. There every comfort of Western culture will be yours. Necessary preparations shall accordingly be made by you as follows:

- You must take with you bedding, clothing, table-ware.
- The number of packages of goods permitted shall not exceed four for each person.
- Each assemblee shall be issued with a card, which on the day of your removal you shall wear on your left breast showing your entrance number.

The Civil Assembly Center, being the best home for those who live in it, must be loved and cherished by all of them. Each person shall take care of his health and live in harmony with each other. There shall be no disputing, quarreling, disturbing or any other improper demeanors.

图1 幸存的西方侨民提供的1943年日军对西方侨民的《收容通知》。从《通知》内容可以看到，当时的收容宣传很有欺骗性。

Picture 1 The 1943 Japanese Army’s “Internment Notice”, provided by an internee. It can be seen from the “Notice” that the information was deceptive.

图 2 西方侨民被集中和押送（1）
Picture 2 The Western residents were escorted collectively(1)

图 3 西方侨民被集中和押送（2）
Picture 3 The Western residents were escorted collectively(2)

图 4 西方侨民被集中和押送（3）

Picture 4 The Western residents were escorted collectively(3)

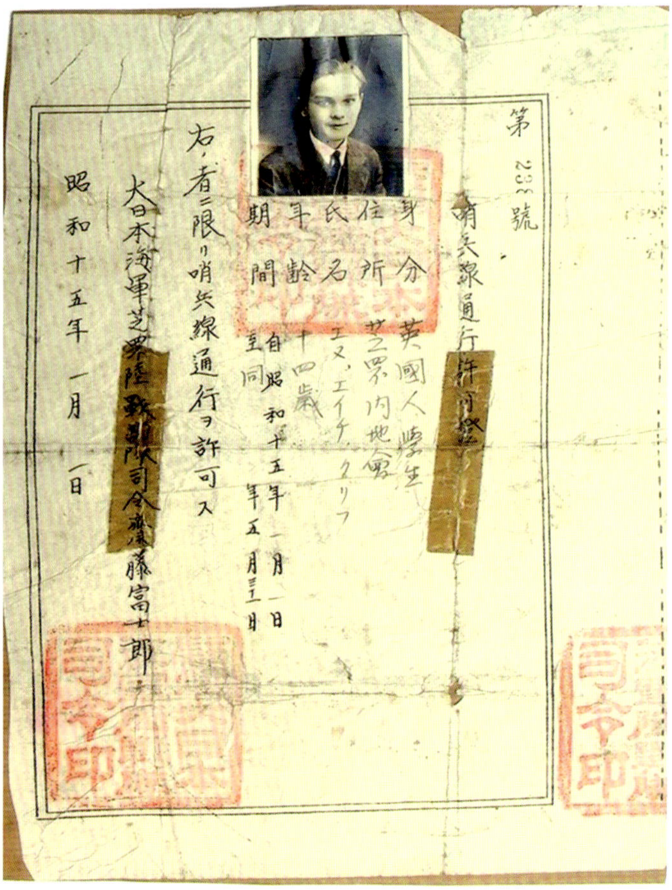

第 號
哨兵線通行許可證
身分 英國人學生
住所 芝罘内地會
氏名 エヌ、エイチ、クリフ
年齢 十四歳
期間 自昭和十五年一月一日 至同 年五月三十一日
右ノ者ニ限リ哨兵線通行ヲ許可ス
大日本海軍芝罘陸戰隊司令 齋藤富士郎
昭和十五年一月一日

图 5 英国人柯喜乐被关押前用过的日军发放的通行证

Picture 5 A pass issued by the Japanese army for Norman Cliff, a British citizen, before his detention

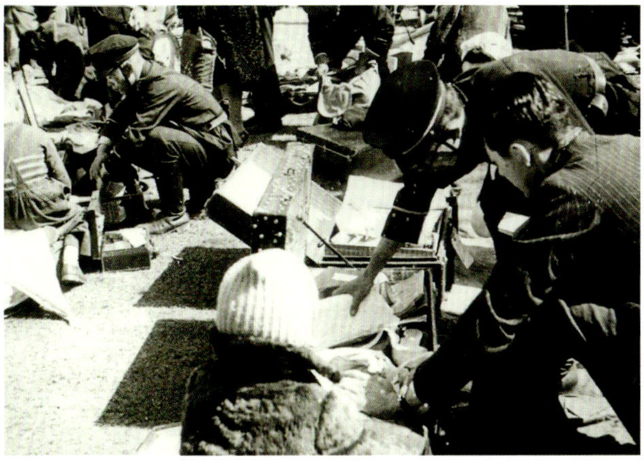

图 6 日本宪兵检查西方侨民的行李物品（1）
Picture 6 Japanese military police inspecting Western residents' luggage (1)

图 7 日本宪兵检查西方侨民的行李物品（2）
Picture 7 Japanese military police inspecting Western residents' luggage (2)

图 8 日本宪兵检查西方侨民的行李物品（3）
Picture 8 Japanese military police inspecting Western residents' luggage (3)

图 9 西方侨民手提被日本宪兵检查过后用粉笔标记的行李箱
Picture 9 Western residents carrying suitcases marked with chalk after being inspected by the Japanese

图 10 西方侨民在车站等待被送往乐道院集中营
Picture 10 Western residents waiting at the station to be sent to Weihsien Camp

第三章　潍县集中营内的基本布局和周边环境

3 Basic Layout and Surrounding Environment of the Camp

日军占领乐道院后，大肆劫掠了这里的医疗和教学设备，将乐道院的教学楼和一排排的病房、宿舍迅速改造成类似牢房的居所。这样，昔日的基督教传教站、学校和医院，变成了集中营。

After the Japanese army occupied the Courtyard of the Happy Way, they plundered the medical and teaching equipment, quickly transforming the teaching buildings, wards and dormitories into a prisoner-of-war camp. The former Christian missionary center, schools and hospital were converted into a concentration camp.

图 1　美国 B–29 轰炸机 1945 年 8 月航拍的潍县集中营
Picture 1　U.S. B-29 bomber took an aerial photography of Weihsien Concentration Camp in August 1945

图 2 集中营位于潍县县城东南方，周边全是农田
Picture 2 The camp was located in the southeast of Weihsien, surrounded by farmlands

图 3 潍县集中营墙外泥泞的道路
Picture 3 Muddy roads surrounding the Weihsien Concentration Camp

图 4　西方侨民绘制的潍县集中营西面的小村庄

Picture 4 A small village in the west of Weihsien Camp, drawn by an internee

图 5 西方侨民用水彩绘制的营外环境

Picture 5 Surrounding area of the camp, drawn by an internee

图 6 西方侨民用水彩绘制的营外环境
Picture 6 Surrounding area of the camp, drawn by an internee

图 7 西方侨民绘制的集中营墓地
Picture 7 The cemetery in the camp, drawn by an internee

图 8 潍县集中营大门仍保留“乐道院”字样

Picture 8 The Chinese characters “乐 道 院”(the Courtyard Happy Doctrine Compound of the Happy Way) still remained on the camp gate

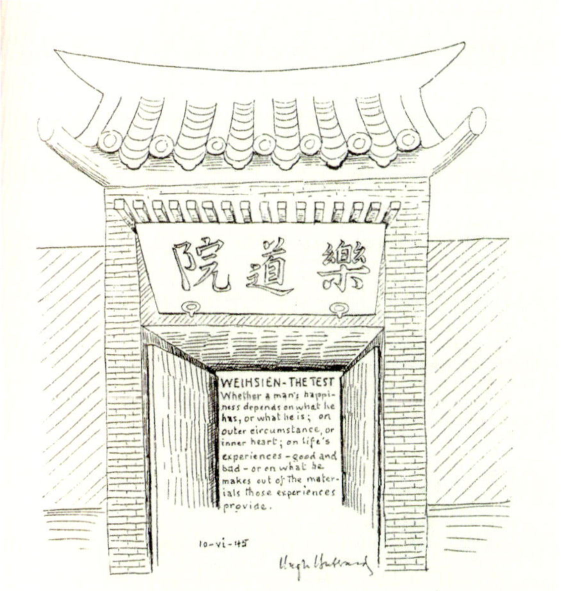

Gateway of Weihsien Presbyterian Mission Compound where the School was interned 1943-5.
Sketch by Hugh Hubbard.
The Chinese characters mean 'Courtyard of the Happy Way'.

图 10 西方侨民胡本德 1945 年 6 月 10 日绘制的潍县集中营正门（前门）。门内英文译成汉语为《潍县·考验》：一个人的快乐，或基于他有什么，或他是什么；基于外界环境或者内心；基于好的或者坏的生活经验；或者基于他从经验中所领悟的。胡本德，1945 年 6 月 10 日，表现了被囚侨民乐观豁达的人生信念

Picture 10 Main entrance (front gate) of Weihsien Concentration Camp drawn by Hugh Hubbard on June 10, 1945. In the picture, it is written, “WEIHSIEN - THE TEST.” Whether a man’s happiness depends on what he has or what he is; on the outer circumstances or the inner heart; on life’s experiences - good and bad - or on what he makes out of the material those experiences provide. Hugh Hubbard on June 10, 1945, which showed this internee’s mental and spiritual strength and optimism

图 9 潍县集中营大门内侧

Picture 9 A view from inside the camp

图 11 潍县集中营警戒塔 -3 区
Picture 11 The guard tower of the camp-district 3

图 12 集中营的东墙
Picture 12 The east wall of the concentration camp

图 13 西方侨民绘制的集中营警戒塔
Picture 13 The guard tower of the concentration camp, drawn by an internee

图 14 集中营营区鸟瞰
Picture 14 Aerial view of the concentration camp

图 15 集中营营区内
Picture 15 Inside the camp

图 16 集中营南墙里日本看守居住的原外国侨民楼房
Picture 16 The former Western resident's house where Japanese guards lived in

图 17 乐道院女子圣经学校楼，集中营时期被日军改造为关押单身男性侨民的住所
Picture 17 The Japanese army transformed the Girls' Bible School into a prison center for the single male residents

图 18 西方侨民绘制的集中营内的大钟
Picture 18 The big bell in the camp, drawn by an internee

图 19 西方侨民绘制的集中营内的球场
Picture 19 Basketball court in the camp, drawn by an internee

图 20 西方侨民绘制的集中营第 32 号营区
Picture 20 Block 32 of the concentration camp, drawn by an internee

图 21 西方侨民绘制的集中营第 23 号营区
Picture 21 Block 23 of the concentration camp, drawn by an internee

图 22　西方侨民绘制的集中营第 23 号营区 9 号室外的阳台

Picture 22　A balcony outside the room number 9 in block 32, drawn by an internee

图 23　西方侨民绘制的集中营第 56 号营区及水塔

Picture 23　Block 56 and the water tower, drawn by an internee

图 24 西方侨民绘制的集中营第 6 号营区
Picture 24 Block 6 of the concentration camp, drawn by an internee

图 25 西方侨民绘制的集中营第 16 号营区
Picture 25 Block 16 of the concentration camp, drawn by an internee

图 26 西方侨民绘制的集中营居住区的楼梯
Picture 26 A staircase in the residential area in the camp, drawn by an internee

图 27 西方侨民绘制的乐道院礼拜堂和集中营居住区
Picture 27 Chapel and residential area in the camp, drawn by an internee

图 28 西方侨民绘制的集中营 1 号厨房外景
Picture 28 Kitchen No.1 in the concentration camp, drawn by an internee

图 29 集中营 2 号厨房外景
Picture 29 Exterior view of kitchen no.2 in the concentration camp

图 30 西方侨民绘制的通往集中营居住区的内门
Picture 30 The inner gate to the residential area in the camp, drawn by an internee

图 32 西方侨民绘制的集中营内的大礼堂（教堂）
Picture 32 Assembly hall (church) in the camp, drawn by an internee

图 31 集中营内的操场
Picture 31 Playground in the camp

第四章　被关押在乐道院的西方侨民

4 Western Residents Imprisoned in the Concentration Camp

自1942年3月起，潍县集中营先后关押了来自美国、英国、澳大利亚、加拿大、法国等国家的两千多名侨民，他们原本居住和工作在中国长江以北各个地区从事各类行业，生活安逸，却因一场战争，命运发生了突变。

Starting in March 1942, Japan transported over 2,000 foreign citizens to the Weihsien Concentration Camp. They originally lived and worked in various areas in the northern region of the Yangtze River in China. The outbreak of the war suddenly changed their fate.

在异国他乡被迫离开温暖的家，被关押的侨民们失去了自由，更让他们担惊受怕的是不知道战争的尽头和他们自己将要面临的命运。

Forced to leave their homes in a foreign country, the imprisoned Western residents lost control over their lives and their freedom. They became very anxious and scared because they did not know what would happen to them and when the war would end.

图 1　被关押在潍县集中营的32名燕京大学外籍教授
Picture 1 Thirty two foreign teachers from Yenching University imprisoned in Weihsien Concentration Camp

图 2 被关押在集中营的烟台芝罘学校师生合影
Picture 2 Imprisoned teachers and students from Yantai Chefoo School

图 3 部分芝罘学校师生在集中营合影
Picture 3 Imprisoned teachers and students from Yantai Chefoo School

图 4 部分芝罘学校师生在集中营留影
Picture 4 Imprisoned teachers and students from Yantai Chefoo School

图 5 从集中营中解救的低年级学生
Picture 5 Junior students rescued from concentration camp

图 6 被关押在集中营的英国奥运冠军埃里克▪利迪尔(右,中文名:李爱锐)

Picture 6 Eric H. Liddell, a British Olympic Champion imprisoned in Weihsien Camp (first from right)

图 7 被关押的汉奎特神父(右)

Picture 7 Imprisoned Father Hanquet (first from right)

图 8 芝罘学校校长布鲁斯一家曾被关押在集中营

Picture 8 Bruce, Principal of the Chefoo School, and his family were imprisoned in the camp

图 9 著名的黑斯医生和母亲在集中营里
Picture 9 Mr. Hess, a famous doctor, and his mother in the camp

图 10 集中营里挤住在一间学生宿舍里的西方侨民一家
Picture 10 A family living in a small student dormitory in the camp

图 11　汤姆森一家，右侧的小男孩为家中长子——布瑞恩，后来被日军关入集中营。1944 年在集中营集合点名时触电身亡，当时布瑞恩只有 17 岁

Picture 11　The Thomson family. The little boy on the right was the eldest son of the family—Brian. He was only 17 when he was electrocuted by an electric fence during a roll call in the concentration camp in 1944

图 12　被关押在集中营的克里斯汀一家

Picture 12　Christines in the camp

图 13 被关押在集中营的孩子们
Picture 13 Children in the camp

图 14 被关押的侨民
Picture 14 Imprisoned Western residents Picture

图 15 集中营里的小女孩
Picture 15 A little girl in the concentration camp

图 16 梅特卡夫一家在集中营
Picture 16 The Metcalfe family in the Camp

图 17 幼小的孩子也未躲过被关押的命运
Picture 17 A young child in the camp

图 18 英国中国内地会戴存仁牧师与 4 个孙子（孙女）一起被关押到集中营，前排右一为玛丽 · 普瑞维特（戴爱美）
Picture 18 Herbert Hudson Taylor, a minister from China Inland Mission, and his four grandchildren were imprisoned together. The first from right is Mary Taylor Previte.

图 19　幼年时期的戴爱美（前右一）、戴爱莲（后右二）、戴绍曾（后左一），戴绍仁（前中）与中国儿童留影

Picture 19 Young Mary Taylor (first from right, front row), Kathleen Taylor (second from right, back row), James Taylor (first from left, back row), John Taylor (middle, front row) and Chinese children

图 20　被关押在集中营的侨民，无奈地站在层层铁丝网前

Picture 20 An internee standing helplessly in front of the barbed wire

图 21 集中营中佩戴标牌的女孩
Picture 21 A girl wearing a tag in the concentration camp

图 22 日军强迫难友佩戴的标志
Picture 22 Japanese soldiers forced the imprisoned to wear such tags

图 23 被囚禁侨民佩戴的分组号牌
Picture 23 Tags with group numbers wore by the internees

第五章　集中营里的生活——强迫劳动

5 Life in the Concentration Camp - Forced Labor

集中营内的生活相当艰苦，日军看守穷凶极恶，规定除80岁以上高龄体弱多病的赫士博士和戴存仁牧师外，其他人不论男女，不管是贵族、官员、专家、学者、商人都必须参加劳动。

每天起床钟敲响后，都得赶紧起床，洗漱后分别到三处食堂吃饭，饭后钟声一响，都要到操场按照划分好的6个队在看守们指定的区域排队点名，用日语报数。入寝钟声敲响后，必须回到房间睡觉，不准在别处逗留。

The life in the concentration camp was very difficult as the Japanese forced all internees to do labor work, except for Dr. Watson McMillan Hayes and minister Herbert Hudson Taylor, who were over eighty years old at the time.

When the bell rang in the morning, they had to get up quickly, wash up and eat in three different dining halls. The bell would rang once again while the internees were having breakfast, signaling that they all had to stop eating; they, then, would go to the playground and line up in the designated area in six teams, before the Japanese would call off their names, and they had to number off in Japanese. At night the bell would ring again, meaning they had to go to their rooms. They were not allowed to wander or stay in other places.

图 1　被关押的侨民等待取水
Picture 1 Internees waiting for water

图 2 侨民在集中营的一个院子里被强迫劳动
Picture 2 Internees working in the yard

图 3 西方侨民画的厨房场景
Picture 3 In the kitchen, drawn by an internee

图 4 西方侨民绘制的排队点名场景（1）
Picture 4 Lining up for roll call, drawn by an internee (1)

图 5 西方侨民绘制的排队点名场景（2）
Picture 5 Lining up for roll call, drawn by an internee (2)

图 6 被囚禁的侨民在锯木头
Picture 6 Internees sawing wood

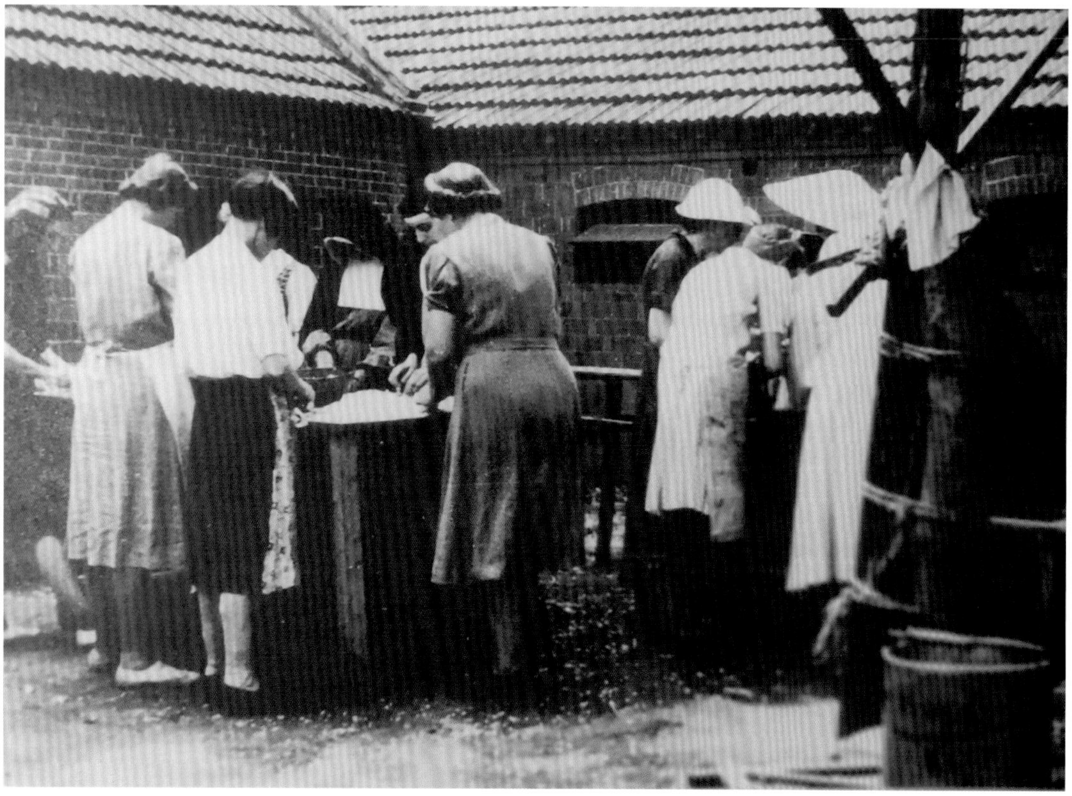

图 7 在厨房劳动
Picture 7 Internees working in the kitchen

图 8 排队取水
Picture 8 Waiting to get water

图 9 西方侨民绘制的集中营里排队取水场景
Picture 9 Lining up for water in the camp, drawn by an internee

图 10 洗衣服
Picture 10 Doing laundry

图 11 前公司高管洗衣服，威廉史·密斯绘
Picture 11 A former company executive doing laundry, by William Smith

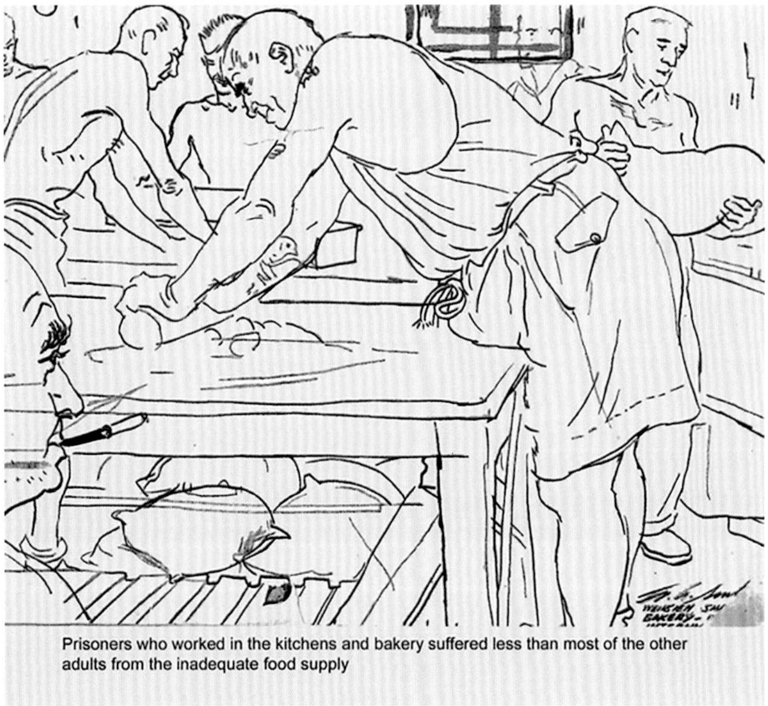

图 12 西方侨民绘制的烘焙场景
Picture 12 Baking, drawn by an internee

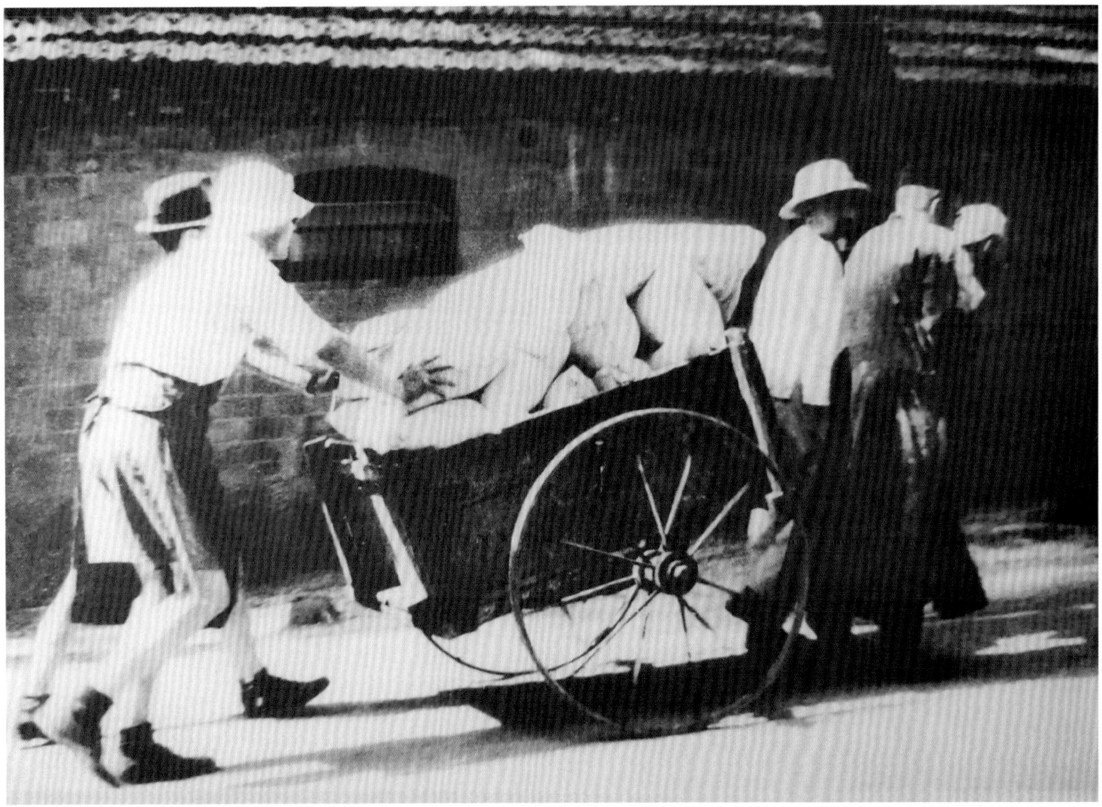

图 13 在集中营搬运面粉的西方侨民
Picture 13 Internees carrying flour in the camp

图 14 西方侨民在修补鞋子
Picture 14 An internee repairing shoes

第六章　集中营内侨民的困苦生活

6 Hardship in the Concentration Camp

在集中营内，除少数家庭单住一间房外，多数混合居住，小平房内每间住几个人，大房间里，几十个人挤在一起，对成年人来说，毫无隐私可言。

侨民们的生活极其艰苦，为了冬天有鞋穿，有些营友在其他季节都打赤脚，踩在冰冷的地上。

集中营内的饮食极差。刚进集中营时，侨民们尚能半饥半饱。到了后期，日本人在饮食上的虐待日趋严重，不少食品都已霉烂变质。侨民们的主食是发霉的高粱粥，排队领取，每人一勺。由于长期饥饿和营养不良，侨民们大多形容憔悴。

In the concentration camp, except for a few families who lived in separated rooms, all families lived together. In each room in the bungalows, several people lived together, and in some large rooms up to dozens of people. Nobody, in fact, had any kind of privacy.

The life in the concentration camp was extremely hard. In order to save their shoes for winter, some internees had to be barefoot in the rest of the year.

The quality of the food was extremely poor. When they first came to the camp, the internees were given enough food. But, later, the Japanese began to ration their meals, while the quality also declined. The camp's basic dietary food was rotten sorghum porridge. They had to line up only to get one spoon of porridge. After a while, many residents of the camp looked miserable because of malnutrition.

图 1 集中营里的一号大食堂

Picture 1 No.1 canteen in the concentration camp

图 2 集中营里拥挤的男宿舍
Picture 2 A crowded men's dormitory in the concentration camp

图 3 西方侨民绘制的居住区宿舍拥挤的住所
Picture 3 A crowded dormitory, drawn by an internee

图 4 宿舍内景
Picture 4 A dormitory

图 5 侨民们在排队洗漱
Picture5 Internees lining up to wash up

图 6 西方侨民绘制的排队打饭场景
Picture 6 Internees lining up for food

图 7 孟義先生祖母在集中营被囚禁时用过的饭碗
Picture 7 The rice bowl used by Mr. Menzi's grandmother during her detention in the camp

图 8 西方侨民用过的饭碗
Picture 8 A bowl used by the internees

第七章　烟台芝罘学校的被囚师生

7 Teachers and Students Imprisoned at Yantai Chefoo School

芝罘学校是“内地会”为方便在华传教士的子女就读而在烟台设立的中小学。1942 年 11 月，日军将该校全体同学和老师强迫集中在 4 所住房里。10 个月后，日军又将他们塞进一艘轮船的统舱里，然后绕过山东半岛，经青岛乘火车押送到潍县集中营。芝罘学校的师生同其他囚徒们一样，生活十分艰苦，男女生分别住在几间大教室里。食品是配给制，少得不足以维持最低的营养。学生们长期饥饿，面黄肌瘦。但学生们在老师的带领下仍按牛津考试的高标准严格要求，坚持学习，表现出了对困境不低头、不屈服的精神。

Chefoo School, which included a primary and a middle school, was set up in Yantai, Shandong Province, by China Inland Mission for the children of the Western missionaries living in China. In November 1942, the Japanese army imprisoned all the students and teachers in four houses. Ten months later, the Japanese transferred them to a ship steerage. Having bypassed Shandong Peninsula, the ship arrived in Qingdao, from which the Japanese army transferred these teachers and students to Weihsien Concentration Camp by train. Like other internees, the teachers and students of Chefoo School had a very difficult life in the camp; the boys and the girls lived separately, in several large classrooms. The quality of food was really low and hardly enough to live on. The Japanese kept the prisoners always hungry. But they were determined and committed to study and increase their academic knowledge. That was a perfect demonstration of their determined spirit and perseverance.

图 1　被解救后的低年级学生与老师合影

Picture 1 Junior students and teachers after being rescued

图 2 烟台芝罘学校女生
Picture 2 Girls from Chefoo School

图 3 老师在带领孩子们做游戏
Picture 3 Children and their teachers playing games

图 4 集中营里孩子们活动的地方
Picture 4 Children did activities in this place

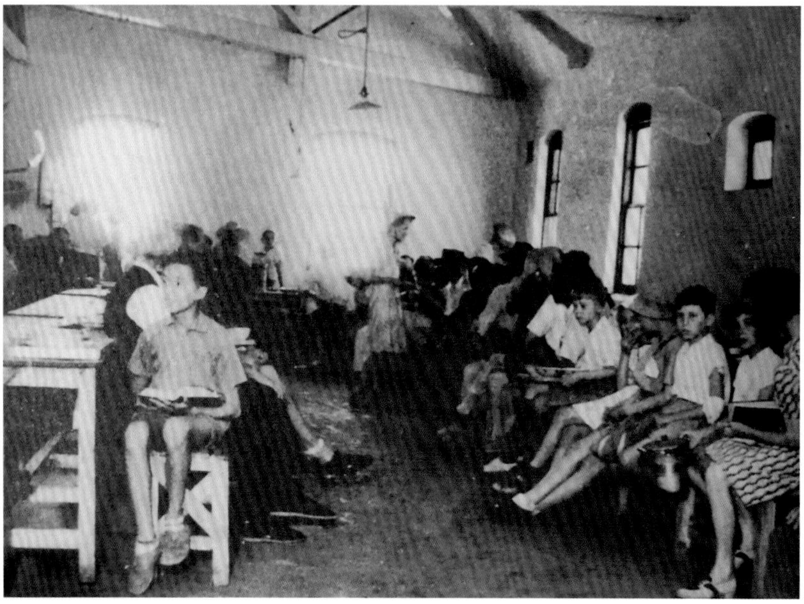

图 5 集中营里老师在辅导孩子们学习
Picture 5 Teachers tutoring students

图 6 被囚禁的孩子们坚持学习
Picture 6 Imprisoned children did not stop studying their lesson

图 7 被关押在乐道院集中营的美国女孩——芝罘学校学生玛丽•普瑞维特（戴爱美），左图为成年的戴爱美女士。老师们在极其艰苦的环境下，无私地向学生们献出自己的爱。玛丽•普瑞维特生日那天，一位老师寻到一个苹果来给她庆祝。这虽不是一件大礼物，但在那样缺衣少食的艰苦条件下，对一个与父母分离的九岁女孩来说却显得十分珍贵

Picture 7 Mary Taylor Previte, an American student of Chefoo School, was imprisoned in Weihsien Camp. The left picture shows Mary in her adulthood. Under extremely hard circumstances, the teachers treated their students with utmost love and kindness. On Mary's birthday, her teacher gave her an apple as a present. Seemingly not a big present, but it was very precious for a 9-year-old girl who was separated from her parents and did not have enough food and clothing

图 8 集中营里的伙食非常低劣，主食是稀的跟水一样的“粥”，正处在生长发育时期的芝罘学校的学生们，得不到成长所需的营养，身心健康受到严重摧残。图为老师将鸡蛋壳研成粉末，一勺勺分给学生们吃，为他们成长中的身体补充钙质

Picture 8 Food in the camp was terrible. The staple food was thin "porridge" like water. The students of Chefoo School could not get enough nutrients. As a result, their physical and mental health were severely damaged. The picture shows that in order to give calcium to young students, a teacher is grinding eggshells. The students will then eat the powder

第八章　集中营里的抗争
——西方侨民自治管理委员会

8 Resistance in the Concentration Camp — Self-governed Committee of Western Residents

侨民们在失去自由的情况下，仍然表现出互相关爱的精神，推选出由 9 人组成的“自治管理委员会”。由于齐鲁大学教务长德位思博士曾在乐道院的广文大学任过校长，熟悉乐道院的情况，大家推选他担任了主任委员。自治管理委员会另外一名负责人是曾任蒋介石顾问的基格神父，中文名为雷震远。他们把集中营分成 4 个组，每个小组选出 9 名代表，由 36 人组成教育、综合、工程、营房、医疗、食品供应、财务、雇工、纪律 9 个委员会，分别负责管理集中营侨民的各项事务，并负责与日本看守进行协调、谈判和抗争。在他们的努力下，侨民可以公开自行组织开展各种学习、工作和文体活动。

Despite losing their freedom, the internees had shown mutual caring to each other. The internees selected nine people to form an “Self-governed Committee”. Dr. L. J. Davies, the academic dean of Shantung Christian University, was elected as the chairman because having been the former president of Shantung Protestant University, he was familiar with the Courtyard. Another director of the Committee was Father R. Jaegher, who served as an adviser to Chiang Kai-shek. His Chinese name was Lei Zhenyuan (雷 震 远). The internees were divided into four groups; each group had nine representatives. The thirty six representatives set up nine departments, that is, education, general management, engineering, barracks, medical care, food supply, finance, employment and discipline. In addition to managing the affairs of the imprisoned civilians, the committee was also responsible for negotiating with the Japanese guards. With their efforts, the internees could finally study, work and do sports.

图 1　侨民推荐的自治管理委员会主任委员　德位思

Picture 1　Dr. L. J. Davies, Chairman of Self-governed Committee

为了争取孩子们在集中营上学以及教徒们做礼拜的权利，德位思博士等同日军看守当局进行了多次交涉谈判。经过努力，日本人只好同意了学生复课、教徒做礼拜等要求。

In order to get the rights of education and worship in the camp, Dr. Deiss and the committee had a number of meetings with the Japanese authorities, who finally agreed to give their consent.

图 2 侨民推荐的自治管理人员
雷震远
Picture 2 R. Jaegher, administrator of Self-governed Committee

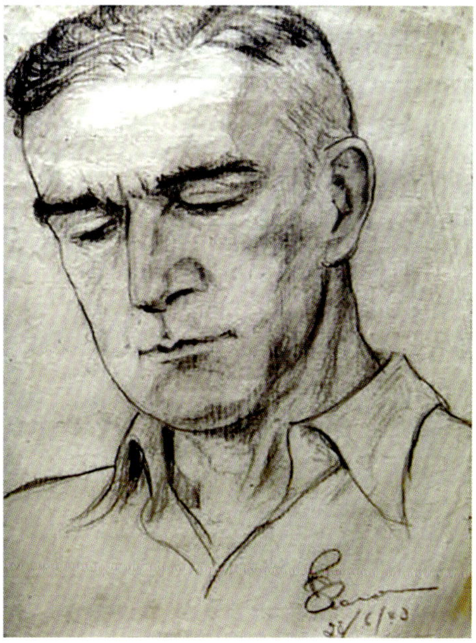

图 3 侨民推荐的自治管理人员画像——纪律委员会主席 J.C. 斯图尔特
Picture 3 Portrait of J. C. Stuart, manager of discipline department, Self-governed Committee

图 4 侨民推荐的自治管理人员画像——教育委员会主席 W. 普瑞尔
Picture 4 Portrait of W. Prior, manager of education department, Self-governed Committee

图 5 侨民推荐的自治管理人员画像——生活委员会主席 M.C. 汉尔顿
Picture 5 Portrait of M. C. Halton, manager of general affairs department, Self-governed Committee

图 6 西方侨民绘制的卡通漫画——剧社
Picture 6 Cartoon comics — dramatic club, drawn by an internee

图 7 侨民绘制的卡通漫画——托尼歌剧
Picture 7 Cartoon Comics — Tony Opera

图 8 西方侨民每周演讲的海报
Picture 8 A poster of internees' weekly lecture

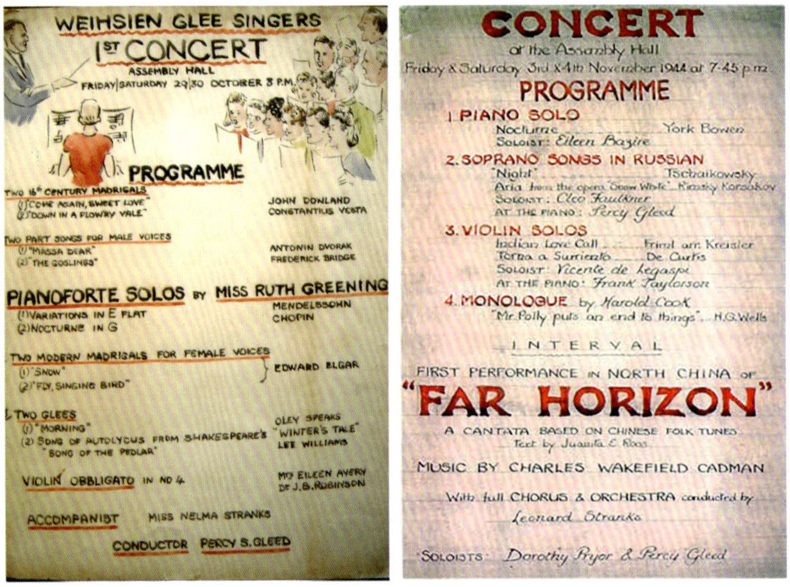

图 9 西方侨民当年举办音乐会的海报
Picture 9 Internees' concert posters

在被押往集中营时，一些颇具才华的音乐家，想尽各种方法把乐器带在身上，以基督教救世军的 15 人铜管乐队为主，加上业余的大、小提琴手，取名救世军乐队的临时乐队成立了。救世军乐队给单调枯燥的营内生活增添了不少乐趣。侨民们还经常组织舞会、喜剧、话剧等表演，庆祝圣诞节和复活节，自娱自乐中等待胜利的那一天。

When transferred to the concentration camp, some musicians did everything they could to bring their instruments. The fifteen-member brass band of the Christian Salvation Army and the amateur cellists and violinists formed a band named The Salvation Army. The band entertained the camp prisoners and broke the dullness of their stagnant, grim life. The internees frequently organized entertaining programs; some sang and danced, some did comic shows, and some staged plays; they celebrated Christmas and Easter and other festivities. They relentlessly tried to keep their spirits up, looking forward to the future.

图 10 军乐队合影
Picture 10 The Salvation Army Band

图 11 “救世军”乐队排练时的情形
Picture 11 The Salvation Army Band rehearsing

图 12 在乐道院地下室发现的当年侨民使用过的旧钢琴（现保存于乐道院潍县集中营博物馆）
Picture 12 An old piano used by internees, found in the Courtyard basement (now in the Courtyard museum)

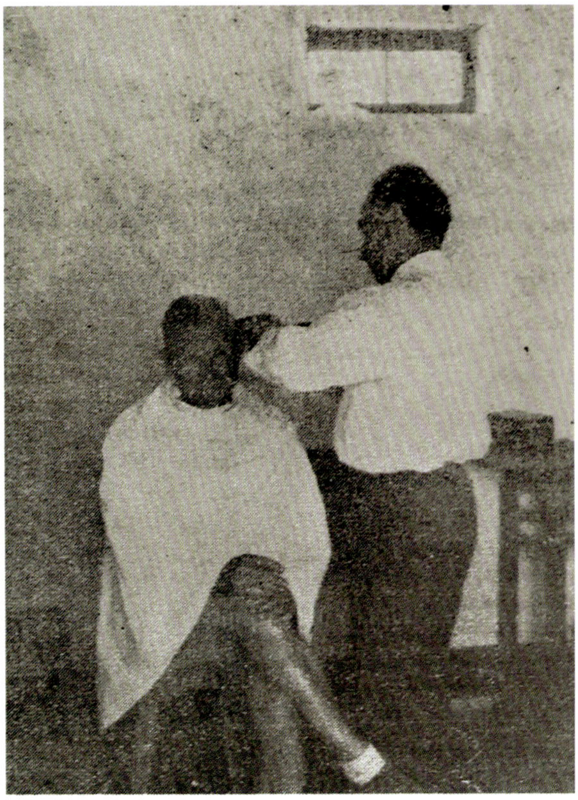

图 13 为侨民理发
Picture 13 A committee member cutting of an internee's hair

图 14 经与日军交涉侨民教徒可以在乐道院教堂做礼拜
Picture 14 After negotiating with the Japanese, the internees were allowed to worship in the Courtyard church

图 15 学生们在压平足球场
Picture 15 Students leveling the football court

图 16　侨民从集中营寄出的圣诞贺卡

Picture 16　A Christmas card sent by an internee from the Weihsien Concentration Camp

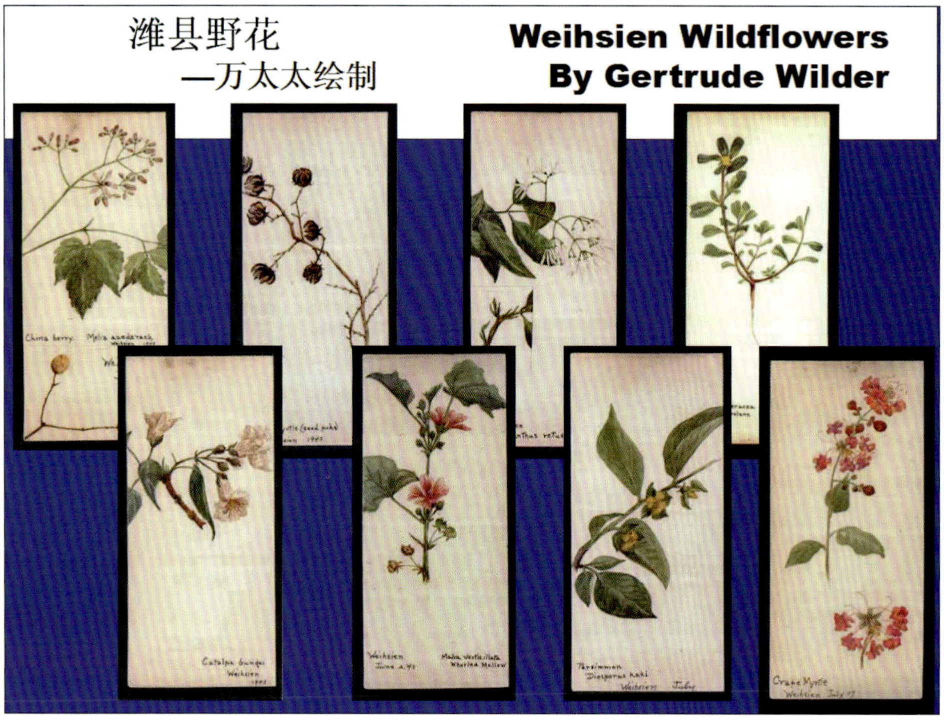

图 17　西方侨民绘制的集中营内的花卉

Picture 17　Weihsien wildflowers drawn by an internee

第九章　逃出集中营

9 Escape from the Concentration Camp

1944 年 6 月 9 日晚，集中营内发生了二人逃走事件。逃出的是通晓中国语言、之前任北平辅仁大学男子附中教师的美国青年恒安石和曾在英国海军担任报务员、退役后在华担任英美烟草公司销售经理的狄兰。此次越狱计划由熟悉当地情况的德位思博士和雷震远神父（曾任蒋介石顾问）策划，通过在集中营的掏粪工张兴泰父子，联系到了潍县抗日武装，趁夜晚日本看守离开岗哨，去检查电网的时机，由身高两米的英国电气专家汤米·韦德充当人梯，狄兰和恒安石先后从院墙跳了出去。成功逃脱后，恒安石和狄兰辗转到达了抗日游击队（ “鲁苏战区挺进第四纵队” ）驻地——平度县孙正村。随后他们分别给美、英驻华使馆写了密信，游击队派人将密信送到重庆美英驻华大使馆。不久之后，援华美军总部迅速调拨一批军用物资和资金，指示他们就地参加中国抗日游击队的工作。

On the evening of 9 June 1944, two internees escaped from the camp. They were Arthur W. Hummel Jr., a young American teacher who spoke Chinese fluently and taught in the Affiliated Boys School of the Fu Jen Catholic University in Beiping, and Laurance Tipton, a former U.K. naval officer and a sales manager at British American Tobacco in China at the time. The escape was planned by Dr. Deiss and the priest R. Jaegher, who were familiar with the local situation. Through the help of Zhang Xingtai and his son, who cleaned up the garbage in the concentration camp, they contacted the Chinese armed forces in Weihsien and informed them of the plan. While the Japanese guards left the watchtower at night to check the electric wire fencing, Tommy Wade, a very tall British electrical expert (about two meters tall), acted as a ladder to help Laurance and Arthur jumped over the Courtyard wall. After escaping from the concentration camp, they went to the station of Chinese guerrillas ('the fourth column in Jiangsu, Shangdong war zone') in Sunzheng Village, Pingdu County, Qingdao. They then wrote letters to the US and UK embassies in the city of Chongqing, which were delivered by the Chinese guerrillas. Soon after, the US Army headquarter in China allocated food and military supplies and funds, and asked them to join the Chinese guerrillas in the fight against the Japanese forces.

图 1 绘画 – 逃离集中营

Picture 1 Escaping from Weihsien Concentration Camp

恒安石：二战结束以后，恒安石回到北京，到联合国善后救济总署工作。1949 年回到美国，在芝加哥大学取得硕士学位后进入美国国务院。1972 年，尼克松访华，中美关系缓和，恒安石出任主要负责中国事务的助理国务卿，直接促成了中美联络处的建立。1981 ~ 1985 年，恒安石担任中华人民共和国成立后的第二任美国驻华大使。他上任后面临的第一个挑战就是谈判解决美国对台湾武器销售的问题。经过恒安石的斡旋努力，1982 年 8 月 17 日，中美两国达成了成为双边关系重要基础的《八・一七公报》，恒安石将此视为他任内的最大成就。在出任美国驻华大使期间，恒安石曾多次到潍坊旧地重游。1985 年，恒安石退休，居住于马里兰州，担任学术界的咨询顾问工作。退休以后，恒安石仍然非常关心美中关系的发展，他说："直到今天我都对中国感到很亲近，有机会就去中国看看"。2001 年 2 月 6 日恒安石因肺气肿在华盛顿去世，享年 80 岁。

图 2 年轻时的恒安石
Picture 2 Arthur William Hummel, Jr.

Arthur William Hummel Jr.: After World War II, Arthur returned to Beijing and worked for the United Nations Relief and Rehabilitation Administration (UNRRA). In 1949, he returned to the United States; after earning a master's degree from the University of Chicago, he began to work in the Department of State. After President Nixon visited China in 1972, the China-US relations eased and Arthur became the state assistant secretary for the Chinese affairs, contributing to the establishment of the China-U.S. liaison office. From 1981 to 1985, he served as the second U.S. ambassador to China. The first challenge he faced during his term was to negotiate how to deal with the issue of selling arms to Taiwan. Through Arthur's mediation and efforts, on August 17, 1982, China and the United States reached the August 17 Communique, which became an important basis for bilateral relations. Arthur William Hummel regarded it as his greatest achievement during his term at office. During his tenure the ambassador in China, he made several trips to Weifang. After the retirement in 1985, Arthur resided in Maryland, serving as an academic consultant. Although retired, he was still very concerned about the development of the US-China relations. "I am very close to China until today and I will visit China if I have a chance," he said. On February 6, 2001, he died of emphysema in Washington at the age of 80.

图 3 狄兰
Picture 3 Laurance Tipton

狄兰，曾在英国海军服役担任报务员。1931 年前后，狄兰来到中国，在英美烟草公司工作。1941 年 12 月 6 日，在天津被日本特务诱捕；1943 年 3 月，随同华北各地的盟国侨民被押送到山东潍县集中营。1944 年 6 月，狄兰与恒安石逃出集中营，来到山东昌邑地方抗日武装驻地，随从这支武装部队跟日军进行了艰苦的周旋，亲眼见证了中国人民不屈不挠的抗战事迹。1945 年抗日战争胜利后，狄兰回国，后被派往印度，居住在孟买。

Laurence Tipton served as a telegraph operator in the British navy. Around 1931, he moved to China to work at British American Tobacco.

On December 6th, 1941, he was captured by a Japanese special agent and, along with other citizens from the allied countries, was transferred to the Weihsien Concentration Camp. Laurence Tipton and Arthur W. Hummel later escaped from the concentration camp and stayed at the Chinese military station. They joined the China's resistance army and fought against the Japanese army during World War II. After the war, Laurence returned to the UK; later, he was relocated to Bombay, India, by British American Tobacco.

图 4　晚年的狄兰

Picture 4　Laurance Tipton in his later years

图 5　狄兰写的回忆录《中国逃亡记》

Picture 5　Chinese Escapade, a memoir written by Laurance Tipton

图 6　1944 年 5 月 4 日，在联系出逃过程中，“鲁苏战区挺进第四纵队”司令王尚志给潍县集中营侨民的信

Picture 6　The letter to the internees from Wang Shangzhi, the commander of the fourth column in Jiangsu, Shangdong war zone, during the planning of the escape

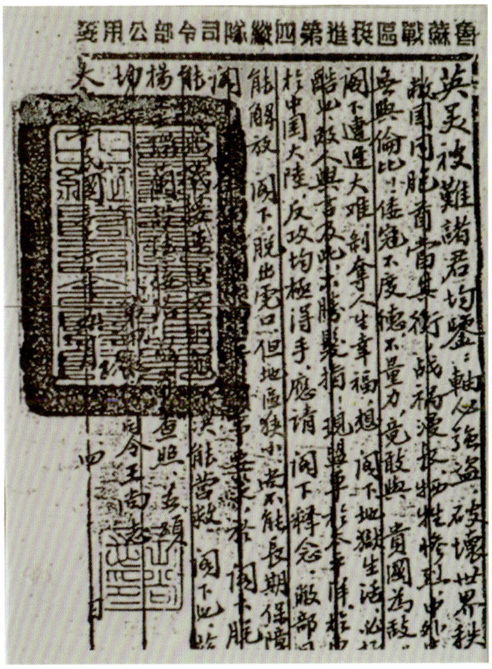

魯蘇戰區挺進第四縱隊司令部公用箋

司令王尚志

图7 协助出逃人员和恒安石、狄兰合影。左起：未知、恒安石、张兴泰、狄兰、刘书云、雷震远、刘腾云、霍伊楚

Picture 7 Arthur William Hummel Jr., Laurance Tipton and the people who assisted them to escape the camp. From left: unknown, Arthur William Hummel Jr., Zhang Xingtai, Laurance Tipton, Liu Shuyun, R. Jaegher, Liu Tengyun and Roy V. Tchoo

图8 逃出集中营的恒安石和狄兰与地方人士合影（后排左一为狄兰，左三为恒安石）

Picture 8 Arthur (third from left) and Laurance (second from right) with the local people after escaping from the concentration camp

第十章　埃里克•利迪尔

10 Eric H. Liddell

埃里克•利迪尔，是出生在天津的苏格兰人。中文名李爱锐，又名李达。他毕业于爱丁堡大学。19 世纪末，他的父母来到中国传教，当时定居在天津。1924 年埃里克荣获奥运会 400 米短跑冠军。后回到中国，在天津的一所中学里当了近 20 年的教师。埃里克意志坚定，决心将所学知识毫无保留地回馈给中国，是一位优秀的教育家。

Eric H. Liddell was of Scottish origins, born in Tianjin, China. His Chinese name was Li Airui (李 爱 锐). He was a graduate of the University of Edinburgh. In the 19th century, his parents came to China as missionaries and settled in Tianjin. Eric won the 400-meter sprint at the Olympic Games in 1924. He then returned to China and worked as a teacher in a middle school in Tianjin for nearly twenty years. Eric was a passionate, dedicated educator, determined to give to China what he had learned.

图 1 埃里克•利迪尔（李爱锐）
Picture 1 Eric H. Liddell

抗战期间，埃里克曾以教徒的身份去河北中部参加敌后抗日活动。太平洋战争爆发，埃里克跟众多外国侨民一样，于 1942 年被日军关进潍县集中营。在集中营三年的生活中，埃里克不畏强暴，忘我工作，帮助难友学习，照顾难友生活，组织各种文体活动，深受侨民们的敬重。但由于身陷困境，生活困苦，营养不良，1945 年 2 月 21 日，年仅 43 岁的埃里克•利迪尔因患脑瘤，得不到有效治疗，病逝在集中营内，而这一天，距离日本宣布战败投降只有 175 天。

During the Sino-Japanese War, Eric went to Hebei Province and took part in the anti-Japanese aggression activities. In 1942, when the Pacific War broke out, Eric was also among the Western citizens who were imprisoned in the Weihsien Concentration Camp by the Japanese forces. During his time in the camp, about three years, he repeatedly showed his courage, caring and kindness. Eric helped other internees study, took care of them and organized sports activities, earning other internees' respect and admiration. On February 21, 1945, because of malnutrition and lack of medical treatment, Eric Liddell died of brain tumor at the age of 43. Just 175 days later, Japan surrendered.

图 2 1903 年，儿时的埃里克·利迪尔
Picture 2 Eric H. Liddell in his childhood, 1903

图 3 埃里克·利迪尔幼时家庭照
Picture 3 Eric H. Liddell's family when he was a baby

图 4 埃里克·利迪尔幼时与家人合影
Picture 4 Young Eric H. Liddell with his family

图 5 埃里克·利迪尔兄妹三人，左二为埃里克·利迪尔
Picture 5 Eric (second from left) with his brother and sister

图 6 年轻英俊的埃里克·利迪尔
Picture 6 Young Eric

图 7 埃里克·利迪尔在爱丁堡大学的毕业照
Picture 7 Eric graduated from University of Edinburgh

图 8 1924 年埃里克·利迪尔在奥运会上夺得 400 米短跑冠军
Picture 8 Eric H. Liddell won the 400m sprint at the Olympics in 1924

图 9 埃里克·利迪尔在运动赛场
Picture 9 Eric H. Liddell in the sports court

图 10 埃里克·利迪尔（右一）与接力队队友（1924 年巴黎奥运会）
Picture 10 Eric Liddell (first from right) and the relay team members (1924 Paris Olympic Games)

图 11　1934 年 3 月 27 日，埃里克•利迪尔与弗劳伦丝•麦肯齐女士在天津的完婚照
Picture 11　On March 27, 1934, Eric married Florence Mackenzie

图 12　1937 年埃里克•利迪尔和妻女在一起
Picture 12　Eric Liddell with his wife and daughters in 1937

图 13 埃里克·利迪尔在中国农村
Picture 13 Eric in the countryside of China

图 14 天津新学书院，埃里克·利迪尔在这里教授自然科学 12 年
Picture 14 Eric taught natural science at Tianjin Xinxue Academy for 12 years

图 15　因爱着中国——被埃里克·利迪尔救助过的中国农民画家送给他的画

Picture 15　Love for China — a painting dedicated to Eric, drawn by a Chinese peasant artist, whom he had saved

图 16　埃里克·利迪尔在集中营里亲自编写的教材

Picture 16　Textbook written by Eric in the concentration camp

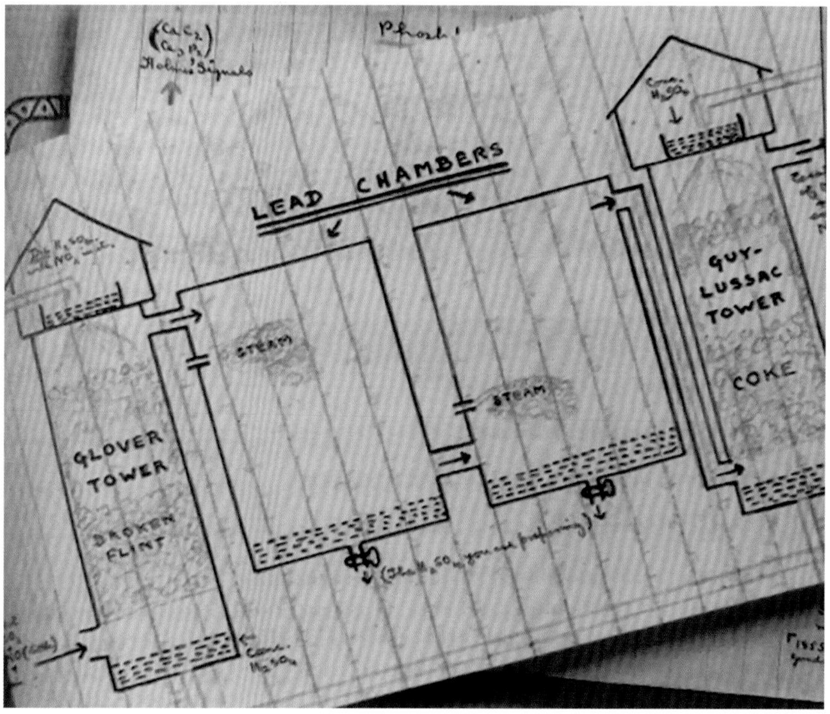

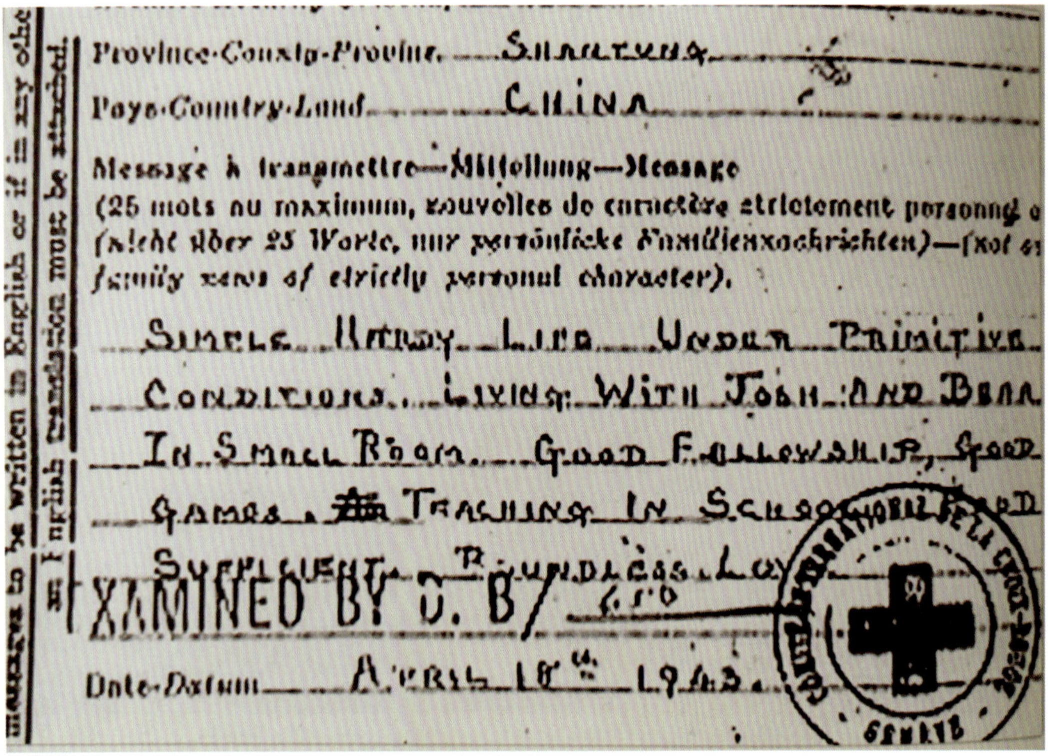
Message to be written in English or if in any other ... English translation must be attached.

Province·Comté·Provinz. SHANTUNG

Pays·Country·Land. CHINA

Message à transmettre—Mitteilung—Message
(25 mots au maximum, nouvelles de caractère strictement personnel ...)
(nicht über 25 Worte, nur persönliche Familiennachrichten)—(not o...
family news of strictly personal character).

SIMPLE HAPPY LIFE UNDER PRIMITIVE
CONDITIONS. LIVING WITH JOAN AND BERN...
IN SMALL ROOM. GOOD FELLOWSHIP, GOOD
GAMES. TEACHING IN SCHOOL ... FOOD
SUPPLEMENT. BOUNDLESS LOV...

EXAMINED BY D. B/

Date-Datum APRIL 18th 1943.

图 17 埃里克·利迪尔在集中营写给家人的信，按日军规定只能有 25 个字

Picture 17 A short letter from Eric Liddell to his family, written in the camp. Due to the restrictions imposed by the Japanese authorities, the letters sent out from the camp could not be more than 25 words

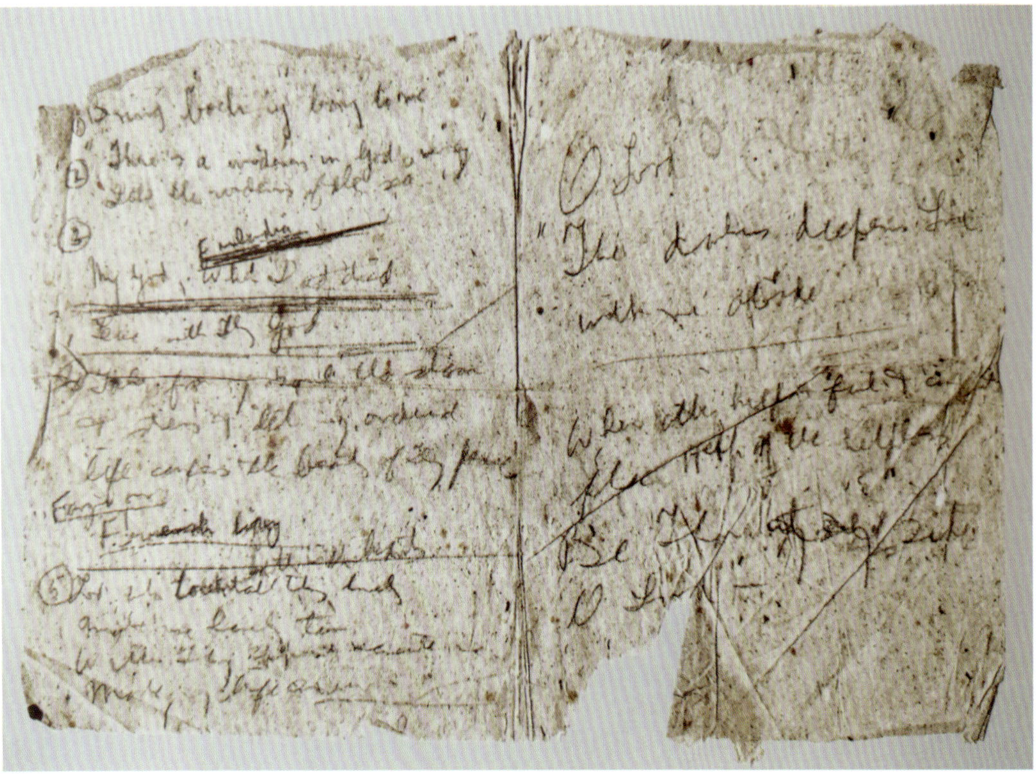

图 18 埃里克·利迪尔去世前在草纸上手写的遗书

Picture 18 Eric Liddell’s last notes before his death

图 19 埃里克·利迪尔在潍县的墓地
Picture 19 The grave of Eric Liddell in Weihsien

图 21 青铜塑像——奔跑着的埃里克。藏于英格兰康宁思路埃里克·利迪尔纪念馆
Picture 21 Bronze statue - The Running Eric, collected in Eric H. Liddell Memorial in Corninx Road, England

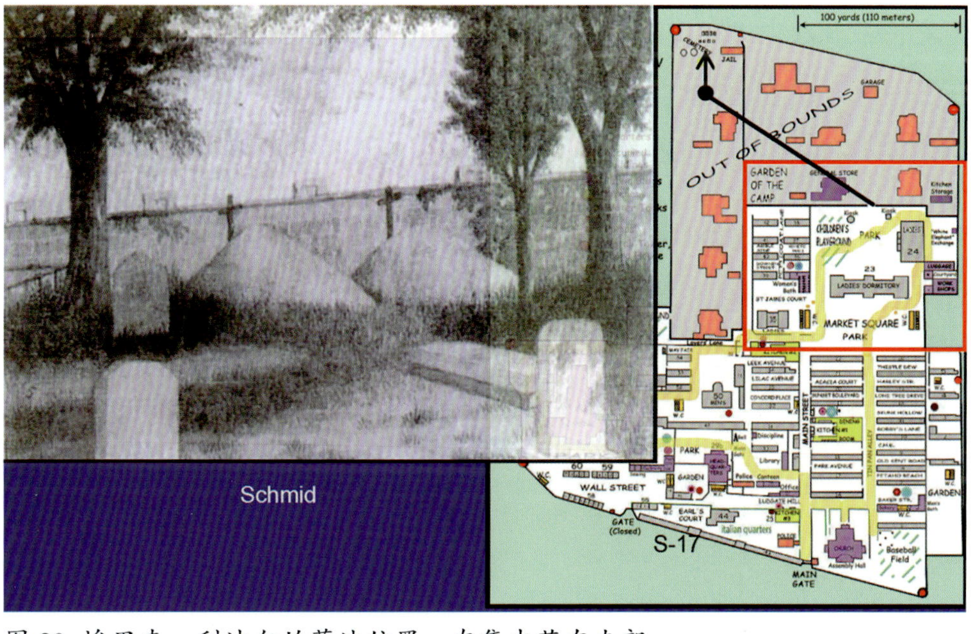

图 20 埃里克·利迪尔的墓地位置，在集中营东南部
Picture 20 The grave of Eric Liddell was at the southeast area of the concentration camp

图 22 1991年，埃里克•利迪尔基金会在潍县设立埃里克•利迪尔纪念碑。这座纪念碑就是用埃里克•利迪尔家乡苏格兰马尔岛的花岗岩制成，碑的正面镌刻有中英文镏金碑文：他们应可振翅高飞，如展翼的雄鹰；他们应可竞跑向前，永不言疲累

Picture 22 In 1991, the Eric H. Liddell Foundation set up a memorial stone in Weihsien.The memorial stone, made of granite from Eric Liddell's hometown Isle of Mull, Scotland, was engraved on the front with gold-plated inscriptions in Chinese: "They shall mount up with wings as eagles; they shall run, and not be weary."

图 23 埃里克・利迪尔纪念雕像，现存于乐道院潍县集中营博物馆

Picture 23 Statue of Eric Liddell, reserved at Weihsien Courtyard of the Happy Way and Concentration Camp Museum

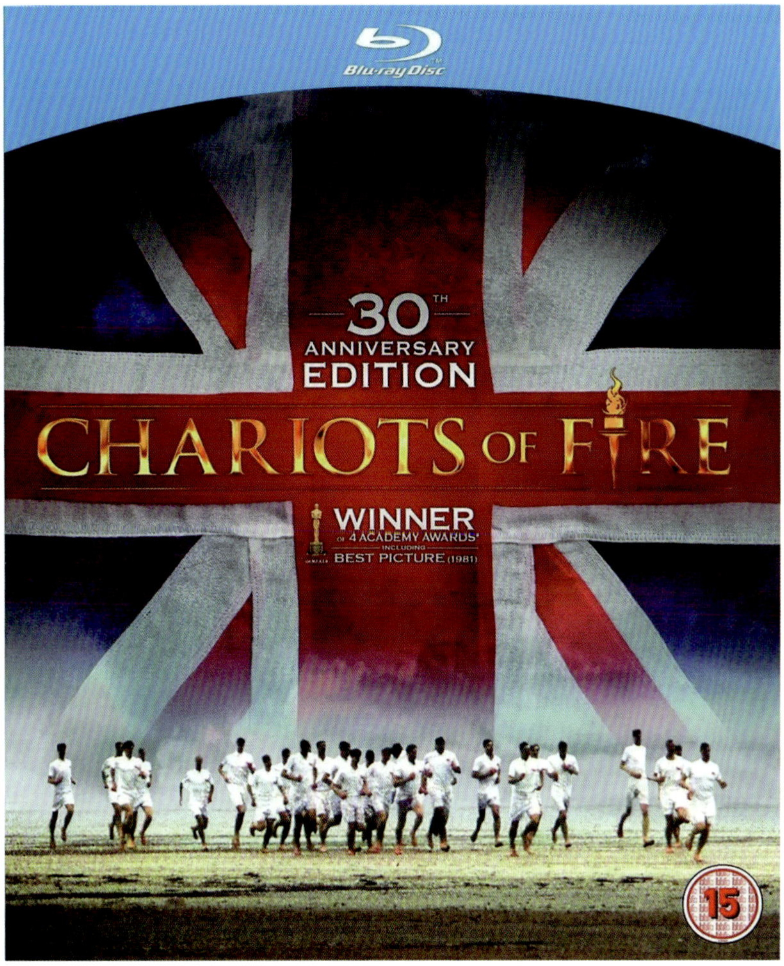

图 24 对于深受人们爱戴、病逝于潍县集中营的英国著名短跑冠军埃里克·利迪尔先生，半个多世纪以来，世界各地的纪念活动从未停止。利迪尔奥运夺魁的故事被拍摄成电影《烈火战车》，1982 年该片荣获第 54 届奥斯卡金像奖。1991 年 1 月，他生前的好友，被他救助过的人们在香港发起了利迪尔纪念基金会

Picture 24 There have been memorial activities all over the world to remember and celebrate the deeply beloved and respected Scottish Olympic champion Eric Liddell since then. The 1982 Oscar Award-winning film, Chariots of Fire, tells Eric's story of winning the gold medal at the 1924 Olympics. In January of 1991, his friends and those who were helped out by Eric established the Eric Liddell Foundation in Hong Kong

图 25 为纪念埃里克·利迪尔出版的一些书籍

Picture 25 Books published to remember Eric Liddell's legacy

第十一章　潍坊人民对乐道院西方侨民的帮助

11 Weifang Local People Helped the Internees

随着战争的深入，乐道院的生活越来越艰苦。食物配给越来越少。在饥饿难忍的情况下，侨民只能买通日本看守和卫兵，代买食品，钱用完了就用高档衣物、高档首饰换取廉价食品，最后大多数侨民都只剩下一身破旧衣服。

从1942年到1945年，潍坊人民曾多次援救和帮助那些身陷囹圄的西方侨民，有的为此献出了宝贵的生命。

As the Second World War intensified, the quality of life in the Courtyard constantly deteriorated. The rationed food became even less plentiful, so the internees began to bribe the Japanese guards of the camp to buy some food for them. Once they ran out of money, they started to trade their expensive clothes and jewellery for low quality food. As a result, most internees ended up dressed in rags.

From 1942 to 1945, the local people of Weihsien frequently helped the imprisoned Western civilians, some losing their lives in the process.

第一节　"黑市交易"

11.1 "Black Market Transaction"

集中营内的食品供应越来越紧张，一些大胆的侨民偷偷将自己的首饰等物品包好，夹上一张此物想换多少食品的字条，趁日本看守不注意时扔出墙外。善良的潍县民众捡到后，总会从墙外扔进超出他们要求的食物。天长日久，这种地下交易逐渐形成规模，侨民们称之为"地下黑市"。正是这种"黑市交易"，一定程度上帮助侨民们度过了那段艰难的岁月。

Considering there was a growing food supply to the camp, some internees would secretly wrap their jewellery and other valuable possessions, with a note showing how much food they wanted in exchange for them; they then would throw the wrapped items out of the walls when the Japanese guards were distracted . The local people then would pick them up and throw food over the walls, usually more than the amount of the food the internees had requested or expected. Over the time, this kind of underground trading became very common; soon, the internees called it the "underground black market". This kind of transaction helped them go through those difficult years and survive.

一日黄昏，当潍县西上虞河的青年韩祥第二次在电网上放置木板，携带食品越墙而入时，被日军看守发现，慌乱中不慎触电死亡。日军看守为了示众，故意让尸体在电网上悬挂了两天两夜。

One evening, when Han Xiang, a young man from Weihsien, placed planks on the wire netting for the second time and decided to climb over the wall to carry in some food, he was discovered by the Japanese guards.

He panicked and was unfortunately electrocuted to death. The Japanese guards deliberately hung the body on the netting fence for two days as a deterrent.

图 1 西方侨民绘制的描绘潍县当地百姓翻越集中营围墙与侨民交换物品的漫画
Picture 1 A cartoon of local people crossing over the camp walls to exchange things with internees, drawn by an internee

图 2 西方侨民绘制的“黑市交易”情景画
Picture 2 “Black Market Transaction” drawn by an internee

图 3 潍县人韩祥触电身亡情景图（拍摄于乐道院潍县集中营博物馆）
Picture 3 A Weihsien young man Han Xiang was electrocuted

第二节　铁床的故事
11.2 The Story of an Iron Bed

图 4　1943 年潍县人韩绪庭与集中营侨民物物交换回的铁床
Picture 4　In 1943, Weihsien native Han Xuting exchanged this iron bed from internees

图 5　铁床的商标，可见“大肯兄弟，伦敦”字样
Picture 5　Bed logo　“ Dakin Brothers, London”

这张床是伦敦大肯兄弟制造公司生产的。原来是一张钢丝床，后来换成木板。潍县集中营的生活艰苦，很多难友用手表、首饰跟老百姓换取食物。这张铁床就是丹麦难友和当地农民韩绪庭做交换后保留下来的。那是 1943 年的春天，一天晚上九时许，韩绪庭来到集中营西墙外，那里有一根长杆，是难友们专门用来和外面交换东西用的。趁着日本兵不在之际，韩绪庭把 2.5 斤白糖和 5 斤鸡蛋吊了进去，里面有人接着。过了十几分钟，长杆子上吊出来一张铁床。床体是拆卸开的，床板一共 3 块。韩绪庭当时很是担心怕被日本兵发现，因为之前有往里面送东西的人被枪杀。韩绪庭战战兢兢地接过床，这张床约 25 公斤重，他家距离集中营 2.5 公里。韩绪庭不敢有丝毫耽搁，扛起铁床，穿过庄稼地，赶紧回去了。保留下来的这张铁床成了那段历史的见证。

The bed was made by Dakin Brothers London Manufacturing Company. It used to be a steel wire bed, which was later converted into a wooden one. There was such a shortage of food in the camp that the internees had to trade their watches and jewellery for food with the locals. In exchange for some food, a Danish internee gave this iron bed to Han Xuting, a local farmer. It was in the spring of 1943. Around nine o'clock in the evening, Han Xuting was waiting outside the west wall of the concentration camp, where there was a long pole, used by internees for exchanging their valuable belongings for food with the local people. When the Japanese soldiers were away, Han Xuting hoisted 1.25 kilograms of sugar and 2.5 kilograms of eggs into the camp. About ten minutes later, an iron bed was hoisted over the wall by the famous long pole. The bed was divided into three parts. Han was worried about being discovered by the Japanese, knowing one of the local people was shot while exchanging food for valuable things. Han Xuting nervously took the bed, which weighed about 25 kilograms. His house was 2.5 kilometers away from the camp. He carried the heavy bed on his shoulders, walking home through the fields. This iron bed became a sort of a witness to those difficult days and the story of the camp and its residents during WWII.

第三节　潍县民众筹款救助被囚侨民
11.3 Local People Raise Money to Aid the Internees

曾经盛传，集中营内有一个神秘电台与外界联系。其实所谓的神秘电台，实际上就是每天出入集中营运送垃圾的清洁工张兴泰父子，通过他们的口信，集中营外的中国军民，在看守不易发现的墙角，经常向集中营内投递食物。虽然当时自己的生活条件也很艰难，但仍然本着人道主义精神，力所能及地救助难民。当地民众还秘密筹集善款，以国际红十字会的名义购买药物和营养品，帮助集中营中的大多数人员幸运地度过了囚禁岁月。

There was a mysterious radio station in the concentration camp, which the camp's internees used to contact the outside world. In fact, the so-called radio station was actually made of flesh and blood. Zhang Xingtai and his son, the two cleaning workers, who went to the concentration camp every day, carried the messages from the camp to the outside world and vice versa. In this way, the Chinese army and local people knew what was happening in the camp, and often delivered food to the camp's residents. Although the Chinese people themselves lived in dire conditions at the time, they nonetheless did whatever they could to help the internees. The local people also secretly raised money to buy medicine and food in the name of the International Red Cross. What they did helped most of the internees survive the difficult life in the camp.

随着战争的深入，集中营里的食物供应日渐减少，大家在沉默中忍受着长期的饥饿，憔悴消瘦，体力枯竭，神情麻木，有人失重 100 多磅。面对如此恶劣的情况，被关押人士代表德位思博士迫切希望能与外界取得联系以求得帮助，可是日本人的监控非常严密，于是他想到了唯一能自由出入集中营的掏粪工张兴泰父子。

As the war escalated, less and less food was supplied to the camp. The imprisoned endured extreme shortage of food for a long period of time which led to their emaciation. Some lost up to 100 pounds. In the face of these dire conditions, Dr. Deiss, the internees' representative became increasingly determined to find a way to contact the outside world and ask for help, but the Japanese were very alert. That was when he first began to think of using the cleaning workers Zhang Xingtai and Zhang Xiwu as messengers, as they could freely enter and exit the camp.

图 6 给西方侨民提供过许多帮助的掏粪工张兴泰、张锡武父子
Picture 6 Zhang Xingtai and his son Zhang Xiwu, two cleaning workers who helped internees

张兴泰父子是附近李家村的农民，当这些外国人在集中营求救时，耿直忠厚的张兴泰没有半点犹豫，冒

着生命危险将信转给了营外原广文中学校长黄乐德牧师。

Zhang Xingtai and his son were farmers, living in the nearby Lijiazhuang Village. When the internees asked for help, Zhang Xingtai did not hesitate, risking his life to transfer a letter to minister Huang Lede, the former principal of Kwangwen Middle School, who lived in Weihsien at the time.

四周的民众得知集中营侨民的惨状后，非常同情，在各自家境并不宽裕的情况下，踊跃捐赠善款，民众和官方共捐款时值美金 10 余万元。这批款项由黄乐德的儿子黄安慰与女儿黄瑞云分三批秘密送往中立国瑞士驻青岛代办处艾格外交官手中，再以国际红十字会的名义购买集中营急需的药物和营养品，分批送往集中营。正是这一批批的救命物资，才使得被关押的 1500 多名西方侨民能够幸运地支撑下来。

After learning about the difficulties of the camp's residents, the local people became very sympathetic to the Western citizens. Although they were themselves very poor, they donated some money. The total donation from the local citizens and the authority was over 100,000 USD at the time. Huang's son, Huang Anwei, and his daughter, Huang Ruiyun, secretly and separately delivered the money to Mr. Eig, a diplomat at the Swiss Representative Office in Qingdao. Mr. Eig then, in the name of the International Red Cross, bought the much-needed medicine and food and sent them to the camp. These supplies were crucial for the survival of the camp's internees, which is estimated to be around 1,500 people at the time.

图 7 “蜜罐”男人——掏粪工张兴泰（西方侨民乌苏拉・西蒙斯 1944 年绘制）
Picture 7 The “honey jar” man – nightman Zhang Xingtai (drawn by Ursula Simmons, a camp's internee, in 1944)

图 8 掏粪工张兴泰赶着驴车运粪的情景画（张美源画）
Picture 8 The nightman Zhang Xingtai driving the donkey cart, drawn by Zhang Meiyuan

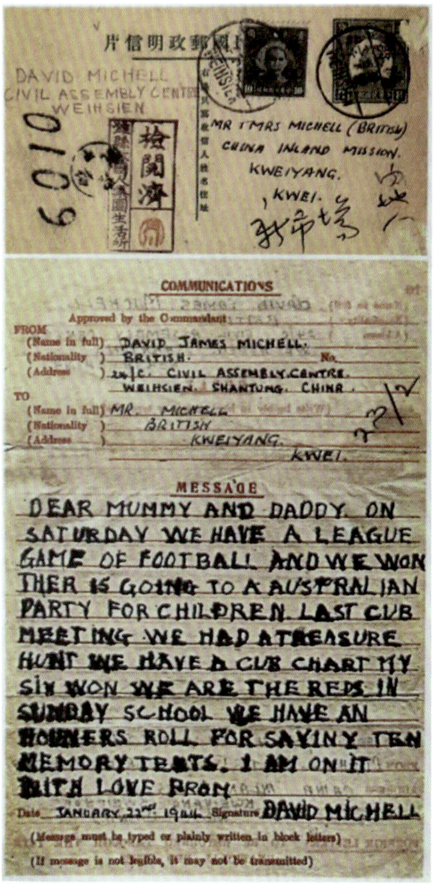

DAVID MICHELL
CIVIL ASSEMBLY CENTRE
WEIHSIEN

MR + MRS MICHELL (BRITISH)
CHINA INLAND MISSION.
KWEIYANG.
, KWEI.

检閲濟

COMMUNICATIONS

Approved by the Commandant

FROM
(Name in full) DAVID JAMES MICHELL.
(Nationality) BRITISH. No.
(Address) 24/C. CIVIL ASSEMBLY CENTRE.
WEIHSIEN. SHANTUNG. CHINA.

TO
(Name in full) MR. MICHELL
(Nationality) BRITISH
(Address) KWEIYANG.
KWEI.

MESSAGE

DEAR MUMMY AND DADDY ON SATURDAY WE HAVE A LEAGUE GAME OF FOOTBALL AND WE WON THER IS GOING TO A AUSTRALIAN PARTY FOR CHILDREN LAST CUB MEETING WE HAD A TREASURE HUNT WE HAVE A CUB CHART MY SIX WON WE ARE THE REDS IN SUNDAY SCHOOL WE HAVE AN HONNERS ROLL FOR SAYINY TEN MEMORY TEXTS. I AM ON IT WITH LOVE FROM

Date JANUARY 22nd 1944 Signature DAVID MICHELL

(Message must be typed or plainly written in block letters)
(If message is not legible, it may not be transmitted)

图 9 通过红十字会转送的西方侨民的信件，都需要经过日军的严格检查。信的内容讲述的是侨民在集中营的日常生活
Picture 9 All the internees' letters were strictly inspected by the Japanese army before being mailed to the Red Cross, which was a transfer station. This letter tells story of the camp life

图 10　帮助过集中营侨民的黄乐德牧师之子黄安慰
Picture 10　Huang Anwei, the son of minister Huang Lede

图 11　瑞士驻青岛领事
Picture 11 Swiss Consul in Qingdao

图 12 生活改善后面带笑容的难友贝西·阿特雷

Picture 12 Internee Bessy smiling after getting food supplies

图 13 生活改善后姑娘们在高兴地打饭

Picture 13 Girls happily waiting for food

图 14 生活条件改善后的侨民

Picture 14 Internees' living conditions improved

第十二章　日本投降、西方侨民获得解救

12 The Surrender of Japan and the Liberated Western Residents

1945 年 8 月，日本宣布无条件投降，潍县集中营盼来了胜利的曙光。1945 年 8 月 17 日，美军援华总部派出代号为“鸭子”行动队的营救小组，驾驶 B-24 型轰炸机，抵达潍县集中营上空。侨民们看清飞机上美军符号及天使标志后，顿时沸腾起来，发了疯一般向院门外冲去（飞机上空投下电台、药品、食品等大批急需物资）。鸭子行动小组 7 位伞兵队员在玉米地和高粱地里集结后，立即整队实施营救。备受 3 年折磨的侨民，在获得自由的那一刻，扑倒在地痛哭不已。降落伞碎片，伞兵身上的纽扣、徽章，甚至女孩剪下他们的一小撮头发，都成了他们收藏的纪念品。

In August 1945, after Japan announced it would accept unconditional surrender, the Weihsien Concentration Camp's residents began to dream being released from a long, horrible confinement. On August 17, 1945, the U.S. military aid headquarters in China sent a B-24 aeroplane carrying a rescue team, in an operation called the "Operation Duck", to the Weihsien Concentration Camp. Upon seeing the sign of American army on the plane, the hopeful internees jumped for joy, and rushed out of the Courtyard gate. The aircraft dropped radio, medicine, food and other supplies for the people captivated in the camp. Subsequently, seven paratroopers landed on the farming fields surrounding the camp and rescued the internees. The internees, who were in confinement for three long years, kneed on the ground and burst into tears as soon as they were set free. The internees collected the fragments of parachutes, buttons on the paratroopers' clothes, their badges, and even the paratroopers' hair cut off by the girls, as souvenirs.

图 1　美军部署代号“鸭子”营救行动
Picture 1　U. S. military deploying Duck Mission

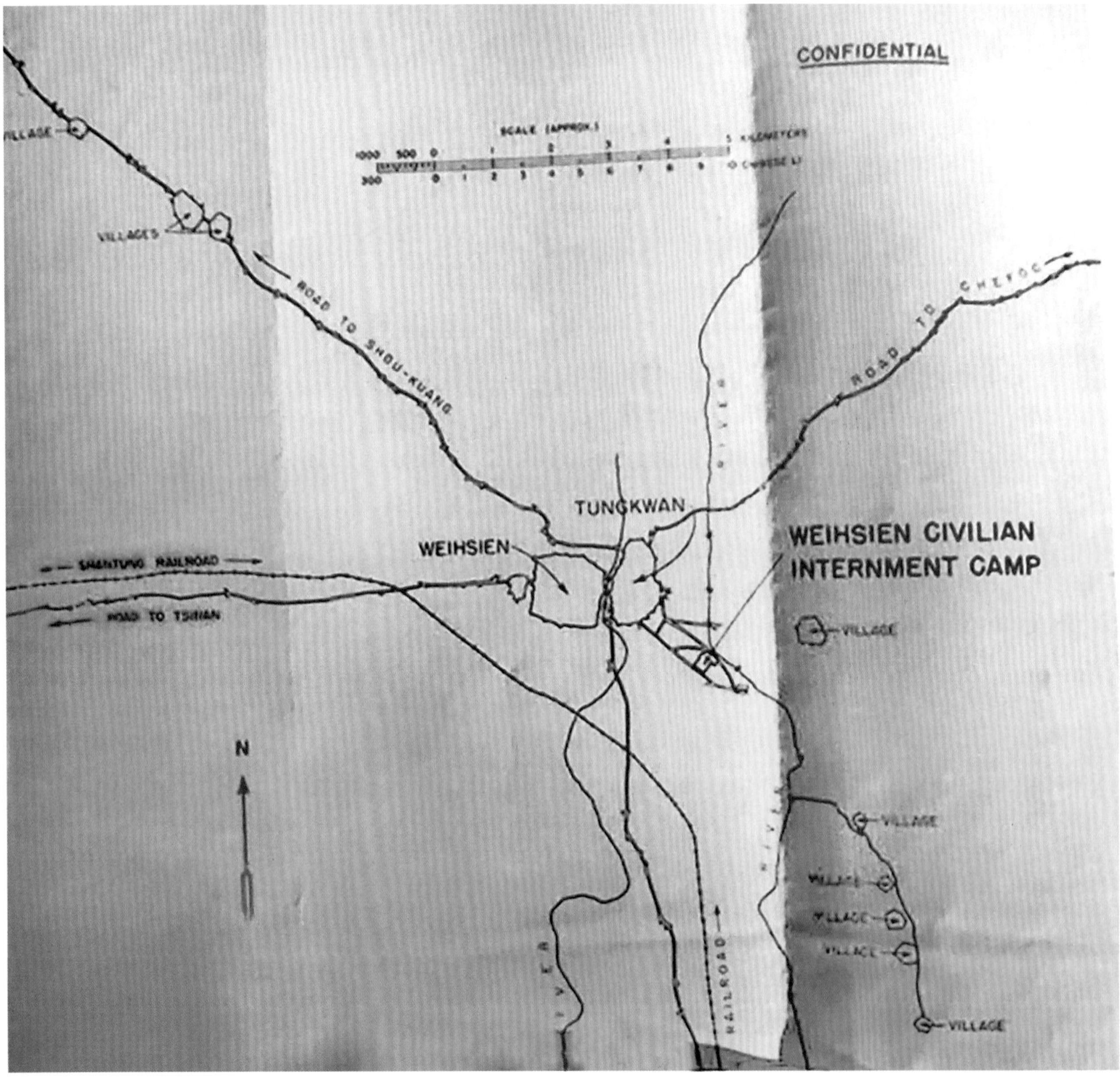

图 2 “鸭子”行动队指挥图（绝密）
Picture 2 Operation Duck command chart (confidential)

图 3 参加“鸭子”营救行动的雷蒙德•汉库莱克和塔德•永木
Picture 3 Operation Duck team members Raymond Hanchulak and Tad Nagaki

图 4 “鸭子”行动队队长斯泰格少校和吉姆•穆尔少尉的合影
Picture 4 Major Stanley A.Staiger, captain of Operation Duck, and Ensign James Moore

图 5 美军空投物资到集中营
Picture 5 The U.S. forces airdropping supplies to the concentration camp

图 6 美国“鸭子”行动队队员跳伞瞬间
Picture 6 Operation Duck team parachuting

图7 “鸭子”行动队4位队员(从左至右分别为:战略情报局少尉吉姆·穆尔、日语翻译塔德·永木、队长斯泰格少校 、医生汉格列治)

Picture 7 Four members of Operation Duck (left to right: Ensign James W. Moore, Office of Strategic Services; Tad Nagaki, Japanese translator; Major Stanley A. Staiger, operation captain; Raymond N. Hanchulak, doctor)

图8 “鸭子”行动队导航员詹姆斯·汉农中尉

Picture 8 1st Lieutenant James J. Hannon, Operation Duck's navigator

图9 “鸭子”行动队无线电报务员皮特·欧力克

Picture 9 Operation Duck member Peter Orlich, radio operator

图 10 “鸭子”行动队队员王成汉
Picture 10 Operation Duck member Wang Chenghan

“鸭子”行动队队员王成汉。1943 年，18 岁的他考入当时的四川大学物理系，1944 年秋天他到庐州参加了“国民革命军青年军”，后来参加了译员培训班，并被 OSS（美国战略情报局）招募进入特别行动组。之后，他在云南开元受训，再回到昆明时被分配到了特别情报组。1945 年 8 月，大学尚未毕业就投笔从戎的王成汉，作为美军 7 人解救小组的翻译，跳伞参加了潍县集中营解放行动。1945 年 10 月，王成汉回到成都后继续上学。

Wang Chenghan, a member of the Operation Duck rescue team. In 1943, the 18-year-old Wang was admitted to the physics department in Sichuan University. He joined the National Revolutionary Army Youth Army in Luzhou in the fall of 1944. After completing an interpreting training course, he was recruited to serve in the Special Action Team by the Office of Strategic Services (OSS). Later, he was trained in Kaiyuan, Yunnan, and was assigned to work in the Special Intelligence Unit which was based in Kunming. In August, 1945, Wang Chenghan, who had not yet graduated from the university, joined the rescue team as an interpreter and took part in the operation which led to the liberation of the Weihsien Concentration Camp. In October 1945, Wang returned to Chengdu to continue his studies.

图 11 美军空投到集中营物资的外包装
Picture 11 Airdropped food from the U.S. force

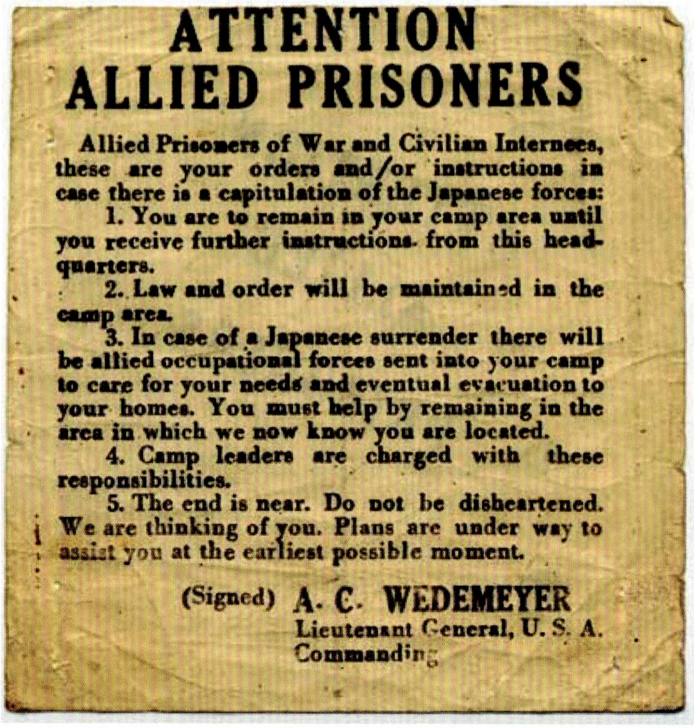

ATTENTION
ALLIED PRISONERS

Allied Prisoners of War and Civilian Internees, these are your orders and/or instructions in case there is a capitulation of the Japanese forces:

1. You are to remain in your camp area until you receive further instructions from this headquarters.

2. Law and order will be maintained in the camp area.

3. In case of a Japanese surrender there will be allied occupational forces sent into your camp to care for your needs and eventual evacuation to your homes. You must help by remaining in the area in which we now know you are located.

4. Camp leaders are charged with these responsibilities.

5. The end is near. Do not be disheartened. We are thinking of you. Plans are under way to assist you at the earliest possible moment.

(Signed) A. C. WEDEMEYER
Lieutenant General, U. S. A.
Commanding

图 12 美国空军空投的传单——提醒侨民注意物资分配
Picture 12 Instructions to the internees airdropped by the US Army Air Force

图 13 美军空投物资飞机飞越集中营第 23 区
Picture 13 The U.S. aircraft delivering relief supplies over the camp Block 23

美軍空降解救樂道院集中營外國僑民及空投救濟物資的 B-24 型飛機

图 14 美军营救潍县集中营难友时使用的 B-24 轰炸机
Picture 14 B-24 bomber, used by the U.S. military for rescuing Weihsien Concentration Camp

图 15 被解救的难友们在欢呼庆祝重获自由
Picture 15 Rescued civilians cheering and celebrating their freedom

图 16 “救世军”管乐队演奏《欢乐之日今来临》
Picture 16 Salvation Army orchestra played Happy Day

图 17 1945 年乐道院集中营解放时的“十字楼”
Picture 17 Cross Building in Weihsien Concentration Camp when it was liberated in 1945

图 18 日本投降后外国侨民代表与中国军政官员合影
Picture 18 Western residents and Chinese officials after the surrender of Japan

图 19 部分难友与营救人员合影（胜利纪念 1945 年 9 月 2 日摄于中国山东省潍县乐道院）

Picture 19 Some Western civilians and rescuers (Chinese words: Celebration of Victory. Taken at the Courtyard of the Happy Way on September 2, 1945)

图 20 1945 年 9 月 11 日雷震远神父和詹姆斯·汉农等庆祝胜利合照（左一为雷震远，左三为詹姆斯·汉农）。

Picture 20 Priest R. Jaegher (first from left) and James Hannon (third from left) celebrating the victory on September 11, 1945

图 21　雷震远与潍县地方军政人员、美军代表合影（右二为雷震远，1945 年 9 月潍县丽芳照相馆拍摄）

Picture 21　R. Jaegher (second from right), Weihsien officials, and representatives of the U.S. Army (by Weihsien Lifang Photo Studio in September 1945)

图 22　难友一家在集中营大门口留影纪念

Picture 22　A family at the concentration camp gate

第十三章　西方侨民离开潍县集中营

13 Western Residents' Departure from the Weihsien Concentration Camp

历经磨难、归心似箭的异国侨民，都想早一天回到祖国与亲人团聚，因当时交通不便，只好按照姓名的第一个英文字母顺序分期分批安排回国，多数人先从潍县乘火车去青岛，再改乘美国军舰。有的因亲人在中国大后方工作，便从潍县二十里堡机场乘美军小型运输机飞赴内地，与离别多年的亲人团聚。

After being liberated, the Western residents wanted to return to their motherland and see their families as soon as possible. Because of the inconvenient transportation at that time, they had to leave in groups according to the order of the first letters in their names. Most civilians took trains from Weihsien to Qingdao and then took American warships to go home. Because some civilians had families working in the rear area of China, they flew there by small U.S. military transport planes from Weihsien Airport and reunited with their families after years of separation.

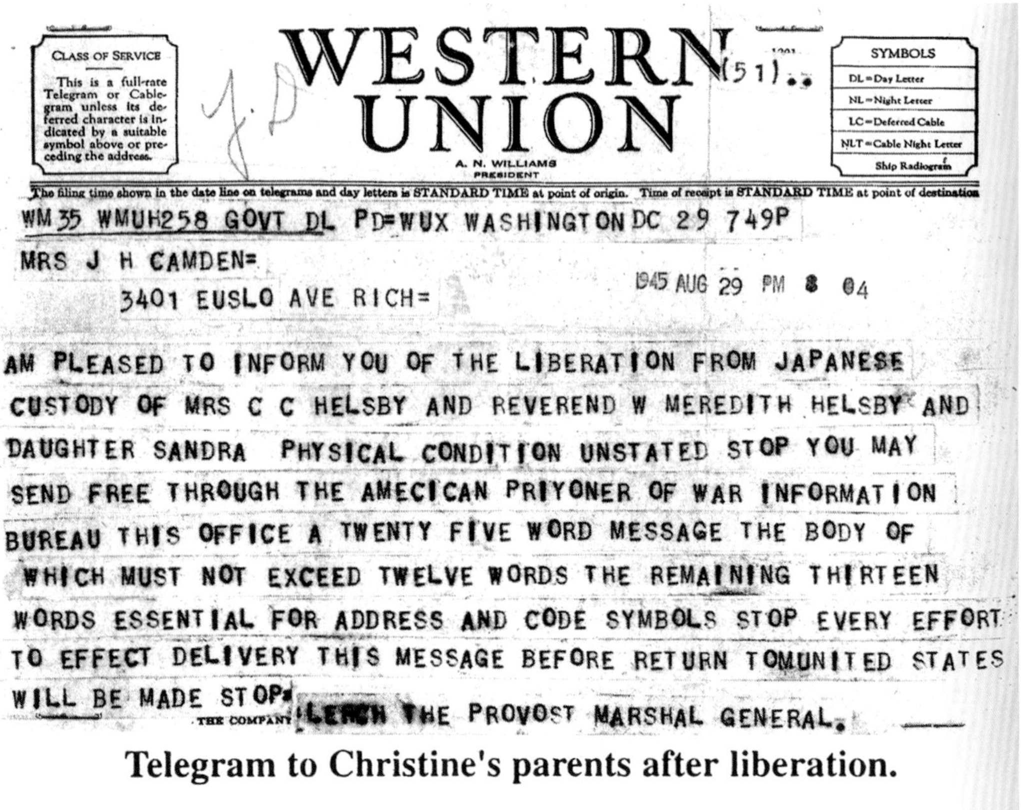

CLASS OF SERVICE
This is a full-rate Telegram or Cablegram unless its deferred character is indicated by a suitable symbol above or preceding the address.

WESTERN UNION

A. N. WILLIAMS
PRESIDENT

SYMBOLS
DL=Day Letter
NL=Night Letter
LC=Deferred Cable
NLT=Cable Night Letter
Ship Radiogram

The filing time shown in the date line on telegrams and day letters is STANDARD TIME at point of origin. Time of receipt is STANDARD TIME at point of destination

WM35 WMUH258 GOVT DL PD=WUX WASHINGTON DC 29 749P

MRS J H CAMDEN=

3401 EUSLO AVE RICH=

1945 AUG 29 PM 8 04

AM PLEASED TO INFORM YOU OF THE LIBERATION FROM JAPANESE CUSTODY OF MRS C C HELSBY AND REVEREND W MEREDITH HELSBY AND DAUGHTER SANDRA PHYSICAL CONDITION UNSTATED STOP YOU MAY SEND FREE THROUGH THE AMECICAN PRIYONER OF WAR INFORMATION BUREAU THIS OFFICE A TWENTY FIVE WORD MESSAGE THE BODY OF WHICH MUST NOT EXCEED TWELVE WORDS THE REMAINING THIRTEEN WORDS ESSENTIAL FOR ADDRESS AND CODE SYMBOLS STOP EVERY EFFORT TO EFFECT DELIVERY THIS MESSAGE BEFORE RETURN TOMUNITED STATES WILL BE MADE STOP= LERCH THE PROVOST MARSHAL GENERAL.

Telegram to Christine's parents after liberation.

图 1　被解救后的西方侨民拍给家人的电报

Picture 1 Telegram sent by Western residents to their family after being rescued

图 2 等待离开潍县的西方侨民
Picture 2 Western residents waiting to leave Weihsien

图 3 等待离开潍县的西方侨民
Picture 3 Western residents waiting to leave Weihsien

图 4 戴爱美（右起第三个）和兄弟姐妹以及其他孩子从集中营被解救，正准备登机与家人团聚
Picture 4 Mary Taylor Previte, (third from right), with her siblings and other children boarding the plane to see their family after being rescued

图 5 西方侨民乘卡车离开集中营
Picture 5 Western residents leaving Weihsien Concentration Camp by trucks

图 6 西方侨民乘卡车离开集中营
Picture 6 Western residents leaving the camp by trucks

图 7 被囚侨民离开潍县

Picture 7 Western residents leaving Weihsien

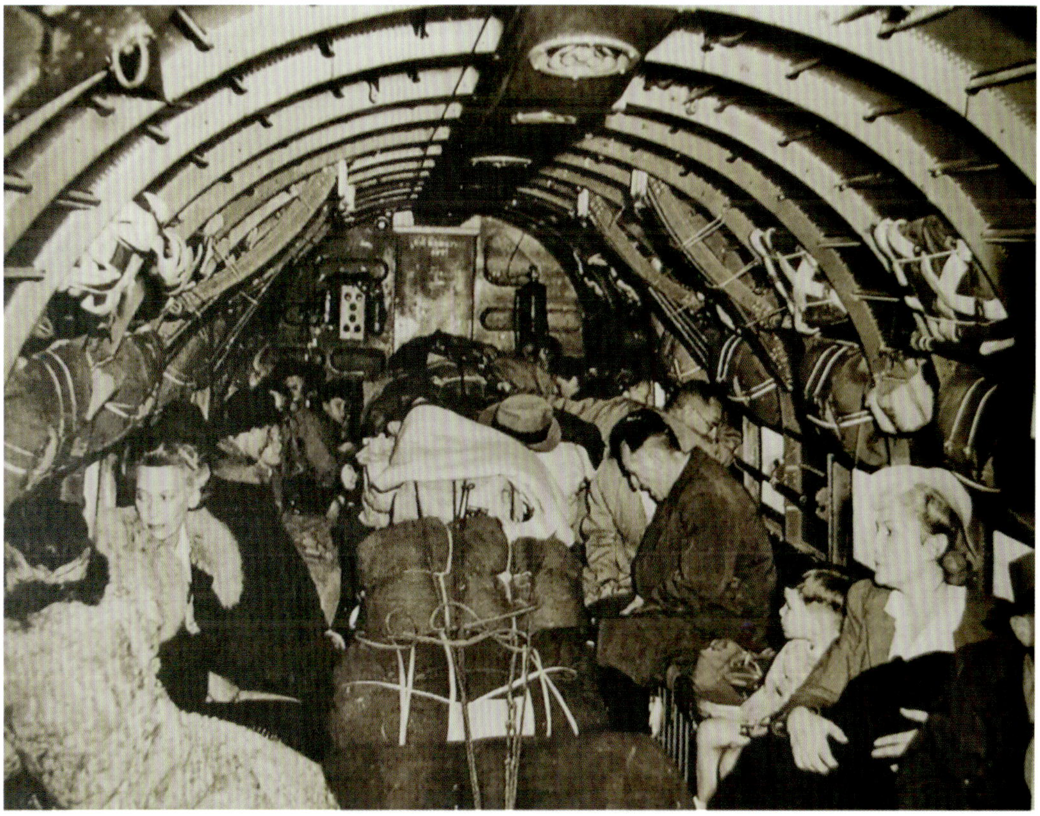

图 8 西方侨民李庞特一家和其他营友坐飞机离开潍县

Picture 8 The Pander family and other families leaving Weihsien by plane

图 9 西方侨民到达青岛
Picture 9 Western residents arrived at Qingdao

图 10 西方侨民到达青岛火车站
Picture 10 Western residents arrived at Qingdao Railway Station

图 11 西方侨民到达青岛
Picture 11 Western residents arrived at Qingdao

图 12 美籍难友玛丽•普瑞维特（戴爱美）及兄弟姊妹四人飞赴中国内地途中在朋友家里欢庆获得自由
Picture 12 Mary Taylor Previte and her brothers and sisters celebrating their freedom at a friend’s house on their way to another region in China

图 13 美籍难友玛丽•普瑞维特（戴爱美）及姐姐凯思琳、弟弟雅各、弟弟约翰与父母团聚后合影。（摄于中国西安）
Picture 13 Mary Taylor Previte and her sister Kathleen, her brother Jacob and John reunited with their parents (taken in Xi’an, China)

图 14 离开潍县集中营后的庞德一家（摄于 1946 年）
Picture 14 The Panders left Weihsien camp (taken in 1946)

第十四章　西方侨民情系潍坊

14 Western Residents' Deep Feelings for Weifang

潍县集中营解放后，被囚禁的人士大多回到了自己的祖国，现在主要散居在美国、英国、法国、加拿大、比利时、挪威、澳大利亚、新西兰、南非等国家。

After the liberation of Weihsien Camp, most of the Western residents returned to their homeland. They would mainly go and live in the United States, the United Kingdom, France, Canada, Belgium, Norway, Australia, New Zealand, South Africa, and so on.

对于集中营中的幸存者而言，潍坊的特殊经历已经成为他们永远的、挥之不去的记忆。既有被羁押失去自由、缺衣少食的痛苦记忆；又有难友团结抗争、潍县人民鼎力相助的珍贵情谊。潍县，成为了集中营幸存难友一辈子魂牵梦系、难以割舍的第二故乡。

For the camp survivors, the Weihsien experience became an unforgettable memory: losing freedom, lack of food and clothes, and of course making precious friendships with the fellow internees and the locals who helped and supported them during those horrible years. Weihsien remained the second hometown for the people imprisoned in the camp.

图 1　1987 年 6 月恒安石先生携夫人回到潍坊乐道院参观访问

Picture 1　In June, 1987, Arthur William Hummel Jr. returned to Weifang with his wife

图 2　恒安石到潍坊昌邑市看望抗日军官郝毓秀时的合影

Picture 2　Arthur William Hummel Jr. visited Chinese army officer Hao Yuxiu in Changyi, Weifang

图 3 美国花旗银行副董事长司马雷与夫人沙德拉·司马雷。司马雷先生的夫人沙德拉·司马雷出生在潍县集中营。为缅怀苦难的过去，1989 年 4 月司马雷夫妇专程来访，受到热烈欢迎。司马雷夫妇为表达对出生地的怀念和对教育的关心，用自己的积蓄在潍坊第二中学设立了奖学金，每年用 1000 美元奖励学校高考前 10 名学生

Picture 3 Vice Chairman of Citibank Shadra and his wife Shadra Simare. Shadra Simare was born in Weihsien Concentration Camp. He and his wife made a visit to Weifang in April, 1989. To express their care for his birth place and the education in Weifang, they set up a scholarship in Weifang No. 2 Middle School (Kwangwen Middle School). The scholarship, which is $1,000 per year, is bestowed to the top ten students in the college entrance examination

图 4 1991 年 6 月 9 日，利迪尔运动场暨纪念碑揭牌仪式在潍坊举行

Picture 4 June 9, 1991, the unveiling ceremony of the Eric H. Liddell Sports Ground and Memorial Stone in Weifang

1995 年 8 月 17 日，来自美国、英国、加拿大、南非、澳大利亚的友好人士露丝•约克逊等 10 多位集中营幸存者及其亲友回到潍县（潍坊），在潍坊二中利迪尔纪念花园举行了抗日战争胜利暨潍县集中营解放 50 周年纪念仪式。

On August 17,1995, Ruth Yorkson along with other camp survivors and their families returned to Weifang from the United States of America, the United Kingdom, Canada, South Africa and Australia. They participated in the 50th anniversary of the Victory of Resistance against the Japan's Aggression and the Liberation of the Weihsien Concentration Camp in Eric H. Liddell Memorial Garden in Guangwen Middle School.

图 5 1995 年 8 月部分西方侨民来潍坊市乐道院参加集中营解放 50 周年纪念活动

Picture 5 Former internees reuniting in the Weifang Courtyard in August,1995 and participating in the ceremony of the 50th anniversary of the camp liberation

图 6　2005 年 5 月，潍坊市代表拜访加拿大多伦多原“芝罘校友会”会长赵爱思先生
Picture 6　The Weifang Officials visiting Mr. Francis Joyce in Toronto, Canada, in May 2005, the former President of Chefoo Schools Association

图 7　2005 年 6 月 12 日，集中营幸存者诺尔曼·柯利夫博士，不顾 80 岁的高龄，再一次踏上了潍坊的土地。图为他在利迪尔纪念碑前默哀
Picture 7　June 12, 2005, the 80-year-old former internee Dr. Norman Cliff visiting Weifang, standing in front of the Eric H. Liddell memorial stone

图 8　诺尔曼·柯利夫博士在讲述那段苦难的经历
Picture 8　Dr. Norman Cliff telling his experience in the camp

图 9 潍坊市举办潍县集中营解放 60 周年纪念活动现场
Picture 9 The 60th Weihsien Concentration Camp Liberation Anniversary in Weifang

2005 年 8 月 17 日，潍坊市委、市政府在乐道院集中营旧址举办潍县集中营解放 60 周年纪念活动。来自美国、英国、加拿大、法国、澳大利亚、新西兰等国家和地区的潍县集中营幸存者及其后裔 100 余人参加了活动。

On August 17, 2005, the 60th Weihsien Concentration Camp Liberation Anniversary was held on the site of the Courtyard camp. Over 100 former internees and their children and families from different countries, including the US, the UK, Canada, France, Australia, and New Zealand, joined the event.

图 10 出席集中营解放 60 周年纪念大会的幸存者和来宾
Picture 10 Camp survivors and guests attending the 60th Weihsien Concentration Camp Liberation Anniversary

图 11　当年为集中营秘密传递消息的掏粪工张兴泰之子张锡宏参加了 60 周年庆典
Picture 11 Zhang Xihong, son of Zhang Xingtai, who secretly delivered messages for the internees, attending the 60th anniversary

集中营解放时年仅 12 岁的戴爱美（玛丽・普瑞维特，时任美国新泽西州众议员）在纪念大会上讲述集中营里的生活和 7 名伞兵解放集中营的情形。

During the anniversary, Mary T. Previte (then-member of the House of Representatives of New Jersey) , who was only 12 years old at the time the concentration camp was liberated, talked about the daily life in the camp as well as the seven paratroopers who rescued them.

图 12　出席集中营解放 60 周年纪念大会的戴爱美女士
Picture 12 Mary T. Previte at the 60th Anniversary of Weihsien Concentration Camp Liberation

图 13　60 周年纪念大会期间，戴爱美女士出席潍县集中营陈列馆揭牌仪式
Picture 13 Mary T. Previte attending the unveiling ceremony of Weihsien Concentration Camp Exhibition Hall during the 60th anniversary

图 14 60 周年庆典活动中，当年被关押的麦克和一位潍坊小姑娘共同敲响“警世钟”
Picture 14 Former internee Michael striking the alarm bell with a Weifang local girl during the 60th anniversary ceremony

图 15 幸存者史蒂芬在 60 周年纪念大会上讲述当年他和埃里克·利迪尔的故事：作为当时一个十几岁的少年，隆冬之际没有鞋穿，埃里克将自己的跑鞋送给了他
Picture 15 Former internee Stephan telling the story of Eric Liddell and himself in the camp: as a teenager at the time, Stephan had no shoes to wear in winter, so Eric gave him his own running shoes.

图 16 2005 年 8 月，在 60 周年纪念活动期间，潍坊人民与潍县集中营难友及其亲友联谊会正式成立
Picture 16 In August of 2005, during the 60th anniversary ceremony, the Council of the Friendship Party between Weifang People and the Former Weihsien Camp Internees was established.

图 17　在纪念潍县集中营解放 60 周年纪念大会上，戴爱美与哥哥戴绍曾相拥而泣

Picture 17　Mary T Previte crying in the arms of her elder brother James Taylor Previte at the 60th anniversary of the Weihsien Concentration Camp Liberation

图 18　60 周年纪念大会上情绪激动的幸存者

Picture 18　The camp survivors unable to hold back their tears during the 60th anniversary ceremony

图 19 集中营幸存者玛丽·布劳顿和她的孩子们来潍坊参加集中营解放 60 周年纪念大会
Picture 19 The Camp survivor Mary Brighton and her children at the 60th anniversary ceremony

图 20 集中营幸存者后代、纽约市立大学人力资源和经济开发部孟羲教授和夫人参加集中营解放 60 周年庆典
Picture 20 Professor Donald (Chinese name Meng Xi), a camp survivor's child, from New York City College Human Resources and Economic Development Department, and his wife attending the 60th anniversary ceremony

图 21 出席潍县集中营解放 60 周年纪念大会的中外来宾
Picture 21 Chinese and foreign guests attending the 60th anniversary ceremony

2015年，在世界反法西斯战争和中国人民抗日战争胜利70周年之际，潍坊市举办了潍县集中营解放70周年纪念大会，一批来自英国、美国、加拿大、新西兰等国家和地区的12位集中营难友及后代共80多人重聚乐道院，纪念重获自由的日子。

The year of 2015 marked the 70th anniversary of the end of the Second World War and the Resistance War against the Japanese Aggression, as well as the Weihsien Concentration Camp Liberation. Twelve former internees and their descendants, totally more than eighty people, from the UK, the US, Canada, New Zealand and other places gathered again in the Courtyard of the Happy Way to commemorate the liberation.

图22 2015年8月17日，潍坊市举办的潍县集中营解放70周年纪念大会会场
Picture 22 The 70th Anniversary Ceremony of Weihsien Concentration Camp Liberation , Weifang, August 17th, 2015

图23 2015年8月，加拿大芝罘校友会代表团访问乐道院集中营，与当年救助过他们的当地村民交谈
Picture 23 Delegation of Canadian Chefoo Alumni Association visiting the con-centration camp site and talking with a local villager who helped them

图 24 2015 年，来潍参加 70 周年纪念大会的集中营难友参观乐道院潍县集中营旧址
Picture 24 Former internees attending the 70th anniversary ceremony and visiting the Courtyard of the Happy Way in 2015

图 25 来潍参加集中营解放 70 周年纪念大会的潍县集中营难友皮特
Picture 25 Peter, a survivor from the camp, visiting the camp site during the 70th anniversary

图 26　来潍参加 70 周年纪念大会的王成汉与埃里克·利迪尔的两个女儿合影
Picture 26 Wang Chenghan and Eric Liddell's daughters at the 70th anniversary

图 27　来潍参加潍县集中营解放 70 周年纪念大会的难友保罗和斯坦利
Picture 27 Camp survivors Paul and Stanley at the 70th anniversary

图 28　来潍参加潍县集中营解放 70 周年纪念大会的幸存者
Picture 28 Camp survivors at the 70th anniversary

图 29 潍县集中营解放 70 周年纪念活动与会代表在乐道院“十字楼”前留影
Picture 29 Participants at the 70th anniversary, in front of the Courtyard's Cross Building

潍县集中营这段宝贵的历史，不仅是潍坊的财富，中国的财富，更是世界的财富！我们要大力挖掘、宣传这段历史，让世界上每个有良知的人知道这段历史，记住这段历史，反思这段历史，为人类和平、互助、友爱的人性光辉刻画下一组永久的史诗！

The story of the Weihsien Concentration Camp, like all other concentration camps set up during WWII, has transcended the city of Weifang or China for that matter; it has affected the people for all around the world. We hope everyone remember this history and learn from it to help build a better world filled with peace, love, mutual cooperation and friendship.

第十五章　与乐道院有关的西方名人

15 Western Celebrities Share Stories of Their Time in the Courtyard

在潍县乐道院 100 多年的风雨历程中，许多西方人在这里驻足、成长、生活、拼搏、工作，有的甚至将生命留在了潍坊这片充满希望的热土上。尽管现在大部分人已经逝去，但他们的事迹永不磨灭，他们的后人更是铭记着祖先曾经洒下过热血和汗水的土地——潍坊。有着厚重历史的乐道院，已经成为中西交流的桥梁。

In more than 100 years of Weihsien Courtyard history, many people from all over the world lived, worked, suffered, sacrificed and struggled there. Some even lost their lives in Weifang. Although most of the camp survivors have passed away, their stories last forever, and their descendants keep their legacies alive. The Courtyard turned into a bridge connecting the West and the East.

一、文会馆的创建者狄考文

15.1 Calvin Wilson Mateer, Founder of Shantung Protestant University

狄考文（1836 ~ 1908），美国宾夕法尼亚州人，美国基督教北长老会传教士，近代教育家、翻译家、慈善家。1863 年底来华，在山东登州传教，开办登州文会馆。1904 年，迁至潍县，与英国浸礼会在青州创办的广德书院合并，改称广文学堂（后改称广文大学）。在中国从事教育数十年，狄考文始终主张向中国社会广泛传播西方的科学和文化，以促进中国的进步。1908 年，这位在山东生活了四十多年的教育家病逝在青岛。

Calvin Wilson Mateer (1836-1908), born in Pennsylvania, the U.S., was a missionary serving the Presbyterian Church in the United States of America, modern educator, translator and philanthropist. He came to China at the end of 1863 and worked as a preacher in Tengchow, Shandong Province, He later set up Tengchow College there. In 1904, the college was relocated to Weihsien and merged with Guangde Academy, which was run by the English Baptist Missionary Society in Qingzhou. This new school was called Kwangwen School (later Shantung Protestant University). During his time working as an educator in China, Calvin Matter had always advocated the dissemination of Western science and culture in order to promote China's progress. In 1908, after having lived in Shandong Province more than four decades, he passed away in Qingdao.

图 1　狄考文
Picture 1 Calvin Wilson Mateer

二、烟台长老会创建者郭显德

15.2 Hunter Corbett, Founder of Yantai Presbyterian Church

郭显德 (1835 ~ 1920），美国宾夕法尼亚州人。基督教美国北长老会教士。1860年，毕业于美国杰斐逊大学。1862年秋，入普林斯顿神学院，次年，受美国长老会派遣来华传教。1864 年 3 月抵达烟台。创建烟台长老会，为首任牧师。此后，在烟台传教半个多世纪。在乐道院创建之前的准备工作中，郭显德倾注了心血。

Hunter Corbett (1835-1920), from Pennsylvania, the United States, was a missionary serving the Presbyterian Church in the United States of America. He graduated from Jefferson College in 1860 before attending Princeton Theological Seminary in the fall of 1862. A year later, he was sent to China by the Presbyterian Church. He arrived in Yantai in March of 1864. Colbert founded Yantai Presbyterian Church and became the first pastor there. He worked for the missionary enterprise for over half a century in Yantai and made great efforts to lay the foundations for establishing the Courtyard of the Happy Way.

图 2 郭显德
Picture 2 Hunter Corbett

图 3 狄乐播
Picture 3 Robert M. Mateer

三、乐道院创建者狄乐播

15.3 Robert M. Mateer, Founder of the Courtyard of the Happy Way

狄乐播 (1853 ~ 1921)，狄考文之弟，美国人。1881 年毕业于普林斯顿大学神学院。同年底，来到中国。此后，在潍县当地教友协助下，建立“乐道院”，用以传教、办学和开办诊所。狄乐播在中国传教近 40 年，于 1921 年 9 月 5 日在潍县去世。

Robert M. Mateer (1853-1921) was the younger brother of Calvin Wilson Mateer. In 1881, he graduated from the Seminary at Princeton University. By the end of 1881, he had moved to China. Later, with the assistance of local missionary friends in Weihsien, he set up the Courtyard of the Happy Way, and built schools and clinics. He worked in China as a preacher for nearly forty years before passing away in Weihsien on September 5,1921.

四、著名甲骨学家方法敛

15.4 Frank Herring Chalfant, Oracle Bone Expert

方法敛（1862 ~ 1914），美国北长老会教士，甲骨学家。1887 年来华，在山东潍县传教。逝于山东。1903 年起，与英国传教士库寿龄大量收藏商代甲骨等中国古代文物。所著《中国古代文字写法》(美国匹兹堡《喀尼各博物院报告》第四卷)，出版于 1906 年，为欧美研究和介绍甲骨文字的第一人。

Frank Herring Chalfant was a missionary serving with the Presbyterian Church in the United States of America, and oracle bone expert. He arrived in China in 1887, living as a missionary in Weihsien, Shandong until his death. Since 1903, he and the British missionary Couling Samuel began to collect a large amount of Chinese antiques from the Shang Dynasty, mainly oracle bones. His book of Early Chinese Characters was published in 1906, making him the first Westerner studying and publicizing the oracle-bone inscriptions.

图 4 方法敛
Picture 4 Frank Herring Chalfant

五、著名汉学家、甲骨学家库寿龄

15.5 Couling Samuel, Famous Sinologist and Oracle Bone Expert

图 5 库寿龄

Picture 5 Samuel Couling

库寿龄（1859 ~ 1922），英国浸礼会教士，著名汉学家、甲骨学家。1884 年来华，在山东青州传教和办学。1904 年其所办广德书院与美国北长老会所办文会馆合并为广文学堂，后改称广文大学（齐鲁大学前身），校址在潍县乐道院。库寿龄曾于1904年在广文学堂任教，1905年赴上海，任亚洲文会名誉干事及编辑，逝于上海。库氏在山东期间，与美国传教士方法敛合伙大量收购自河南经潍县古董商人转运来的甲骨，将自己经手的甲骨摹写编成《库方二氏藏甲骨卜辞》一书，后于 1935 年由商务印书馆出版。库氏又有《河南之卜骨》等有关中国考古学的文章，并编写《中国百科全书》，1917 年在上海和牛津大学分别出版，在世界上产生了广泛影响。

Samuel Couling (1859 - 1922) was a missionary serving with the English Baptist Missionary Society, famous Sinologist, and oracle bone expert. 1884, Couling started missionary work and opened schools in Qingzhou, Shandong. His Guange Academy merged with Tengchow College into Shantung Protestant University which was located at the Weihsien Courtyard. In 1904, Samuel Couling taught at Shantung Protestant University. A year later, in 1905, he was appointed as the honorary director-general and editor of the Royal Asiatic Society in Shanghai. He died in Shanghai in 1922. Together with fellow missionary Frank Herring Chalfant, Samuel purchased large amounts of oracle bones re-sold by the Henan antiquaries at Weihsien. He compiled a depiction of the oracles in A Study of Clan Pedigree Inscription on the Oracle Bone published by the Commercial Press in 1935. Samuel Couling wrote several articles about archaeology in China such as Oracle Bone in Henan. He also compiled The Encyclopedia of China which was published by Shanghai and Oxford University press in 1917. It became an international best-seller.

六、山东大学堂总教习、华北神学院院长赫士

15.6 Watson Mcmillen Hayes, Provost of Shandong University and Dean of North China Theological Seminary

图 6 赫士

Picture 6 Watson McMillen Hayes

赫士（1857 ~ 1944），美国人。基督教北长老会教士。1882 年受美国长老会差遣来华，在山东传教。1883 ~ 1895 年任教于山东登州文会馆，1896 ~ 1901 年任该校馆主（校长），创办山东第一家报纸《时报》，还创办了山东最早的乡村邮政事业。1901 年创立山东大学堂（山东大学前身），受到清政府嘉奖；1904 年到广文学堂任职，1906 年到青州葛罗神学院任总教习，1917 年到济南齐鲁大学神科任教授，后任神学院院长。1919 年在潍县创办华北神学院，1922 年迁址山东滕县。1941 年末，侵华日军强行接管华北神学院，赫士被关押到潍县乐道院集中营，1944 年病逝于集中营，享年 87 岁。

Watson Mcmillan Hayes (1857 - 1944), was a missionary, who served with the Presbyterian Church in the United States of America. Watson came to China in 1882 and did missionary work in Shandong.

From 1883 to 1895, he taught at Tengchow College, between 1896 and 1901, was the president of the college. He founded Times (Chinese:《时报》), the first newspaper in Shandong, and established the first rural postal service in Shandong. Hayes also received an award from the Qing government for establishing Shandong Imperial College (later Shandong University). In 1904, he worked at Shantung Protestant University. Later, in 1906, he was appointed as the academic dean at Qingzhou Gotch-Robinson Theological College. In 1917, he started working in Shantung Christian University as the theology lecturer and dean of the seminary. He founded the North China Seminary in 1919, and moved the school to Teng County, Shandong in 1921. In 1941, Japanese army took over the school, and Hayes was imprisoned in Weihsien Concentration Camp. He died that at the age of 87 in the camp in 1944.

七、美国北长老会中国总干事卫礼士

15.7 Ralph C.Wells, Director General of the Presbyterian Church of the United States in China

卫礼士，美国人。于1904年至1925年在乐道院中学任职，是乐道院学校历史上任职时间最长的校长。他除主持校务工作外，还教英语课，担任体育指导，教学生打球、做体操。他对学生既和蔼可亲又严格要求。1925年，卫礼士调到上海，担任美国基督教北长老会中国总干事。1933年，回广文中学参加了该校建校50周年校庆。

图7 1933年参加广文中学校庆时的卫礼士（中）
Picture 7 Ralph C.Wells (middle) at the 50th anniversary of Kwangwen Middle School in 1933

Ralph C.Wells was an American citizen, working as the middle school principal in the Courtyard from 1904 to 1925. He was the longest-serving principal in the history of the Courtyard. In addition to managing the school affairs, he also taught English, PE, and sports. He was a very kind but strict teacher. In 1925, he went back to Shanghai after he was appointed as the general secretary of the American Presbyterian Mission North in China. He attended the 50th anniversary of Kwangwen Middle School in 1933.

图8 伯尔根
Picture 8 Paul D. Bergen

八、广文大学校长柏尔根

15.8 Paul D. Bergen, President of Shantung Protestant University

柏尔根（1860 ~ 1915）：美国基督教北长老会传教士，1893年到登州文会馆任教，1901年接替赫士出任监督一职。1904年，随文会馆一同迁至潍县，担任广文学堂（后改称广文大学）监督和第一任校长。1915年病逝于潍县。现山东大学内仍有保存完好的“柏尔根楼”，即为纪念其杰出贡献而命名。

Paul D. Bergen (1860-1915), was also a missionary serving with American Presbyterian Mission, North. In 1893, he began teaching at Tengchow College. Later, in 1901, he succeeded Watson Mcmillan Hayes as the college's superintendent. In 1904, he was appointed as the superintendent and first president of Shantung Protestant University. In 1915, after a long illness, he died in Weihsien. Shandong University built Bergen Hall in memory of his great contribution.

九、齐鲁大学教务长德位思

15.9 Dr. Davies, Academic Dean of Cheeloo University

德位思：1867 年生于美国芝加哥市，1892 年来中国，先后在济南和烟台传教。1906 年任广文大学校长，1917 年任齐鲁大学教务长。太平洋战争爆发后，被日军关入潍县集中营，侨民推选他为“侨民自治管理委员会”主任委员。

Dr. L. J. Davies, born in Chicago in 1867, came to China in 1892. He carried out missionary work in Ji'nan and Yantai. He became the president of Shantung Protestant University in 1906 and the academic dean of Shantung Christian University in 1917. The Japanese army arrested and transferred him to the Weihsien Concentration Camp during World War II. He was elected as the directer of the Western Residents Autonomous Management Committee in the camp.

图 9 德位思
Picture 9 Dr. L. J. Davies

十、燕京大学筹建人之一、副校长路思义

15.10 Henry Winters Luce, Founder and Vice President of Yenching University

图 10 路思义
Picture 10 Henry Winters Luce

路思义（1868 ~ 1941）：美国人，1897 年 9 月，受美国基督教北长老会派遣，与妻子伊丽莎白一同来到中国，在登州文会馆担任物理教师。在他和柏尔根博士的联络、推动与筹划下，1904 年，广文学堂在潍县乐道院建立，首任校长由柏尔根博士担任，路思义为副校长。路思义还是燕京大学的筹建人和副校长。1927 年秋，路思义因健康原因辞去燕京大学职务，回到美国，1941 年 12 月去世。

Henry Winters Luce (1868-1941), was an American missionary serving the Presbyterian Church in the United States of America. Henry and his wife Elizabeth came to China in September of 1897. He was a physics teacher at Tengchow College. Dr. Bergen and Henry Luce established Shantung Protestant University in the Weihsien Courtyard in 1904. Dr. Bergen and Henry Luce were elected as the first president and vice-president of the university, respectively. Henry was also the founder and vice-president of Yenching University. Due to some health concerns, he later resigned from his position in Yenching University and went back to the United States in the autumn of 1927. He died in December of 1941.

十一、美国传媒大亨、《时代周刊》创始人亨利·鲁斯

15.11 Henry Luce, American Media Tycoon and Founder of Time Magazine

亨利·鲁斯（1898 ~ 1967）：路思义之子，1898 年生于山东蓬莱。6 岁随父母到潍县乐道院生活，后考入美国耶鲁大学。创办美国《时代周刊》《财富》《生活》杂志，成为美国文化出版界巨商，享誉世界。

Henry Luce (1898 - 1967), the son of Henry Winters Luce, born in Penglai, Shandong in 1898. He lived in Weihsien Courtyard with his parents from the age of six. He later studied at Yale University. By founding the magazines like Time, Fortune and Life, Henry Luce became a mogul in the publishing industry and won worldwide reputation.

图 11 亨利·鲁斯
Picture 11 Henry Luce

图 12 基格
Picture 12 R. Jaegher

十二、曾任蒋介石顾问的雷震远

15.12 Raymond J. De Jaegher , Former Adviser to Chiang Kai-shek

雷震远：天主教神甫，曾担任蒋介石的顾问。太平洋战争爆发后，被日军关入潍县集中营。在集中营期间，被侨民推选为“侨民自治管理委员会”委员。

R. Jaegher was a Catholic priest and former adviser for Chiang Kai-shek. His Chinese name is Lei Zhenyuan (雷震远). The Japanese army imprisoned him in the Weihsien Concentration Camp. He was elected as a member of the Western Residents Autonomous Management Committee in the camp.

十三、教育家、奥运冠军埃里克·利迪尔

15.13 Eric H. Liddell, Educator and Olympic Champion

埃里克•利迪尔（1902 ~ 1945），苏格兰人，1902 年 1 月 16 日出生在中国天津，中文名李爱锐，又名李达。著名田径运动员，基督教新教传教士。埃里克·利迪尔曾在 1924 年巴黎奥运会上摘得 400 米跑金牌并打破世界纪录。大学毕业后返回天津任教，同时还参与了天津民园体育场的设计和改建。抗日战争期间被日军抓入潍县集中营，并在抗战胜利前夕病逝于集中营。埃里克·利迪尔意志坚定，是一位优秀的教育家。现在香港建有埃里克·利迪尔基金会。

图 13 埃里克•利迪尔
Picture 13 Eric H. Liddell

Eric H. Liddell (1902 - 1945) was born from Scottish parents in Tianjin, China on January 16, 1902. His Chinese name is Li Airui

(李 爱 锐). He was a protestant missionary and a celebrated athlete, winning the 400-meres gold medal and breaking the world record at the 1924 Paris Olympics. After graduating from university, he returned to Tianjin as a teacher. He also contributed to the designing and reconstruction of the Tianjin Minyuan Stadium. He was imprisoned in Weihsien Concentration Camp by the Japanese army and died just 175 days before the liberation of the camp. Eric was also an excellent educator. Years later, the Eric H. Liddell Foundation was established in Hong Kong.

图 14 恒安石
Picture 14 Arthur William Hummel

十四、原美国驻华大使恒安石

15.14 Arthur William Hummel, Jr, Former U.S. Ambassador to China

恒安石：美国外交官。1920 年 6 月出生在中国山西省汾阳县，他的父亲恒慕义是位传教士，曾在中国传教多年。二十世纪四十年代，恒安石来到北京后，曾一度在辅仁大学男子附中教授英文。太平洋战争爆发后，恒安石因为是美国公民而被当时占领北平的日本军队关押起来，并被送到山东潍县集中营。恒安石千方百计和外面的游击队联系，最后在游击队的帮助下，他与一名同伴在 1944 年 6 月 9 日成功越狱。他于 1949 年回到美国，后来进入美国国务院，开始了职业外交官的生涯。1981 年至 1985 年恒安石任美国驻中国大使。

Arthur William Hummel was an American diplomat. He was born in Fenyang County, Shaanxi Province, China, in June of 1920. His father was a missionary who worked in China for many years. Arthur came to Beijing in the 1940s, and was and an English teacher at the Affiliated Boys School of Fu Jen Catholic University. After the outbreak of the Pacific War, because of his American citizenship, he was arrested by the Japanese army, who had occupied Beijing at the time, and was sent to the concentration camp in Weihsien, Shandong. He made every effort to communicate with the Chinese guerrillas. Finally, on June 9, 1944, with the help of the guerrillas, he and another internee escaped from the camp. In 1949, he returned to the United States and later joined the State Department, where he began a career as a diplomat. He served as the U.S. Ambassador to China from 1981 to 1985.

2001 年 2 月 6 日，恒安石在华盛顿逝世，享年 80 岁。一个世纪以来，他和他的家族与中国结下不解之缘，经历了中美关系的风风雨雨。

Arthur Hummel passed away in Washington on February 6, 2001 at the age of 80. For a century, he and his family had been tightly bound to China and gone through the ups and downs of China-US relations.

第三编

Chapter 3

乐道院的红色记忆

The Courtyard of the Happy Way at the Time of Revolutionary Movements

乐道院的历史是一部风云激荡的历史。从1921年中国共产党成立到1949年中华人民共和国成立，潍县土地上的每一场革命活动都与乐道院息息相关。由于乐道院是美国传教士狄乐播创办，属美国人管辖，地方当局不便干涉，这为革命活动的开展提供了相对安全的环境。

The history of the Courtyard of the Happy Way is a turbulent one. From the founding of the Communist Party of China (CPC) in 1921 to the founding of the People's Republic of China in 1949, each revolutionary movement in Weihsien was closely related with the Courtyard. Because it was set up by American missionary Robert M. Mateer and was run by the Americans, the local authorities could not interfere with the affairs of the Courtyard. It became a safe place for the activities of a variety of movements.

乐道院开办的教育机构，从文华馆、广文大学到文华、文美中学和广文中学，吸引了众多进步知识分子和青年学生，培养了大批优秀人才，涌现出了许多站在革命运动前列的仁人志士。

The schools run by the Courtyard, from Wenhua Academy, Shantung Protestant University to Wenhua and Wenmei Middle Schools and Kwangwen Middle School, attracted many young students and educated a large number of excellent people for the revolutionary movements.

乐道院的医疗机构——潍县基督教医院，为抗日军民提供了急需的医疗救护，并为革命培养了许多医务人员。

Weihsien Christian Hospital, the hospital in the Courtyard, provided much-needed medical aid to the Chinese army and people during the WWII and trained many medical workers for the movements.

乐道院为中国革命事业做出的贡献，我们永志不忘。

The contributions made by the people in the Courtyard to China’s movements will never be forgotten.

第一章　五四时期乐道院的革命活动

1 The Courtyard of the Happy Way during the May Fourth Movement

图 1　五四运动时，北京大学学生向天安门进发

Picture 1　Peking University students marching towards Tian'anmen Square during the "May 4th Movement"

1919 年 5 月 4 日，以北京爱国学生的示威游行为起点，一个以"外争国权、内惩国贼"为口号的爱国民主运动在全国爆发。

On May 4, 1919, a democratic movement broke out throughout the country, which grew out of student protests in Beijing with the slogan of "securing our sovereignty and punishing the traitors".

于培绪（1901 ~ 1928），字赞之，又名茂宁，化名伯涛，山东昌邑人。1919 年考入文华中学，在校时积极参加学生运动，因创办《醒华报》揭露帝国主义的侵略本性，被迫辍学。

Yu Peixu (1901 - 1928), was a native of Changyi, Weihsien. In 1919, Yu was admitted to Wenhua Middle School. Later, he took part in student movements. He was forced to drop out of school because he founded the newspaper Wake-up Call to China whose aim was to expose the aggression done by imperialism.

图 2 于培绪
Picture 2 Yu Peixu

1924 年考入齐鲁大学，1925 年由关向应、丁君羊介绍加入中国共产党。成为齐鲁大学的第一位学生党员。

In 1924, Yu Peixu was admitted to Shantung Christian University; a year later, in 1925, he joined the Communist Party of China. At the time, he became the first student Party member of Shantung Christian University.

1927 年，根据省委意见到泰安任中共泰安县苏维埃支部委员会组织委员，并直接领导了翠英中学的革命活动，后被推选为执行委员会书记。1928 年，省委派其回家乡昌邑饮马地区组织发动农民革命，建立起昌邑第一个党支部。12 月 25 日，黄凤歧部下偷袭饮马，于培绪不幸被捕，英勇就义，年仅 27 岁。

In 1927, he was appointed as the member of the Tai'an County Soviet Branch Committee of the Communist Party, responsible for organizing and ushering the revolutionary activities in Cuiying Middle School. Later, he was elected as the secretary of the executive committee. In 1928, the provincial Party committee sent him back to his hometown, Yinma, Changyi, to organize a peasant movement and set up the first Party branch in Changyi. On December 25, Yu Peixu was arrested and executed by Kuomintang army (National Revolutionary Army). He was only 27 years old.

1919 年 5 月 12 日，文华中学与潍县公私立学校纷纷成立“学生联合会”。文华中学学生于培绪领导全县学生罢课，上街游行、散发传单、张贴标语，创办《醒华报》，宣传发动群众。联合社会各界人士，组织国货维持会，查烧日货，长达一年之久。

On May 12th, 1919, Kwangwen Middle School and other schools in Weihsien set up “students unions”. Yu Peixu, as a student of Wenhua Middle School, guided students strikes and demonstrations, distributed leaflets and put up banners in the streets. In order to mobilize the masses, he founded the Wake-up Call to China. He also organized a National Products Protection Association which invited people to boycott Japanese goods, which lasted for a year.

图 3 抵制日货
Picture 3 Boycotting Japanese goods

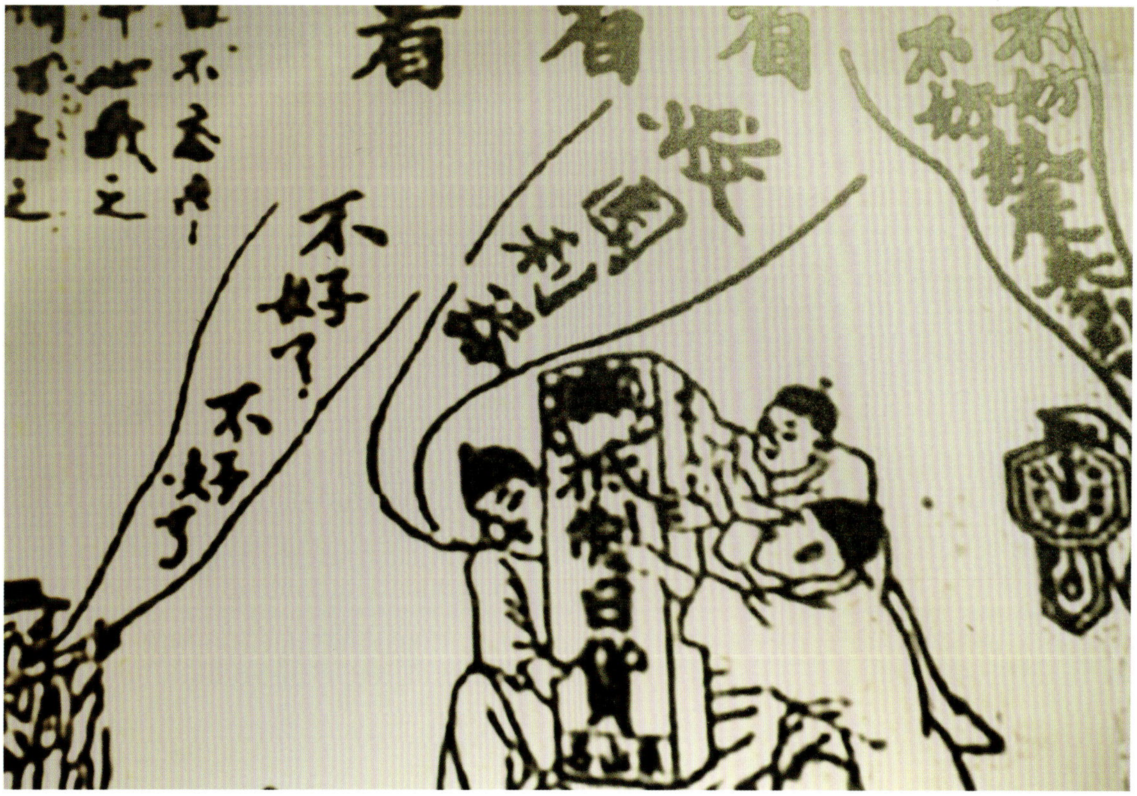

图 4 抵制日货宣传画
Picture 4 A poster of boycotting Japanese goods

第二章　党成立早期乐道院的革命活动

2 The Courtyard of the Happy Way during the Early Years of CPC

1921 年 7 月，中国共产党第一次全国代表大会在上海举行，王尽美、邓恩铭代表济南中国共产党早期组织参加会议。次年，中共直属济南支部成立。

In July 1921, the first National Congress of the CPC was held in Shanghai. Wang Jinmei and Deng Enming attended the meeting as representatives of The early organization of the Communist Party of China in Jinan. In the following year, the Ji'nan Party branch, which was directly under the CPC, was established.

王尽美（1898 ~ 1925）原名瑞俊，字灼斋，山东诸城人。中国共产党创始人之一，山东共产党组织的缔造者和早期领导人。1921 年春，与邓恩铭等同志发起创建了山东第一个党组织——济南中国共产党早期组织，同年出席第一次全国代表大会，后担任中共山东省地方执行委员会书记。因积劳成疾，1925 年 8 月在青岛病逝。

Wang Jinmei (1898 - 1925), born in Zhucheng, Weihsien, was one of the founders of the CPC, and the founder and the first director of Shandong communist organizations. In the spring of 1921, he, along with Deng Enming and other comrades, initiated the foundation of Shandong's first Party organization - The early organization of the Communist Party of China in Jinan. At the same year, he attended the first National Congress, later serving as the secretary of the local executive committee of CPC in Shandong Province. He fell sick from overwork, and died in Qingdao in August, 1925.

图 1　出席中共一大的山东代表王尽美

Picture 1 Wang Jinmei attended the first National Congress of CPC as a representative of Shandong

1923 年 5 月，经王尽美介绍，曾在文华中学读书的庄龙甲正式加入中国共产党，并任济南第一师范党支部书记。庄龙甲在学校寒暑假期间，回到乐道院学校，向进步学生宣传马列主义，向校友们赠送进步书刊，传播反帝反封建的革命道理。

In May 1923, Wang Jinmei asked Zhuang Longjia to join the CPC. Zhuang Longjia, who had studied in Wenhua Middle School, was appointed as the secretary of the CPC committee of Provincial First Normal School in Ji'nan. During the winter and summer vacations, he would go back to the Courtyard school to give lectures on Marxism-Leninism, promoting revolutionary concepts such as anti-imperialism and anti-feudalism.

庄龙甲，字麟森（1903 ~ 1928），生于山东省潍县庄家村。1923 年 5 月加入中国共产党，是中共山东省早期党员、中共潍坊地区早期组织创始人。1923 年至 1928 年先后担任中共山东省立第一师范学校支部书记、中共潍县支部书记、中共潍县地方执行委员会书记、中共潍县县委书记、省委农民运动特派员等主要职务。先后创建了山东省第一个农民协会、第一个县级党组织、第一个革命武装组织。1928 年 10 月被敌人杀害。

图 2 庄龙甲
Picture 2 Zhuang Longjia

Zhuang Longjia (1903-1928) was born in Zhuangjia Village, Weihsien. In May 1923, he joined the CPC. As an early member of CPC in Shandong Province, he founded the early Party organizations in Weifang. From 1923 to 1928, he served as the secretary of the Party branch of Provincial First Normal School in Ji'nan, secretary of the Weihsien Party branch, secretary of the Weihsien Party Committee, secretary of the local executive committee of CPC in Weihsien, and commissioner of the peasant movement of the provincial Party committee. He established the first peasant association in Shandong, the first county-level Party organization as well as the first revolutionary armed organization. In October 1928, he was killed by the Kuomintang.

图 3 庄龙甲在省立一师与师生合影（前排右二）
Picture 3 Zhuang Longjia (front, second from right) with his students in Shandong Provincial First Normal School

1925 年 1 月，受党的派遣，庄龙甲回家乡潍县开展革命活动。庄龙甲经常深入到乐道院，和学生、工人广泛接触，使乐道院成为党组织的重要活动阵地。庄龙甲在文华、文美两个学校的进步学生中发展团员、党员，先后介绍文华中学学生郑官升、王仰之、王宇澄、延鑫、刘浩等人加入青年团。1925 年 8 月，成立了文华中学团支部，后成立党支部，王仰之为书记。后又发展文美中学孙肇修（陈少敏）、董汝勤、谭静、刘好义、葛文英、高炎之、牟秀珍等 20 余人参加了团组织，建立文美女中团支部。1927 年春又建立了党支部，由牟秀珍担任书记。

In January 1925, CPC transferred Zhuang Longjia back to his hometown, Weihsien, to organize and guide the revolutionary activities. Zhuang often went to the Courtyard of Happy Way to meet the students and workers, turning the Courtyard into a crucially important place for the Party's activities. He recruited new Communist Youth League members and Party members from the students in Wenhua School and Wenmei School. A Youth League branch was established in Wenhua Middle School in August, 1925. Subsequently, the

CPC branch was also set up, with Wang Yangzhi as the secretary. Later, the League branch of Wenmei Middle School was established. More then twenty students joined the League. In the spring of 1927, the Party branch was established, with Mu Xiuzhen as the secretary.

潍县党组织还注意在乐道院工人中培养骨干力量。吸收电工牟光仪入党，吸收乐道院医院的扈梅村、傅锡泽、傅乃武、金素兰等先后加入共青团或共产党。 打更老人谭念仁、给美国牧师做工的李长秀，都成了入党积极分子。乐道院党团组织成为一支强大的领导力量。

The Weihsien Party organization also attracted much attention among the workers who worked in the Courtyard. Mu Guangyi, an electrician, and some medical workers, who worked in the Courtyard hospital, joined the Party and the League. Tan Nianren, a night watchman, and Li Changxiu, who served an American pastor, were the applicants for Party membership. The Party and the League organizations in the Courtyard became a powerful leading force for the movements.

图 4 1925 年庄龙甲和部分山东党团员合影
Picture 4 Zhuang Longjia and some Party and League members in Shandong, 1925

图 5 陈少敏
Picture 5 Chen Shaomin

陈少敏（1902～1977），原名孙肇修，山东寿光人。1923年加入了邓恩铭等组织的秘密工会。1926年考入文美女子中学，1927年加入中国共产主义青年团，后转为中共党员。历任中共江西省委妇女部长、中共河南省洛阳特委书记、中共鄂中区委书记兼新四军鄂豫挺进支队政治委员、中共豫鄂边区区委书记、新四军第五师副政治委员等职。1945年6月，在中共"七大"上被选为候补中央委员。1945年10月，任中共中央中原局组织部长。

Chen Shaomin (1902-1977) was born in Shouguang, Weifang. In 1923, she joined the secret labor union founded by Deng Enming. In 1926, she was admitted to Wenmei Middle School. In 1927, Chen Shaomin joined the Communist Youth League of China, later, becoming a member of the CPC. She served as the minister of Women of Jiangxi Provincial Party Committee and the secretary of Special Committee in Luoyang, Henan Province, the secretary of the CPC Central Hubei District Committee and the political member of the Hubei-Henan advanced detachment of the New Fourth Army, the secretary of the Henan-Hubei Border Region Party Committee and the deputy political member of the Fifth Division of the New Fourth Army. In June 1945, she was elected as the alternate member of the Central Committee at the Seventh National Congress of the CPC. In October 1945, she became the organization minister of the Central Plains Bureau of the CPC Central Committee.

中华人民共和国成立后历任中共第八届中央委员、全国纺织工会主席、全国总工会副主席。

After the founding of New China, she served as the member of the Eighth CPC Central Committee, Chairman of the National Textile Union and vice-president of All China Federation of Trade Union (ACFTU).

董汝勤 (1910 ~ 1971)，山东安丘人。1927 年，在文美中学求学时加入中国共产主义青年团，并任团支部书记。1929 年转为中国共产党党员。历任中共青岛市委秘书、秘书长、北平市革命互济会主任、冀中区十地委宣传部长、中共霸县县委书记、中共冀中区委第一地委书记等职。中华人民共和国成立后历任北京市民政局长、中央政法委员会办公厅城市组组长、全国人大常委会办公厅人民接待室主任、第三届全国人大代表、全国人大常委会机关党组成员等职。

Dong Ruqin (1910-1971) was born in Anqiu, Weifang. In 1927, while studying in Wenmei Middle School, she joined the Communist Youth League of China, serving as the secretary of the League branch. In 1929, Dong Ruqin was admitted to the CPC. She served as the secretary and then secretary-general of Qingdao Municipal Committee of the CPC, director of the Beiping Revolutionary Mutual Aid Association, propaganda director of the Tenth Prefectural Party Committee of central Hebei, secretary of the Baxian County Party Committee and secretary of the First Prefectural Party Committee of central Hebei. After the founding of New China, she served as the director of Beijing Municipal Civil Affairs Bureau, head of the City Group of the General Office of Committee of Political and Legislative Affairs, director of the Petition Reception Office of the General Office of the Standing Committee of the National People's Congress, deputy to the Third National People's Congress and Party member of the National People's Congress Standing Committee.

图 6 董汝勤
Picture 6 Dong Ruqin

张眺（1901 ~ 1934），字鹤眺，原名星芝，笔名耶林，山东潍县人。1921 年，任寒亭高等小学校长。1927 年在文华中学任教师，期间加入中国共产党。大革命失败后，与党失去联系，遂赴上海、杭州寻找党组织，并在杭州组建“波播社”“一八艺社”等进步团体。1930 年，参加左翼文化运动，先后任“美联”“左联”的党团书记。1932 年，任江苏文委书记，后受中央派遣，去江西苏区工作，任闽浙赣苏维埃政府教育部长兼共产主义学校校长。1934 年 11 月不幸牺牲。

Zhang Tiao (1901-1934), was a Weihsien native. In 1921, he was appointed as the headmaster of Hanting Higher Primary School. In 1927, while working as a teacher in Wenhua Middle School, he joined the CPC. After the failure of the Great Revolution, he lost contact with the Party. He, therefore, went to Shanghai and Hangzhou to find the Party organization. Later, he set up progressive associations in Hangzhou. In 1930, he participated in the left-wing cultural movement and successively served as the Party and League secretary of "Alliance of the Leftist Artists" and "China League of Left-Wing Writers". In 1932, he served as the secretary of the Jiangsu Cultural Commission. The Central Committee, then, sent him to work in the Soviet area of Jiangxi Province. Later, he was appointed as the Education Minister of the Soviet Government of Fujian, Zhejiang and Jiangxi Province as well as the head of the Communist school. He sacrificed himself in November 1934.

图 7 张眺
Picture 7 Zhang Tiao

扈梅村（1906～1968），山东潍县人，又名扈本尧。1926年加入中国共产党。同年6月，任中共潍县地方执行委员会组织委员。1928年考入北平燕京大学。抗日战争爆发后回到潍县。

Hu Meicun (1906-1968), was a Weihsien native. He joined the CPC in 1926. In June of the same year, he served as an organizing member of the local executive committee of CPC in Weihsien. In 1928, he was admitted to Yenching University in Beijing. After the outbreak of War of Resistance against Japanese Aggression, he returned to Weihsien.

1938年初，参加了党领导的八路军鲁东游击队。同年去延安，在边区政府建设厅工作。北平解放后，先后任北京市企业局、工业局、公用局、化工局副局长，皮革工业科学技术研究所副所长等职。

In early 1938, he joined the eastern Shandong guerrilla of the Eighth Route Army. In the same year, he went to Yan’an, working in the Construction Office of the border region government. After the liberation of Beiping, he served as the deputy director of the Beijing Bureau of Enterprise, Industry Bureau, Public Utilities Bureau and Chemical Industry Bureau, as well as the deputy director of the Leather Industry Science and Technology Research Institute.

图8 扈梅村
Picture 8 Hu Meicun

图9 牟光仪
Picture 9 Mu Guangyi

牟光仪，1917年考入文华中学，1920年因参加进步活动被校方劝退。1924年，牟光仪回到乐道院当电工，其间结识了潍县共产党领导人庄龙甲、王全斌，并加入中国共产党。他把“电机重地、外人不得入内”的标识贴在电机房外，并把钥匙交给进步学生，电机房成为周围县市区党团组织的秘密活动中心。电机房既是党的文件和物品存放中心，还是印刷秘密刊物的基地。时任青岛团地委书记的关向应来潍县视察，电机房成为联络点、接待处。庄龙甲等县委领导在这里汇报情况、研究工作。

Mu Guangyi was admitted to Wenhua Middle School in 1917. In 1920, because of his involvement in revolutionary activities, he was dismissed from the school. In 1924, Mu Guangyi returned to the Courtyard of the Happy Way, working as an electrician. In the Courtyard, after meeting Zhuang Longjia and Wang Quanbin, directors of the Communist Party of Weihsien, he joined the CPC. By putting a sign outside the generator room, saying “Electric Machinery Site. No Admittance!”, and handing the room’s key over to the progressive students, Mu Guangyi turned the generator room into a secret center for the Party and Youth League activities of the surrounding counties, cities and districts organizations. The generator room was not only used for storing the Party’s documents and belongings but also for printing its secret publications and pamphlets. When Guan Xiangying, then Secretary of the local committee of the Qingdao Youth League, visited Weihsien, the generator room was used as a contact point and reception office. Multiple directors of the Communist Party of Weihsien, such as Zhuang Longjia, also worked in that room.

图 10 关向应
Picture 10 Guan Xiangying

图 11 张同俊
Picture 11 Zhang Tongjun

关向应（1902 ~ 1946），辽宁省大连市金州区人，满姓瓜尔佳氏，是中国共产党早期军事领导人，是无产阶级革命家、军事家。

Guan Xiangying (1902-1946), born in Dalian, Liaoning Province, was an early military director of the CPC, a proletarian revolutionary and strategist.

张同俊 (1907 ~ 1975)，山东潍县人。1925 年 10 月，在济南齐鲁大学读书期间加入中国共产主义青年团，1926 年转为中国共产党党员。同年 6 月，任中共潍县地方执行委员会宣传委员。1931 年至 1934 年，任中共燕京大学支部书记、中共北平西郊区委书记、河北省委宣传干事等职。1935 年被捕后脱党。中华人民共和国成立后曾任潍坊市建设局代理局长。

Zhang Tongjun (1907-1975) was born in Weihsien. In October 1925, he joined the Communist Youth League of China while studying in Shantung Christian University. In 1926, he was admitted to CPC. In June of the same year, he was appointed as the publicity commissar of the CPC local executive committee in Weihsien. From 1931 to 1934, he served as the secretary of the CPC Branch in Yanjing University as well as the Beijing western suburbs, and the publicity officer of Hebei Party Committee. In 1935, he lost contact with the Party after he was arrested. After the founding of the People's Republic of China, he served as the acting director of Weifang Construction Bureau.

关向应同志当时为共青团济南地委负责人。1925 年底，关向应曾与在齐鲁大学读书的共产党员张同俊商议到潍县开展团的工作问题。1926 年 1 月，两人受省委委派来到潍县，张同俊安排关向应同志住在乐道院电机房牟光仪处。在潍期间，关向应与庄龙甲一起在乐道院听取了文华中学团支部的工作汇报，召开了有文华中学团员张长盛、田蜀生、周怀之、王宇澄、孙葵书和文美女中的团员共十几人参加的会议，关向应同志为团员青年讲述了国内革命形势、阶级斗争理论和党的纪律，最后教唱《国际歌》，此后文华中学的进步力量发展很快。

Guan Xiangying was in charge of Ji’nan Committee of the Communist Youth League. At the end of 1925,

Zhang Tongjun, a communist student from Shantung Christian University, discussed with Guan Xiangying to organize the Communist Youth League's activities in Weihsien. In January 1926, they were assigned to serve in Weihsien by the provincial party committee. Guan Xiangying lived with Mu Guangyi in the generator room in the Courtyard. Guan and Zhuang Longjia, along with with a dozen League members, attended a meeting in the Youth League branch of Wenhua Middle School. Guan Xiangying delivered a speech about the revolution in China, the theory of class struggle and the Party's disciplines; he also taught them how to sing The Internationale. That was a turning point and a critical moment in the revolutionary activities of Wenhua Middle School.

1926 年 4 月，省地执委委员丁君羊来潍县召开党的骨干分子会议，部署建立中共潍县地方执行委员会工作。

In April 1926, Ding Junyang, a member of the Provincial Executive Committee, organized a meeting of the Weihsien Party's core members to set up the local executive committee.

图 12 丁君羊
Picture 12 Ding Junyang

图 13 1926 年春丁君羊在乐道院校长办公楼召开党的会议
Picture 13 In the spring of 1926, Ding Junyang held a Party meeting in Principal's Office Building of the Courtyard.

1926 年文华中学成立了马列主义读书会。《向导》《新青年》《共产主义 ABC》等进步书刊公开陈列，供人借阅，在学生中自由研讨、争论。

In 1926, The Marxism-Leninism Reading Association was established in Wenhua Middle School. The Guide, the New Youth, ABC of Communism and other progressive books and periodicals were on display for people to study.

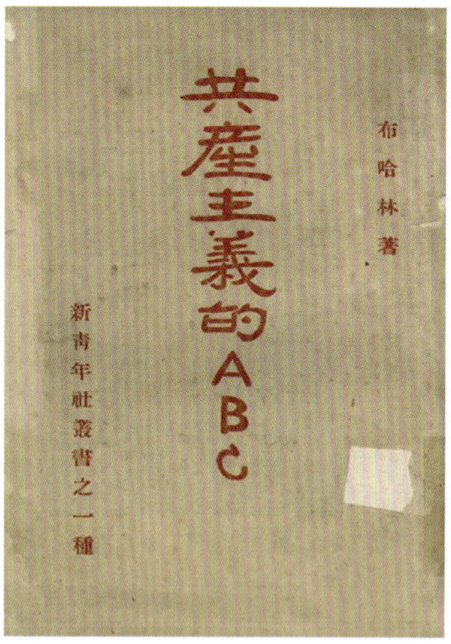

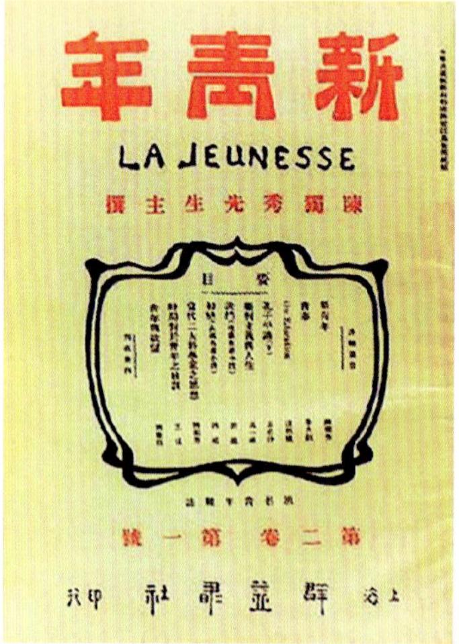

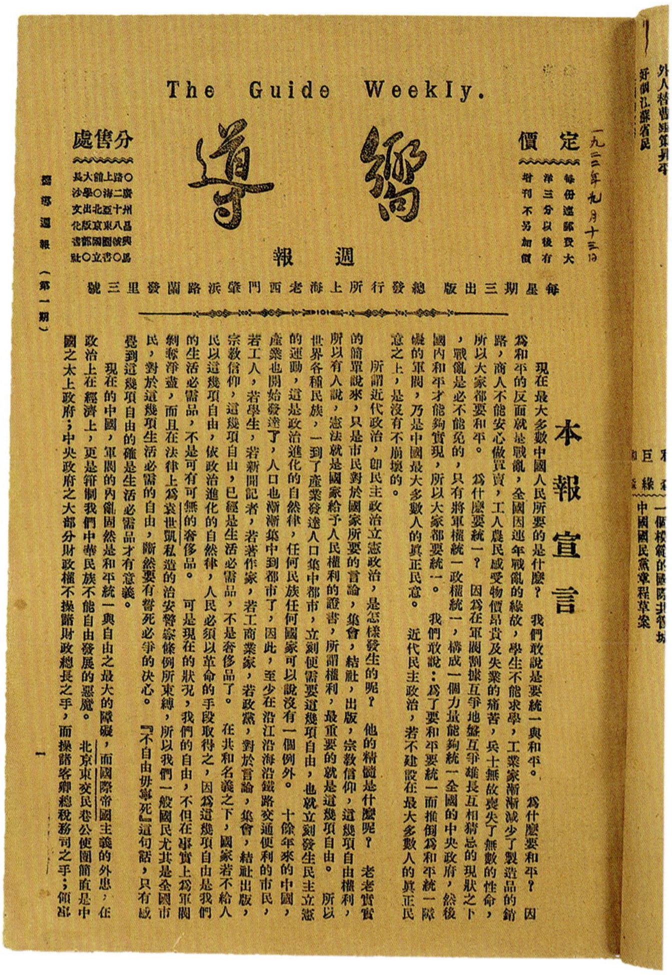
The Guide Weekly.

嚮導週報

一九二二年九月十三日

每星期三出版　總發行所上海老西門肇浜路蘭發里三號

本報宣言

現在最大多數中國人民所要的是什麼？我們敢說是要統一與和平。爲什麼要和平？因爲和平的反面就是戰亂，全國因連年戰亂的緣故，學生不能求學，工業家漸漸減少了製造品的銷路，商人不能安心做買賣，工人農民感受物價昂貴及失業的痛苦，兵士無故喪失了無數的性命，所以大家都要和平。爲什麼要統一？因爲在軍閥割據互爭地盤互爭雄長互相猜忌的現狀之下，戰亂是必不能免的，只有將軍權統一政權統一，構成一個力量能夠統一全國的中央政府，然後國內和平才能夠實現，所以大家都要統一。我們敢說：爲了要和平要統一而推倒爲和平統一障礙的軍閥，乃是中國最大多數人的真正民意。近代民主政治，若不建設在最大多數人的真正民意之上，是沒有不崩壞的。

所謂近代政治，即民主政治立憲政治，是怎樣發生的呢？他的精髓是什麼呢？老老實實的簡單說來，只是市民對於國家所要的言論，集會，結社，出版，宗教信仰，這幾項自由權利，所以有人說，憲法就是國家給予人民權利的證書，所謂權利，最重要的就是這幾項自由。所以世界各種民族，一到了產業發達人口集中都市，立刻便需要這幾項自由，也就立刻發生民主立憲的運動，這是政治進化的自然律，任何民族任何國家可以說沒有一個例外。十餘年來的中國，產業也開始發達了，人口也漸漸集中到都市了，因此，至少在沿江沿海沿鐵路交通便利的市民，若工人，若學生，若新聞記者，若著作家，若工商業家，若政黨，對於言論，集會，結社出版，宗教信仰，這幾項自由，已經是生活必需品，不是奢侈品了。在共和名義之下，國家若不給人民以這幾項自由，依政治進化的自然律，人民必須以革命的手段取得之，因爲這幾項自由是我們的生活必需品，不是可有可無的奢侈品。可是現在的狀況，我們的自由，不但在事實上爲軍閥剝奪淨盡，而且在法律上爲袁世凱私造的治安警察條例所束縛，所以我們一般國民尤其是全國市民，對於這幾項生活必需的自由，斷然要有誓死必爭的決心。『不自由毋寧死』這句話，只有感覺到這幾項自由的確是生活必需品才有意義。

現在的中國，軍閥的內亂固然是和平統一與自由之最大的障礙，而國際帝國主義的外患，在政治上在經濟上，更是箝制我們中華民族不能自由發展的惡魔。北京東交民巷公使團簡直是中國之太上政府；中央政府之大部分財政權不操諸財政總長之手，而操諸客卿總稅務司之手；領

嚮導週報（第一期）　一

图 14　文化中学马列主义读书会的进步书籍
Picture 14　Books in the Marxist-Leninist Reading Club of Wenhua Middle School

第三章　乐道院曾经成为中共潍县县委驻地

3 The Courtyard of the Happy Way becomes Residence of Weihsien Committee of the CPC

大革命失败以后，白色恐怖日益严峻。1928 年 10 月，庄龙甲同志不幸被捕，壮烈牺牲。1932 年，共产党员乔天华因政治身份暴露，转移至广文中学。在校任图书馆管理员兼美术教师，以此为掩护，从事党的地下工作。1933 年，山东省委指示乔天华，恢复被敌人破坏的潍县党组织。乔天华依靠地下党组织的力量，成立了潍县中心县委，并担任县委书记。

After the failure of the Great Revolution, the “white terror” alarmingly spread. In October 1928, Zhuang Longjia was arrested and murdered. In 1932, Qiao Tianhua, a member of the Communist Party, was transferred to Kwangwen Middle School after his political identity was revealed. He worked as a librarian and art teacher in the school which he used as a cover for his underground activities for the CPC. In 1933, the Shandong Provincial Party Committee instructed Qiao to rebuild the Weihsien Party organization that was dismantled by the Kuomintang. Relying on the power of the underground party organization, Qiao established the Weihsien Central County Party Committee and served as the county Party committee secretary.

图 1　乔天华

Picture 1　Qiao Tianhua

乔天华（1902 ~ 1989）原名乔永祥，平度乔家村人。1931 年 10 月加入中国共产党。1932 年，代理中共烟台特支书记。同年冬，任中共青岛市委青年委员兼左联党团书记。1933 年夏，任中共潍县中心县委书记。1934 年 10 月被捕，1937 年 8 月由济南出狱，回平度宣传抗日救国思想，组织发动群众，组建抗日队伍。抗日战争期间，先后组建抗日游击小组、小七支队、抗日救国会、莱平大队等七支抗日队伍，计 3000 余人，均被改编充实到抗日主力部队，为扩大抗日力量做出了杰出的贡献。整个抗战时期，他亲自带领队伍参战 20 余次，多次取得战斗的胜利。1939 年，任中共胶、即、平工委军事部长。1943 年春，任平北县政府县长兼县大队长。1944 年，去胶东区党委党校学习，1945 继续担任平北县长。中华人民共和国成立后，在山东省农业厅果树处任处长。1957 年被错划为右派，1978 年平反。离休之后享受厅局级待遇。

Qiao Tianhua (1902-1989) was born in Pingdu, Qingdao. He joined the CPC in October 1931. In 1932, he was appointed as the acting secretary of Yantai Special Branch of CPC, later serving as the member of Qingdao Municipal Party Committee and secretary of the China League of Left-Wing Writers. In 1933, he was assigned as the secretary of Central Party Committee of Weihsien. In October 1934, he was arrested. He was released from prison in Ji'nan in August 1937. He returned to Pingdu to organize people and build an partisan militia to fight against the Japanese forces. During the War, he managed to build seven fighting organizations, with a total number of 3,000 fighters. These militia groups later joined the principal force and played a crucial role in the resistance against the Japanese occupation. During the War, he successfully led his troops in over twenty battles against the Japanese forces, inflicting serious damage upon the enemy. In 1939, he was appointed as the minister of Military affairs of CPC in Jiaozhou, Jimo and Pingdu. In the spring of 1943, he served as the head of Pingbei County government. After the founding of PRC, he served as the director of Fruit Trees Office, Shandong Department of Agriculture. In 1957, he was wrongly classified as a rightist, which eventually led to his exoneration in 1978.

共产党员孙世禄在1933年博兴起义失败后，转移到广文中学，在校长办公室当文书，积极开展党的地下工作。与乔天华共同创办《春笋》旬刊，撰写社会调查论文，宣传革命，为革命做出了积极贡献。

After the failure of the Bohsing Uprising in 1933, Sun Shilu, a member of the Communist Party, was transferred to Kwangwen Middle School as a copy clerk in the principal's office, where he carried out his underground activities for the Party. Together with Qiao Tianhua, Sun Shilu founded the magazine Bamboo Shoots. He wrote social investigation papers, promoted revolutionary ideas and made invaluable contributions to the revolution.

图2 孙世禄
Picture 2 Sun Shilu

第四章　中华民族解放先锋队潍县队部驻扎乐道院

4 National Liberation Vanguard Stations in the Courtyard of the Happy Way

抗日战争时期，乐道院一度曾经是中华民族解放先锋队潍县队部的驻地。中华民族解放先锋队（简称“民先”)是在中国共产党领导下以抗日民主为奋斗目标的先进青年的群众性组织。1936年2月在北平成立。1937年，潍县共产党员王一之、丁子新，发展“民先”队员30余人，正式成立“民先”潍县队部，积极开展抗日救亡运动。

During the War of Resistance against Japanese Aggression, the Courtyard of the Happy Way turned into a kind of refuge for the Vanguard of National Liberation of China (or simply “the Vanguard”). The Vanguard was a mass organization consisted of progressive young people whose objectives, under the leadership of the Communist Party of China, were resisting the Japanese aggression and advocating democracy. The Vanguard was founded in Beijing in February 1936. In 1937, under the supervision of Wang Yizhi and Ding Zixin, members of the CPC in Weihsien, over thirty individuals were admitted to the Vanguard, formally establishing Weihsien branch of the Vanguard. It made remarkable contributions in the fight against the Japanese forces and saving the country.

图 1　中华民族解放先锋队

Picture 1　The Vanguard of National Liberation of China

丁子新，抗日战争和解放战争期间是潍县地下革命组织的负责人。中华人民共和国成立后，丁子新同志曾任广文中学的政府代表和教务处主任。

Ding Zixin was a directer of the underground revolutionary organization in Weihsien during the Sino-Japanese War and the War of Liberation. After the founding of PRC, Ding Zixin served as the government's representative and academic affairs director of Kwangwen Middle School.

图 2 丁子新
Picture 2 Ding Zixin

图 3 “民先”队员组织宣传抗日救国思想
Picture 3 Vanguard member advocating the resistance against Japanese aggression

“民先”队员陈秉忱。早在青年时期，就具有革命思想，1937年参加中华民族解放先锋队。中华人民共和国成立后随毛泽东主席出访苏联，回国后调任中央军委办公厅秘书处长、干部处长、档案处长等职。1957年11月调任中共中央办公厅秘书室副主任。1979年3月调任中共中央办公厅政研室顾问、毛泽东主席图书管理组组长。为纪念毛泽东主席九十诞辰，他选编了《毛泽东手书古诗词选》等三本书。

Chen Bingchen was a Vanguard member. Since his youth, he was drawn to revolutionary movements, joining the Vanguard in 1937. After the founding of New China, Chen Bingchen accompanied Chairman Mao Zedong in his state visit to the Soviet Union. He, later, was served as the secretary-general, director of personnel administration and director of archives office of the Central Military Commission. In November 1957, he was appointed as the deputy director of Secretary Office, General Office of the CPC Central Committee. Since March 1979, he served as a consultant with the Political Research Office of the CPC Central Committee General Office and director of Chairman Mao Zedong's Library Management Office. To commemorate the 90th birthday of Chairman Mao, he edited three books including Selected Ancient Poems in MAO Zedong's Calligraphy.

图4 陈秉忱
Picture 4 Chen Bingchen

1938年，日军占领潍县前夕，“民先”潍县队部由撞钟园小学进驻乐道院。由于美国为中立国，当地政府对乐道院无管辖权，使乐道院对抗日组织和“民先”的游击活动起了很好的保护作用。同时，这里还是“民先”组织与八路军七支队的联络站。

1938年下半年，“民先”组织完成了历史使命，大部分队员加入了八路军鲁东游击队八支队，少数加入了五支队。

In 1938, before the occupation of Weihsien by the Japanese forces, the Weihsien Vanguard militia groups entered the Courtyard of the Happy Way from Zhuang-zhong-yuan Primary School. Since the United States was a neutral country at the time, the local government had no jurisdiction over the Courtyard. So the Courtyard became a sanctuary for the guerrilla's activities. The Courtyard was also used as a liaison station between the Vanguard and the Eighth Route Army.

In the second half of 1938, the Vanguard forces joined the guerrilla of Eighth Route Army in the east of Shandong.

图5 撞钟园小学
Picture 5 Zhuang-zhong-yuan Primary School

第五章　乐道院救治抗日军民伤病员

5 Treatment of Wounded Soldiers and Civilians in the Courtyard of the Happy Way

1924 年建成的乐道院医疗机构——潍县基督教医院，是胶东一带一所规模大、档次高的医院。医疗设施齐全、医护人员水平较高，医院还开办了护士学校，培养自己的护理人员。

The Weihsien Christian Hospital, built in the Courtyard of the Happy Way in 1924, was a large, modern hospital in the east of Shandong Province. It was equipped with modern medical facilities, highly-educated and experienced medical staff as well as a nursing school for training its own nursers.

抗战期间，根据地医疗条件十分简陋，伤病员只能冒险偷偷送来乐道院救治，加之战斗频繁，伤员较多，救治任务很重。中美医护人员暗中救治八路军伤病员。日本宪兵队和汉奸经常到医院搜查抗日军民。医护人员冒着生命危险，千方百计掩护伤病员，甚至把伤病严重的人员藏在外国人的住宅里养伤。

During the Sino-Japanese War, since the military bases did not have adequate and proper medical equipment and staff, the sick and the wounded were secretly transferred to the Courtyard's hospital to receive better treatment. Because of the large number of the wounded, it was an arduous task for the hospital's doctors and the medical staff. The Chinese and American medical staff had to give medical treatment to the Eighth Route's wounded soldiers in secret. The Japanese forces and the Chinese collaborators often inspected the hospital to find and arrest the anti-Japanese army members and civilians. The medical workers risked their lives, doing everything possible to save the sick and the wounded, including hiding the seriously-injured in the foreigners' homes.

潍县名医张众航。乐道院医生张众航被抗日游击队“请”到潍县北根据地医治伤病员，后遭到日本人刑讯逼供。

Zhang Zhonghang was a famous doctor in Weihsien. During his service in the Courtyard's hospital, the northern Weihsien base's guerrillas asked him to treat their wounded fellow soldiers. He was later was tortured to make confessions by the Japanese.

图 1 张众航
Picture 1 Zhang Zhonghang

在乐道院学医的丁梦皎，全家都去了胶东革命根据地，后成为解放区医院的骨干。

Ding Mengjiao studied medicine in the Courtyard hospital. He and his family went to Jiaodong revolutionary base and later became the backbone of military hospitals.

图 2 曾在潍县乐道院医院学医的丁梦皎夫妇

Picture 2 Ding Mengjiao, who studied medicine in the Courtyard, and his wife

第六章　潍县战役中的乐道院

6 The Courtyard of the Happy Way during the Weihsien Battle

1945 年抗战胜利，国民党反动派占据潍县城，大举进攻解放区，组织还乡团，疯狂屠杀我干部群众。面对敌人的猖狂进攻，中国人民解放军华东野战军山东兵团在许世友司令员指挥下，决定发动潍县战役。

When the War of Resistance Against Japanese Aggression ended in 1945, the Kuomintang reactionaries occupied Weihsien, attacked the liberated areas and massacred the CPC members. Shandong Corps of the East China Field Army of the PLA, guided by Commander Xu Shiyou, decided to launch a battle in Weihsien.

1948 年 4 月，潍县战役打响。广文中学主教学楼上的大钟楼是当时潍县地区的最高建筑，在钟楼上可用望远镜直接观察到城内外的敌军部署，了解攻城部队的进展情况。因此攻城开始以后，聂凤智司令员带领攻城部队指挥部便进驻广文中学教学楼，在这里指挥了著名的潍县战役。

In April, 1948, the Weihsien Battle broke out. Being the highest building in Weihsien at the time, the bell tower on the main teaching building in Kwangwen Middle School, was used for monitoring the enemy's deployment by telescope. Once the siege began, Commander Nie Fengzhi led the headquarters of siege troops stationed in the teaching building and the ensuing Weihsien Battle.

图 1 许世友
Picture 1 Xu Shiyou

图 2 聂凤智
Picture 2 Nie Fengzhi

图 3 潍县战役中的解放军炮兵部队
Picture 3 The PLA artillery troop in Weihsien Battle

图 4 潍县战役结束后，功臣们披红戴花，受到表彰
Picture 4 Soldiers wearing red flowers and receiving awards after Weihsien Battle

图 5 潍县战役胜利后，9 纵 79 团荣获“潍县团”称号。（前排左起：副政委马晴波、政委陶庸、团长彭辉、兵团政治部组织部长李新华；后排左起：副团长隋克荣、政治处主任李辉）
Picture 5 After the victory of Weihsien Battle, the 79th Regiment, 9th Column was awarded the honorable title of Weihsien Regiment. (Front from left: Vice Political Commissar Ma Qingbo, Political Commissar Tao Yong, Regimental Commander Peng Hui, Head of the Political Department Li Xinhua; Back from left: Deputy Regimental Commander Sui Kerong, Director of the Political Office Li Hui)

第七章　华东大学在乐道院诞生

7 Birth of East China University in the Courtyard of the Happy Way

1948年，人民解放战争进入历史性转折，夺取全面胜利已经为期不远。为了给全国解放做准备，华东局决定，以临沂山东大学为基础，在潍坊市组建华东大学，并任命韦悫任校长，张勃川、李宇超任副校长，校址就设在潍县乐道院内。筹备工作从5月开始，大批干部从各解放区集中到潍坊。在这里，聚集了一大批领导干部和知名专家教授。6月份，各地选拔的学员600余人陆续抵达乐道院。9月份正式开学授课。设有政治经济、文学艺术、教育三个临时研究班和两个预科部。1948年11月，华东大学从潍县迁往济南。

In 1948, the Liberation War entered a turning point. In order to prepare for the national liberation, the East China Bureau of the CPC decided to appoint Wei Que as president, Zhang Bochuan and Li Yuchao as vice presidents to set up East China University in Weifang. The campus was located in the Courtyard of the Happy Way. The organizing process started from May. A large number of CPC cadres and notable scholars attended the inauguration of the university. In June, more than six hundred students selected from all over the country arrived at the Courtyard campus. The courses officially began in September. There were three temporary programs in politics & economy, literature & art, and education, as well as two preparatory departments. In November 1948, the campus was relocated to Jinan.

华东大学存在不到3年，在潍坊的时间仅7个月。但短短的时间培养了4000多名革命干部，有力地支援了人民解放战争，这些干部后来都成了建设新中国的骨干力量。

East China University had a very short life, not more than three years, including a short brief of time, i.e., seven months in Weihsien. But within this very short period of time, it trained more than four thousand revolutionary cadres who supported the People's Liberation War, later becoming a powerful force in building the New China.

华东大学在乐道院的历史上留下了光辉的篇章。

East China University had left a glorious chapter in the Courtyard's history.

图 1 华东大学主教学楼
Picture 1 Main Teaching Building of East China University

图 2 1948 年 9 月，华东大学开学典礼
Picture 2 East China University opening ceremony in September 1948

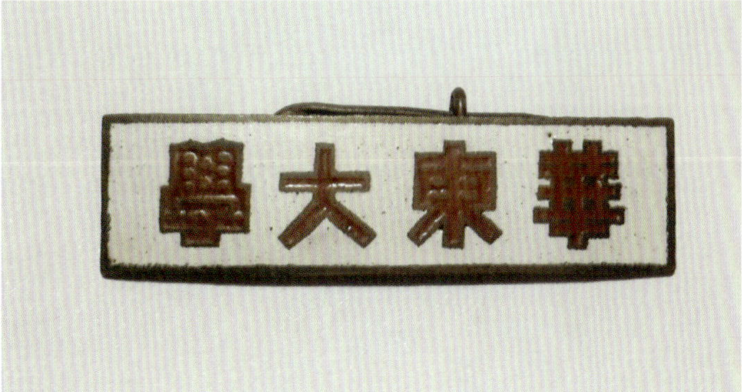

图 3 华东大学校徽
Picture 3 East China University badge

图 4　校长韦悫，著名教育家、上海解放后任副市长、中华人民共和国成立后曾任教育部副部长

Picture 4　President Wei Que, a famous educator, served as vice mayor of Shanghai, and vice president of the Education Ministry after the founding of PRC

图 6　教务处长刘雪苇，在延安抗大当过教员，毛泽东主席著作里几次提到他，后任华东局宣传部文艺处长

Picture 6　Academic director Liu Xuewei, served as teacher in Chinese People's Anti-Japanese Military and Political College as well as the director of Publicity Department of East China Bureau. Chairman Mao mentioned him several times in his books

图 5　副校长张勃川，后调外交部任司长、驻外大使

Picture 5　Vice President Zhang Bochuan, later served as director-general of the Ministry of Foreign Affairs and ambassador to foreign countries

图 7　李清崑，笔名李澄，山东潍县（今潍坊）人，北京大学哲学系教授，1948 年考入华东大学

Picture 7　Li Qingkun, from Weihsien, professor of Philosophy in Peking University. He was admitted to East China University in 1948

图 8　丁伟志，山东潍县（今潍坊）人。1948 年考入华东大学读书。先后在华东大学、山东大学工作，后任中国社会科学院副院长

Picture 8　Ding Weizhi, a Weihsien native, Shandong Province, was admitted to East China University in 1948. He worked in East China University and Shandong University and later served as vice-president of the Chinese Academy of Social Sciences

第八章　潍县解放后的乐道院医院

8 The Hospital after the Liberation of Weihsien

1948 年 4 月，在潍县战役期间，解放军华东野战军和中共山东分局首长来看望伤员时，发现这所医院实力雄厚，当即决定接管医院，并迅速扩大规模，为即将开始的淮海战役提供大规模医疗方面的准备。1948 年 12 月起，乐道院医院先后派出 30 余名医生和附设护校学生，加入为支援淮海战役而设立的坊子临时医院，先后 3 批接收救治了 2323 名伤员。

In April 1948, during the Weihsien Battle, the directors of the PLA East China Field Army and the Shandong Bureau of the CPC paid a visit to the wounded soldiers in the Courtyard's hospital. During the visit, they noticed that it was a well-equipped and modern hospital. They immediately decided to take over the hospital, expanding it to provide large-scale medical care for the upcoming Huai-hai Campaign. Since December 1948, the Courtyard's hospital had sent more than thirty doctors and students from its affiliated nursing school to support the Fangtze temporary hospital during the Huai-hai Campaign, and totally treated 2,323 wounded.

图 1　1948 年潍县解放后乐道院医院全体职工合影
Picture 1　Courtyard hospital staff after Weihsien's liberation in 1948

1948 年 4 月医院被人民政府接管，改为“潍坊特别市乐道院医院”，张冠增为院长、张汉民为副院长。1949 年 1 月 1 日，又改为“潍坊特别市市立医院”。以后几易其名，最终于 1984 年改称“潍坊市人民医院”。

In April 1948, the People's Government took over the hospital and changed its name to "Weifang Special City Courtyard Hospital", appointing Zhang Guanzeng as the president, and Zhang Hanmin as the vice-president. It was renamed again as "Municipal Hospital of Weifang Special City" on January 1, 1949, and once again in 1984, as "Weifang People's Hospital".

1949 年 10 月 1 日，全院职工集会庆祝中华人民共和国成立，并举行隆重升旗仪式，会后全体职工合影留念。

On October 1, 1949, the hospital staff gathered to celebrate the founding of the People's Republic of China, which included a grand national flag raising ceremony.

图 2 1949 年 10 月 1 日，医院全体职工庆祝中华人民共和国成立合影。背景为十字楼正门

Picture 2 On October 1, 1949, the hospital staff gathered at the Cross Building to celebrate the founding of the People's Republic of China

张冠增，生于1912年，山东寿光人。1931年考入北平燕京大学，后转入协和医科大学。在校期间接受进步思想，参加中国共产党领导的抗日组织。毕业后在北平人民医院任医师。1945年因病返回潍县在昌乐中学任英语教员。抗日战争胜利后参与潍县基督教医院的恢复工作。1947年冬，解放战争节节胜利，教会人士和美籍人员纷纷逃离，张冠增以自己的威望主持医院，代行院长职务，积极准备迎接解放，为保全医院呕心沥血。1948年潍县解放后，他被委任为潍坊特别市乐道院医院院长。1948年9月，参加中国人民解放军，历任白求恩学院教师、山东省立医院外科主任、医务主任、副教授、副院长。1978年晋升为教授、主任医师。张冠增曾先后率领医院医护人员参加济南战役和中国人民志愿军伤员的医疗工作，为革命战争做出了贡献。

Zhang Guanzeng was born in Shouguang, Shandong in 1912. He was admitted to Yenching University in 1931, and later was transferred to Peking Union Medical College. At school, he joined anti-Japanese aggression organization led by the CPC. After graduation, he worked in Beiping People's Hospital as a physician. In 1945, because of some health problems he returned to Weihsien and worked as an English teacher in Changle Middle School. After Sino-Japanese War, he participated in the restoration of Weihsien Christian Hospital. In the winter of 1947, before the final victory of Liberation War, the missionaries and the American staff left the Courtyard. Zhang took charge of the hospital and served as the acting president. He worked hard to keep the hospital during the war. In 1948, after the liberation of Weihsien, he was selected as the president of the Weifang Special City Courtyard Hospital. In September 1948, he joined the Chinese People's Liberation Army, working in Bethune College as a teacher. He also worked as the head of the surgical department, medical director, associate professor and vice president of Shandong Provincial Hospital. In 1978, he was promoted to the position of the professor and chief physician. Zhang and his medical staff participated in Ji'nan Battle and treated the wounded soldiers of the Chinese People's Volunteer Army.

图3 张冠增，1948年任潍坊特别市乐道院医院院长

Picture 3 Zhang Guanzeng served as the president of Weifang Special City Courtyard Hospital

张汉民，生于1918年，山东潍县(今潍坊)人。1940年，考入北平燕京大学，1942年转入北京大学医学院，1945年毕业。1947年在潍县基督教医院任外科医生。潍县解放前夕与院长张冠增共同筹划保护医院，迎接解放。1948年潍县解放后被委任为潍坊特别市乐道院医院副院长。1950年代理院长，同年加入中国共产党。1951年任昌潍专署卫生科科长兼昌潍地区中心卫生院院长、昌潍医士学校校长。1954年，调任山东省卫生厅医疗预防处副处长、处长。1970年，任中医处处长。1980年，任山东省中医药研究所党委书记。

Zhang Hanmin was born in Weihsien in 1918. He was admitted to Yenching University in 1940, transferred to Peking University Medical College in 1942 and graduated in 1945. In 1947, he was a surgeon at Weihsien Christian Hospital. On the eve of the liberation of Weihsien, he and President Zhang Guanzeng made plans to protect the hospital. After the liberation of Weihsien in 1948, he was appointed as the vice president of the Weifang Special City Courtyard Hospital. In 1950, serving as the hospital's acting president, he joined the CPC. Since 1951, he was the head of Changwei Health Department, president of Changwei Central Hospital, and principal of Changwei Medical School. Since 1954, he served as the deputy director and later director of Medical Prevention Office of Shandong Health Department. Since 1970, he served as the director of Traditional Chinese Medicine Office. Since 1980, he served as the secretary of the Party Committee of Shandong Traditional Chinese Medicine Institute.

图 4 张汉民，1948 年任潍坊特别市乐道院医院副院长

Picture 4 Zhang Hanmin served as vice president of Weifang Special City Courtyard Hospital in 1948

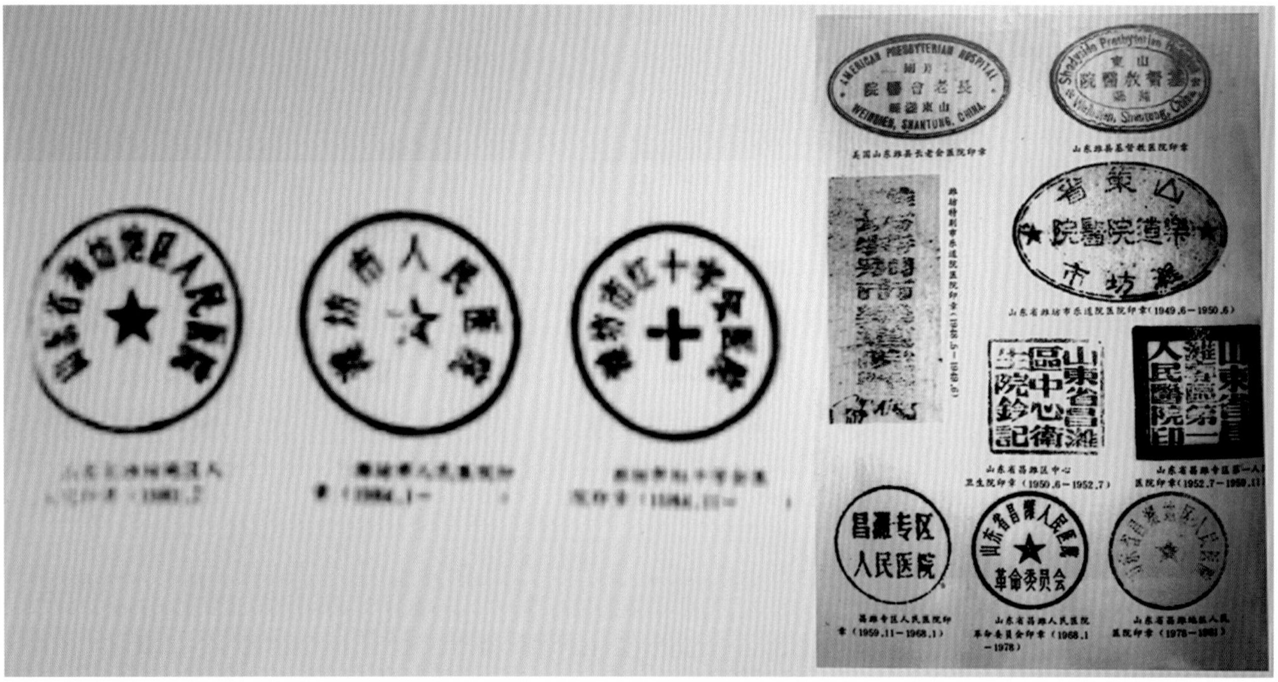

图 5 这些历史遗留下来的印章印迹显示了从潍县乐道院基督教医院到潍坊市人民医院的演变历程
Picture 5 The old seals show the evolution from Weihsien Christian Hospital to Weifang People’s Hospital

第四编 Chapter 4

新时代的乐道院

Chapter 4 The Courtyard of the Happy Way in the New Era

潍县乐道院暨西方侨民集中营旧址现存 7 处近代建筑，建筑面积约 4894 平方米。该旧址是潍坊市国际交往和文化交流的重要窗口，是开展爱国主义和革命传统教育的重要阵地，也是二战期间西方侨民与中国人民团结反抗日本法西斯的正义斗争及国际主义精神的象征。

Currently, there are seven buildings in the former site of Weihsien Courtyard of the Happy Way and Concentration Camp, covering 4,894 square meters. It is a symbolic figure of communication and cultural exchanges on an international level in Weifang; it is also a symbol of the shared struggles of the Western residents and the Chinese people in their fight for defending the motherland, and for democracy through the revolutionary movements. It markedly demonstrates the importance of international cooperation between the Western residents and Chinese people in their fight against Japan's militarism during WWII.

新时代迎来新使命，乐道院潍县集中营博物馆将在潍坊城市总体规划下，实施潍县乐道院旧址复原保护、文物征集、史料发掘、学术研究，推动陈列展览再上新台阶，构建富有历史底蕴、反映时代精神的优秀传统文化传承创新区，打造具有民众亲和力、社会感召力和国际影响力的文物保护利用典范案例，有效发挥文化旅游、国际交流和宣传教育作用，为弘扬爱国主义、国际主义精神，培育和树立社会主义核心价值观，为中外文明交流互鉴和人类命运共同体建设做出积极贡献。

Under the overall plan of Weifang, the new mission of Weihsien Courtyard and Concentration Camp Museum is to protect and restore the Courtyard old site, collect cultural relics and historical materials, and perform academic researches. The museum aims to build an excellent traditional cultural inheritance and innovation zone, and create a model of cultural relic protection and utilization with social appeal and international influence. The museum is expected to serve the people in cultural tourism, international exchange and education, and make contributions to the exchange and mutual learning between Chinese and foreign civilizations, and a community with shared future for mankind.

图 1 新落成的潍县乐道院暨西方侨民集中营旧址景区东门

Picture 1 East gate of Weihsien Courtyard of the Happy Way and Concentration Camp Museum

第一章　现存建筑

1 Existing Buildings in the Courtyard

中华人民共和国成立前的潍县乐道院，占地 200 余亩，内有大小建筑 70 余座，总建筑面积达 83200 平方米。中华人民共和国成立后，旧址作为学校和医院使用，60 年代以来部分建筑相继被拆除。目前仅存 7 处建筑，分别为原乐道院医院楼（“十字楼”）、原潍坊市人民医院专家一号楼（原乐道院校长办公室）、专家二号楼（原乐道院女子圣经学校、乐道院医院护士学校楼）、文华楼（现存于广文中学内）、文美楼（现存于广文中学内）以及平房两排（原乐道院医院病房区域）。

Before the founding of PRC, the Courtyard covered an area of more than thirteen hectares, containing over seventy buildings with a total construction area of 83,200 square meters. After the founding of New China, it was used as a school and a hospital. Since the 1960s, some buildings have been dismantled. The seven existing buildings are as follows: the former Courtyard Hospital Building (also known as the Cross Building), the former No.1 Experts' Building of Weifang People's Hospital (the former Courtyard principal's office), No.2 Experts' Building (the former Girls' Bible Academy and Courtyard Hospital Nurse School), Wenhwa Building (now in the campus of Kwangwen Middle School), Wenmei Building (existing in the campus of Kwangwen Middle School), and two rows of one-story houses (the former Courtyard Hospital wards).

图 1 原乐道院医院大楼（“十字楼”），现为乐道院潍县集中营博物馆展馆
Picture 1 Former Courtyard Hospital Building (Cross Building), now the exhibition hall of Weihsien Courtyard and Concentration Camp Museum

图 2 曾作为乐道院医院病房区的平房，现为乐道院潍县集中营博物馆办公和游客服务区
Picture 2 Former hospital wards, now the office and tourist service area of the Museum

图 3 乐道院现存历史建筑——文华楼（位于广文中学内）
Picture 3 Wenhwa Building (now in the campus of Kwangwen Middle School)

图 4 乐道院现存历史建筑——文美楼（位于广文中学内）
Picture 4 Wenmei building (now in the campus of Kwangwen Middle School)

图 5　乐道院现存历史建筑——原乐道院校长办公室（位于潍坊市人民医院西侧家属院内）
Picture 5 Former Courtyard principal's office

图 6　乐道院现存历史建筑——原乐道院女子圣经学校楼（位于潍坊市人民医院西侧家属院内）
Picture 6 Former Girls' Bible Academy

第二章　旧貌新颜

2 New looks on the old site

为理顺潍县乐道院暨西方侨民集中营旧址的产权和管理体制，更好地对历史建筑进行修缮和保护，充分发挥其历史价值、警示教育作用和中西文化友谊见证的桥梁作用，中共潍坊市委、潍坊市人民政府于2019年5月，将潍县乐道院暨西方侨民集中营旧址所属建筑集中划归市文化和旅游局，由市博物馆统一管理。市文旅局和博物馆先后与市人民医院、广文中学等单位进行对接协调，完成了乐道院7处历史建筑资产移交、文物文献移交、相关国有资产移交等历史遗留问题；解决了房屋腾空、办公场地、不动产转移登记、土地确权等一系列工作难题。

In May, 2019, in order to settle the property rights and the management system of the Courtyard's old site, better repair and protection of the historical buildings, and giving full play to its historical and educational value, Weifang Culture and Tourism Bureau and Weifang Museum was appointed to be in charge of the Courtyard buildings by the Weifang Communist Party Committee and the Municipal Government. With the help of Weifang People's Hospital and Kwangwen Middle School, the transfer of assets, relics and documents of seven historical buildings was completed. In the meantime, a series of problems such as real estate transfer registration and land ownership was resolved as well.

产权关系和管理体制理顺后，经过1年多的紧张筹备，在市委、市政府的正确领导和各级各部门的大力支持下，潍县乐道院暨西方侨民集中营旧址面貌焕然一新。2019年9月16日，乐道院暨西方侨民集中营旧址被中宣部命名为全国爱国主义教育示范基地，成为山东省2019年唯一一处获评的全国爱国主义教育示范基地，是潍坊市首个全国爱国主义教育示范基地；2019年10月16日，潍县乐道院暨西方侨民集中营旧址被国务院公布为第八批全国重点文物保护单位。

Through over a year of preparation, under the supervision of the Municipal Party Committee and the Municipal Government, the former site of Weihsien Courtyard and Concentration Camp took on an entirely new look. On September 16, 2019, it was listed as a National Demonstration Base of Patriotic Education by the Central Publicity Department, becoming the only one as such in Shandong Province in that year and the first one in Weifang. On 16 October 2019, it was listed as a State Protected Cultural Heritage Site by the State Council.

图1　历史建筑修缮施工现场——“十字楼”
Picture 1　Renovating the Cross Building

图 2 历史建筑修缮施工现场——“十字楼”
Picture 2 Renovating the Cross Building

图 3 乐道院景区东门施工现场
Picture 3 Construction site of the Courtyard's east gate

图 4 乐道院潍县集中营展厅布置现场
Picture 4 Embellishing the Courtyard's exhibition hall

图 5 潍县乐道院暨西方侨民集中营旧址景区大门（建于 2020 年）
Picture 5 Main gate of the Weihsien Courtyard of the Happy Way and Concentration Camp Museum (built in 2020)

图 6 潍县乐道院暨西方侨民集中营旧址景区道路
Picture 6 The road leading to the museum

图 7 乐道广场内的《和平 · 友谊》铸铜雕塑纪念碑
Picture 7 The “Peace, Friendship” monument, made of bronze statutes, in the Courtyard square

图 8 乐道广场内的《和平 · 友谊》铸铜雕塑纪念碑（局部）
Picture 8 The “Victory, Friendship” monument

图 9　潍县乐道院暨西方侨民集中营旧址景区内的“警世钟”，钟体刻有铭文：铭记历史，警钟长鸣；勿忘国耻，和平永存

Picture 9　The “Warning Bell” in the Courtyard engraved with the words, “Remember the history, and keep the alarm bell ringing; Remember the national humiliation and may peace last forever.”

图 10　乐道院潍县集中营博物馆办公和游客服务区入口的月亮门

Picture 10　The moon gate at the entrance of the museum office and tourist service center

图 11　复原的潍县乐道院正门（位于乐道院潍县集中营博物馆办公和游客服务区内）

Picture 11 Restored front gate of the Courtyard (located in the museum’s service area)

图 12 乐道院浮雕墙（位于乐道院潍县集中营博物馆办公和游客服务区内）
Picture 11 Restored front gate of the Courtyard (located in the museum’s service area)

图 13 乐道院潍县集中营博物馆十字楼、办公和游客服务区鸟瞰
Picture 13 Aerial view of the Cross Building, museum office and tourist service area

图 14 乐道院潍县集中营博物馆展区的荣誉牌（从左至右依次为：中宣部命名的“全国爱国主义教育示范基地”、国务院公布的“全国重点文物保护单位”、中国博物馆协会授予的“国家一级博物馆”牌）
Picture 14 Honor boards of the museum (left to right: “National Demonstration Base of Patriotic Education”, named by the Central Publicity Department, “State Protected Cultural Heritage Site”, designated by the State Council, and “National First-Class Museum”, awarded by the China Museum Association)

乐道院潍县集中营博物馆，展馆设在“十字楼”，一层为乐道院的发展介绍，包括乐道院产生的历史背景、发展历程以及乐道院的教育、医疗、宗教传播等；二层为潍县集中营时期展陈；负一层为世界反法西斯陈列。

The museum exhibition hall is located in the Cross Building. The first floor provides a brief introduction to the Courtyard of the Happy Way, including its history as well as the functions of the schools, hospital, and church; the second floor is the Weihsien Concentration Camp exhibition; the basement is the anti-fascist war exhibition.

图 15 乐道院潍县集中营博物馆一层序厅（局部）
Picture 15 Introduction Hall on the first floor of the museum

图 16 乐道院潍县集中营博物馆一层序厅（局部）
Picture 16 First floor of the museum

图 17 乐道院潍县集中营博物馆二层西方侨民集中营展览
Picture 17 Concentration Camp Exhibition Hall on the second floor

图 18 乐道院潍县集中营博物馆二层西方侨民集中营展陈（局部）
Picture 18 Concentration Camp Exhibition Hall

图 19 乐道院潍县集中营博物馆二层西方侨民集中营展陈（局部《西方侨民及其后裔的手模墙》）
Picture 19 Concentration Camp Exhibition Hall (handprints of the Western residents and their later generations)

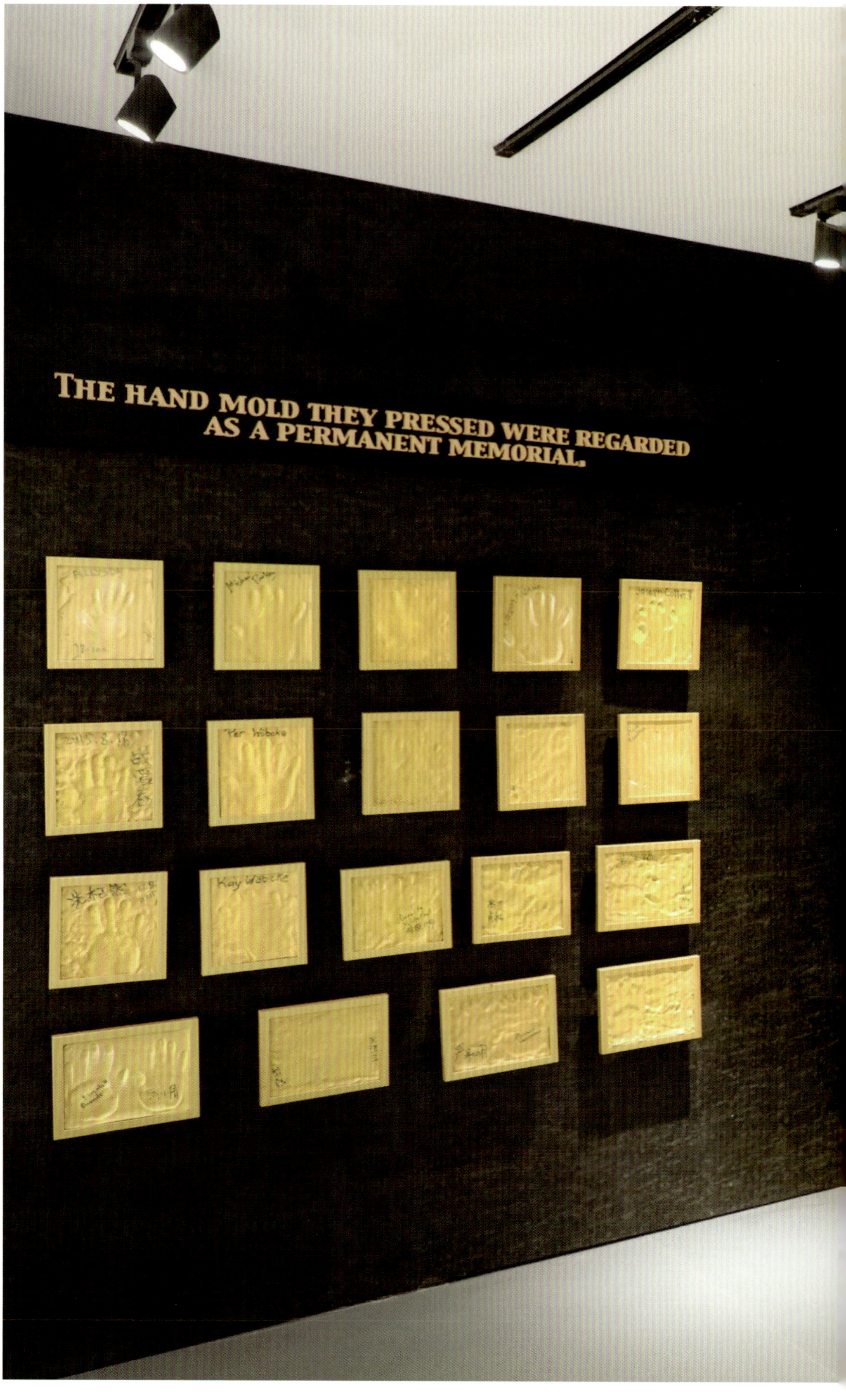

西方侨民难友及其后代到访潍坊市时
摁下的作为永久纪念的手模

图 20 乐道院潍县集中营博物馆负一层世界反法西斯陈列
Picture 20 The World Anti-Fascist War Exhibition on the sub-basement

图 21 乐道院潍县集中营博物馆负一层世界反法西斯陈列（展厅内部）
Picture 21 The World Anti-Fascist War Exhibition

第三章　乐道院潍县集中营博物馆开馆和揭牌仪式

3 Opening Ceremony of Weihsien Courtyard of the Happy Way and Concentration Camp Museum

2020 年 9 月 3 日是中国抗日战争胜利纪念日暨世界反法西斯战争胜利 75 周年纪念日。当天，中共潍坊市委在潍县乐道院暨西方侨民集中营旧址举行乐道院潍县集中营博物馆开馆仪式，并为“全国爱国主义教育示范基地”“全国重点文物保护单位”揭牌。百年沧桑乐道院，迎来新的使命。

September 3, 2020 was the anniversary of the victory of China in the Second Sino-Japanese War and the 75th anniversary of the end of World War II. During the opening ceremony of the Weihsien Courtyard of the Happy Way and Concentration Camp Museum at the former site of the Courtyard, the “National Demonstration Base of Patriotic Education” and “State Protected Cultural Heritage Site” were unveiled by the Municipal Party Committee of Weifang. Coming through a century of ups and downs, the Courtyard of the Happy Way ushered in a new path.

9 月 3 日上午 11 点，乐道院潍县集中营博物馆“十字楼”楼前广场上一曲《友谊地久天长》随风悠扬。随后在雄壮的国歌声中，五星红旗在广场上冉冉升起。接下来，一段三分钟的视频把人们带回百年的历史记忆中，重温了乐道院的前世今生。

At 11 AM September 3, the song “Auld Lang Syne” was played in the square in front of the Cross Building. Later, as the national anthem was being played, the flag of China was gradually raised. Finally, a three-minute video took the audience back to a century of challenges, making them relive the past and present of the Courtyard.

中共潍坊市委常委、宣传部部长初宝杰主持仪式。中共潍坊市委书记、市人大常委会主任惠新安，潍坊市人民医院原院长、著名放射学家、享受国务院特殊津贴专家夏宝枢，南京国际和平城市联合申报人、南京大学教授刘成分别致辞。仪式期间，受新冠疫情影响，二战期间被关押在潍县集中营的外国侨民幸存者及其家属不能来到现场，他们也送来了视频祝福。中宣部宣教局副局长冷志明、省文旅厅党组成员、副厅长王廷琦分别致辞。中宣部、省委宣传部、省文化和旅游厅、潍坊市委有关领导和专家为乐道院潍县集中营博物馆“全国爱国主义教育示范基地”和“全国重点文物保护单位”揭牌。随后，与会人员参观了乐道院潍县集中营博物馆。

Chu Baojie, a member of the Standing Committee of the CPC Weifang Municipal Committee and minister of the Publicity Department, presided over the ceremony. Hui Xin’an, Secretary of the Weifang Municipal Party Committee and director of the Standing Committee of the Municipal People’s Congress, Xia Baoshu, former president of Weifang People’s Hospital and a renown radiologist, Liu Cheng, joint applicant of Nanjing International City of Peace and a professor at Nanjing University, Wang Tingqi, a member of the

Party Leadership Group and the deputy director of the Provincial Department of Culture and Tourism, and Leng Zhiming, the deputy director of the Publicity and Education Bureau of the Central Publicity Department, were among the speakers. Due to the outbreak of Covid-19, the foreign survivors and their families detained in Weihsien Concentration Camp during WWII were unable to attend the ceremony; however, they sent their blessings via video messages. The "National Demonstration Base of Patriotic Education" and the "State Protected Cultural Heritage Site" of Weihsien Courtyard of the Happy Way and Concentration Camp Museum were unveiled by the authorities from the Publicity Department of the CPC Central Committee, the Publicity Department of the Provincial Party committee, the Provincial Department of Culture and Tourism, and the Weifang Municipal Party Committee. Afterwards, the participants visited the museum.

图 1 仪式现场举行升国旗仪式
Picture 1 National flag raising ceremony

参加仪式的还有中国文化遗产研究院、中国文物报社、山东大学、南京城墙保护管理中心、山东艺术学院的相关专家；潍坊市直各有关部门领导、市文化和旅游局各部门负责人，各县市区博物馆馆长，潍坊市人民医院、广文中学代表，新闻媒体记者和部分热心市民。

The participants included experts from China Cultural Heritage Research Institute, China Cultural Relics Newspaper, Shandong University, Nanjing City Wall Protection Management Center, and Shandong University of Arts, heads of relevant departments directly under Weifang City, heads of departments of Municipal Culture and Tourism Bureau, directors of the other museums in Shandong Province, representatives of Weifang People's Hospital and Kwangwen middle school, reporters and some local residents.

图 2 仪式现场，乐队合唱《让世界充满爱》
Picture 2 Singing the song, "Fill the World with Love"

图 3 中共潍坊市委书记、市人大常委会主任惠新安同志致辞

Picture 3 Hui Xin’an, Secretary of the Weifang Municipal Committee of the CPC and Director of the Standing Committee of the Municipal People’s Congress, delivering a speech

图 4 中共潍坊市委常委、宣传部部长初宝杰同志主持仪式

Picture 4 Chu Baojie, member of the Standing Committee of the CPC Weifang Municipal Committee and Director of the Publicity Department, presiding over the ceremony

图 5 南京国际和平城市联合申报人、南京大学教授刘成致辞
Picture 5 Liu Cheng, joint applicant of Nanjing International City of Peace, and professor of Nanjing University, delivering a speech

图 6 潍坊市人民医院原院长、著名放射学家、享受国务院特殊津贴专家夏宝枢致辞
Picture 6 Xia Baoshu, a notable radiologist and former president of Weifang People's Hospital,, making a speech

图 7 与会领导和嘉宾为“全国爱国主义教育示范基地”和“全国重点文物保护单位”揭牌
Picture 7 Participants and guests unveiling the “National Demonstration Base of Patriotic Education” and “State Protected Cultural Heritage Site”

在开馆揭牌仪式当天下午，举办了“珍爱和平，构建人类命运共同体，申办国际和平城市”专题学术会议。南京国际和平城市联合申报人、南京大学教授刘成，中国文化遗产研究院中国世界文化遗产中心副主任燕海鸣，山东大学历史文化学院教授刘家峰、胡卫清，潍坊市博物馆研究馆员孙敬明等专家分别作了会议发言。

In the afternoon, the academic conference on “Cherish Peace, Build a Community with a Shared Future for Mankind, and Bid for an International City of Peace” was held. Professor Liu Cheng, Yan Haiming, the deputy director of China World Cultural Heritage Center, Chinese Academy of Cultural Heritage, Liu Jiafeng, Hu Weiqing, professors at the School of History and Culture of Shandong University, Sun Jingming, a research librarian at Weifang Museum, and other experts delivered speeches.

乐道院潍县集中营博物馆使命光荣，将充分发挥“全国爱国主义教育示范基地”“全国重点文物保护单位”和“国家一级博物馆”这三块国家级金字招牌优势，立足世界反法西斯战争胜利75周年的活动主题，通过举办开馆仪式和学术研讨活动，挖掘保护潍县乐道院暨西方侨民集中营旧址历史，使其与城市记忆、国家记忆、全球记忆融为一体，提升广大人民群众对珍爱和平、构建人类命运共同体思想的认知，形成弘扬爱国主义、国际主义精神的浓厚氛围。

The Weihsien Courtyard of the Happy Way and Concentration Camp Museum is the first national patriotic education demonstration base in Weifang. It opened on the 75th anniversary of the end of WWII. The museum will fully demonstrate the advantages of the three national golden signs, i.e. “National Demonstration Base of Patriotic Education”, “State Protected Cultural Heritage Site”, and “National First-Class Museum”. In accordance with the theme of the 75th anniversary of the end of WWII, an opening ceremony and several academic seminars were held by the museum, celebrating the history of the Weihsien Courtyard of the Happy Way and Concentration Camp, which integrated them with the memory of the city, the country and the world. This was a great occasion to enhance people’s awareness of cherishing peace and building a community with a shared future for mankind, which help to promote the spirit of patriotism and internationalism.

第四章 潍坊市成为国际和平城市

4 Weifang becoming an International City of Peace

2021 年 1 月 16 日，国际和平城市协会主席弗雷德·阿门特先生发来邮件，祝贺潍坊成为国际和平城市，并定于 2021 年 2 月 3 日，向全球正式发布公告。继南京之后，潍坊成为中国第二个、全球第 308 个加入国际和平城市协会的城市。该组织是全球唯一得到联合国正式认可的和平城市协会，致力于连接、促进和鼓励全球开展和平活动，实现世界和平的梦想。加入国际和平城市组织，是向全世界表明近 1000 万潍坊人民牢记战争创伤、创造和平未来的决心。成为国际和平城市的潍坊，将为构建亚洲乃至世界持久和平、推动构建人类命运共同体做出积极贡献。

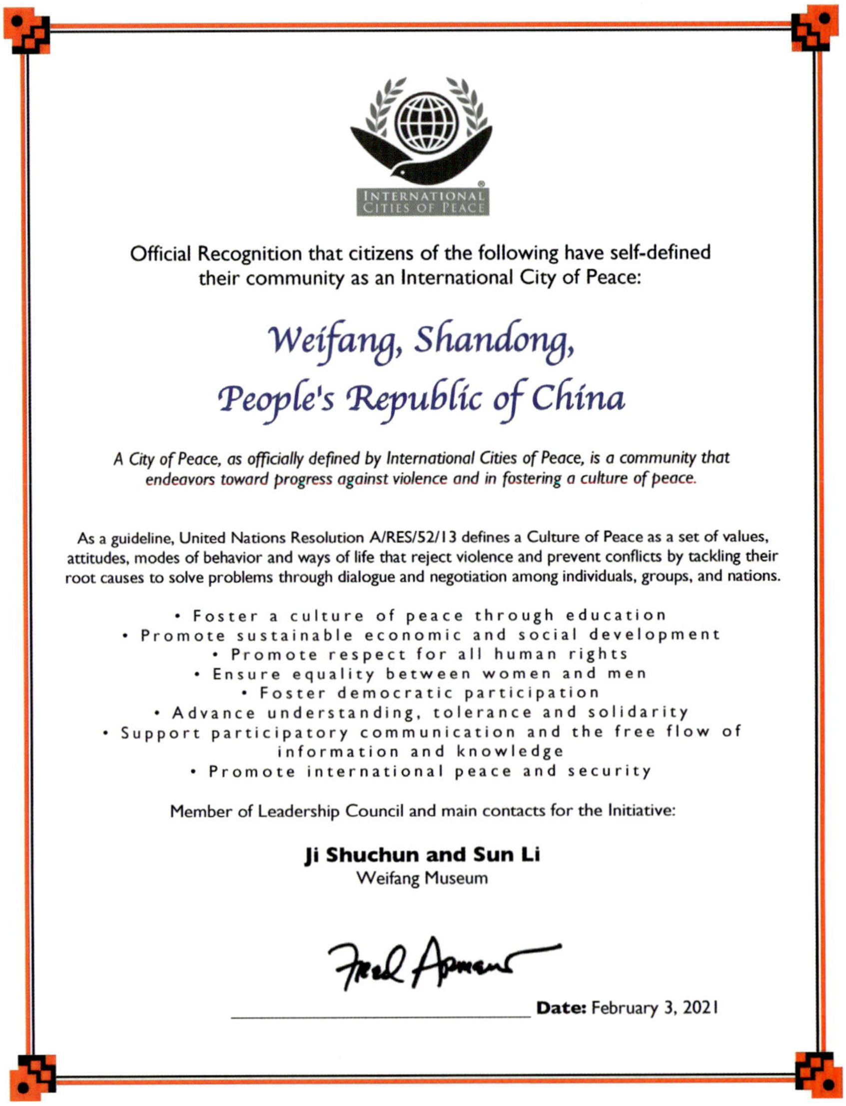
INTERNATIONAL CITIES OF PEACE

Official Recognition that citizens of the following have self-defined their community as an International City of Peace:

Weifang, Shandong, People's Republic of China

A City of Peace, as officially defined by International Cities of Peace, is a community that endeavors toward progress against violence and in fostering a culture of peace.

As a guideline, United Nations Resolution A/RES/52/13 defines a Culture of Peace as a set of values, attitudes, modes of behavior and ways of life that reject violence and prevent conflicts by tackling their root causes to solve problems through dialogue and negotiation among individuals, groups, and nations.

- Foster a culture of peace through education
- Promote sustainable economic and social development
- Promote respect for all human rights
- Ensure equality between women and men
- Foster democratic participation
- Advance understanding, tolerance and solidarity
- Support participatory communication and the free flow of information and knowledge
- Promote international peace and security

Member of Leadership Council and main contacts for the Initiative:

Ji Shuchun and Sun Li
Weifang Museum

Date: February 3, 2021

图 1 国际和平城市协会授予潍坊国际和平城市证书

Picture 1 The Weifang International City of Peace certificate awarded by International Cities of Peace Association

On January 16, 2021, J Fred Arment, the directer of International Cities of Peace Association, sent an email to congratulate Weifang on becoming an International City of Peace, which is scheduled to be officially announced on February 3, 2021. After Nanjing, Weifang is the second city in China, and the 308th in the world, to join the International Cities of Peace. This association is the only cities of peace organization officially recognized by the United Nations. It is committed to connecting, promoting and encouraging peace activities around the world, and to realize the dream of world peace. Joining the International Cities of Peace shows the determination of nearly 10 million people of Weifang to remember the trauma of war and create a peaceful future. As an International City of Peace, Weifang will contribute to build lasting peace in Asia and around the world, and a community with a shared future for humanity.

INTERNATIONAL CITIES OF PEACE

官方承认以下城市的公民自愿定义
其社区为国际和平城市：

中国山东省潍坊市

国际和平城市协会对和平城市的官方定义是
为反对暴力和促进和平文化事业不断做出努力的社区。

联合国第A /RES/52/13号决议将和平文化定义为：通过个人、团体和国家之间的对话和谈判处理问题根源，从而解决问题，防止冲突以及拒绝暴力的价值观、态度、行为方式和生活方式。

- 通过教育促进和平文化
- 促进经济与社会可持续发展
- 促进对所有人权的尊重
- 确保男女平等
- 促进民主参与度
- 促进理解、宽容和团结
- 支持参与式交流以及信息和知识的自由流动
- 促进世界和平与安全

领导委员会成员及主要联络人：

吉树春，孙丽
潍坊市博物馆

日期：2021年2月3日

图 2　国际和平城市证书中文版
Picture 2 The Weifang International City of Peace certificate in Chinese

第一节　潍坊申请创建国际和平城市的经过
4.1 Weifang Establishing an International City of Peace

和平城市，是指在特定的城市行政区内，继承城市的和平传统，倡导和平与和解，联合政府、高校、社会团体和城市市民，以和平为城市发展理念，融合历史、记忆、遗迹中的和平元素，通过和平维护、和平创建、和平构建的途径，实现多维度的和平项目创建，全面提升城市发展并推动国际和平的一种城市形态。和平城市共有十个类型，潍坊属于第四类型，即“该城市遭受过战争的创伤并利用历史遗产致力于和平建设”。国际和平城市协会，是全球唯一得到联合国教科文组织正式认可的和平城市协会，具有联合国经济及社会理事会（联合国六大主要机构之一）特别协商地位。该组织成立于 2009 年，总部设在美国俄亥俄州代顿市，现由六大洲 60 多个国家 307 个和平城市构成，致力于连接、促进和鼓励全球开展和平活动的城市，实现世界和平的梦想。

City of Peace, is a city where the government, schools, organization and citizens connect together to develop a peaceful environment and advocate peace and reconciliation; a city of peace is an environment built based on the concept of peace through the ways of peace maintenance and peace projects, improving the city development, and promoting international peace. There are ten types of cities of peace; Weifang belongs to the fourth type, that is, “Cities which, having been destroyed in war, have used this tragedy to dedicate themselves to work for peace”. International Cities of Peace is the only cities of peace association officially recognized by UNESCO in the world. It achieved Special Consultative Status with the United Nations Economic and Social Council (one of the six major United Nations bodies). ICP, founded in 2009, with headquarters in Dayton, Ohio, USA, has 307 member cities in more than sixty countries on six continents. It is committed to connecting and encouraging cities around the world to promote peace activities and realize the dream of world peace.

一、申请创建国际和平城市的背景
1.1 The Background of Applying for International City of Peace

和平与发展依然是当今世界的主题，但负面因素依然不断增加。2017 年 1 月 18 日，习近平总书记在日内瓦发表题为《共同构建人类命运共同体》的主旨演讲，深刻、全面、系统地阐述人类命运共同体理念，提出“让和平的薪火代代相传”。通过和平方式解决国际争端越来越受到国际社会的重视，营造和平文化，共同面对挑战，化解冲突，建设和平已成为当今时代潮流下的一种国际共识。

Peace and development are still the main themes of today’s world, but negative factors are on the rise. On 18 January 2017, President Xi Jinping delivered a keynote speech entitled “Building a Community with a Shared Future for Mankind” in Geneva, elaborating on the concept of such a community, and calling for “passing on the torch of peace from generation to generation”. The international community has paid more and more attention to settling international disputes through peaceful means. It has become an international consensus to create a culture of peace, joining hands to face challenges, resolving conflicts and building world peace.

潍坊历史悠久，文化底蕴深厚，文物资源丰富，是山东省的文物大市，以潍县乐道院暨西方侨民集中营旧址、坊子德日建筑群、大英烟草公司旧址、二十里堡火车站、胶济铁路等富含和平因素的近现代历史文化遗产，既见证了潍坊近代中西文化交流的进程，也凸显了潍坊城市文化品格的博大和深厚。作为二战时期亚洲最大外国侨民集中营——潍县乐道院集中营所在地，潍坊这座城市的人民更懂得和平的珍贵。潍坊申请创建国际和平城市有助于彰显中国的和平形象，对于构建亚洲乃至世界持久和平、推动构建人类命运共同体具有特殊重要的意义。

Weifang enjoys a profound culture and a long history, and rich in cultural relics resources. In recent century, the city's cultural heritage include such historical sites as the former site of the Weihsien Courtyard of the Happy Way and Concentration Camp, Fangtze German and Japanese Building Group, the old site of British Tobacco Company, Ershilipu Railway Station, and Jiaozhou-Ji'nan Railway. These place have been witness to a series of cultural exchanges between China and the West as well as the development of the city's inclusive culture. As the place where more than two thousand European and American residents were interned during WWII, the people of Weifang know and recognize the value of peace more than many people around the world. Weifang's application to become an International City of Peace helps to demonstrate China's hope of peace; it is also of special significance to build lasting peace in Asia and the rest of the world, and a community with a shared future for mankind.

图 3 坐落于潍坊市坊子区的德日历史建筑群——坊茨小镇
Picture 3 Fangtze Town, a German-Japanese historical building group located in Fangzi District, Weifang

图 4 坊茨小镇内的历史建筑
Picture 4 Historic buildings in Fangtze Town

图 5 坐落于潍坊市奎文区的大英烟厂旧址
Picture 5 The former site of British Tobacco Company in Kuiwen District, Weifang

图 6 大英烟厂旧址内的铁路遗迹
Picture 6 Railway remains in the former site of British Tobacco Company

二、申请创建国际和平城市过程

1.2 The Process of Applying for an International City of Peace

南京作为中国首个国际和平城市，是经过 20 年持续努力、两年精心筹备申请，于 2017 年创建成功。潍坊自 20 世纪 90 年代依托乐道院・潍县集中营旧址开展相关和平纪念活动、2005 年市政府拨专款对集中营旧址进行维护修缮、2019 年正式提出创建国际和平城市目标、到 2021 年 1 月 16 日创建成功，也历经 30 年积淀和努力。主要创建经过如下：

Nanjing, the first City of Peace in China, was officially recognized as an International City of Peace in 2017. It took them twenty years to do the preparation and two years to get their application processed. Weifang has also gone through thirty years of efforts; it first started in the 1990s, when the first peace activities took place in the site of Weihsien Courtyard of the Happy Way and Concentration Camp. In 2005, the municipal government allocated special funds to maintain and repair the concentration camp site. In 2019, the city formally put forward the goal of building an International City of Peace. On January 16, 2021, it was officially admitted. The whole process was as follows:

——2019 年 5 月，中共潍坊市委决定“理顺乐道院产权体制，乐道院所属建筑划归市博物馆统一管理”，并提出乐道院・潍县集中营旧址争创“全国爱国主义教育示范基地”的目标和潍坊市创建“国际和平城市”的构想。

—— In May of 2019, the Weifang Municipal Party Committee made the decision to reorganize the property rights of the Courtyard which paved the way to transfer the responsibility of preserving the buildings to Weifang Museum. The Committee also proposed a broader goal, that is, to establish the old site of the Courtyard and the concentration camp as “a National Demonstration Base of Patriotic Education”, which would contribute to building Weifang as an “International City of Peace”.

——2019 年 9 月 16 日，潍县乐道院・西方侨民集中营旧址成为山东省当年唯一获评全国爱国主义教育示范基地的单位；10 月 16 日，潍县乐道院・西方侨民集中营旧址成为第八批国家重点文物保护单位。这座历经百年沧桑的建筑正在以全新的面貌聚焦人们的视线，同时也为国际和平城市的创建筑牢了基础、鼓舞了信心。

—— On September 16, 2019, the old site of the Courtyard and the concentration camp was listed as a National Demonstration Base of Patriotic Education by the Central Publicity Department, becoming the only city as such in Shandong Province in that year; On 16 October 2019, it was listed as a State Protected Cultural Heritage Site by the State Council. The brand new look of the century-old buildings drew people’s attention; in the meantime, it provided a solid foundation for building an International City of Peace.

——2019 年 10 月，市委、市政府正式组建潍坊市和平城市创建工作领导小组，领导小组负责协调推进潍坊市国际和平城市创建工作，组织深度挖掘和平文化内涵并开展相关活动，研究解决创建过程中的重点问题。领导小组下设办公室，副市长马清民兼任办公室主任，葛晓东、田素英、吉树春兼任办公室副主任。

——By October 2019, the Weifang Municipal Party Committee and the Weifang Government had established the Weifang City of Peace management team which shall be responsible for preparing and coordinating the International City of Peace application procedure. It would also organize and supervise the in-depth exploration of Weifang culture, and resolve any issues in the process. The management team members were vice mayor Ma Qingmin serving as the director, and Ge Xiaodong, Tian Suying and Ji Shuchun serving as the deputy directors.

——2019 年 10—12 月，创建团队根据国际和平城市创建要求，组织开展和平场馆建设、学术研究、文物征集、档案整理、和平教育等系列活动，并开始撰写中英文版申请报告。

—— From October to December 2019, the Weifang City of Peace team organized a series of activities, including the peace exhibitions, academic research, collection of cultural relics, archiving, and peace education; it also began to prepare the application report, both in Chinese and English.

——2020 年 12 月 7 日，创建团队正式向国际和平城市协会提交中英文申请报告。

—— On December 7, 2020, the team officially submitted the application report to the International Cities of Peace Association.

——2020 年 12 月 25 日，国际和平城市协会主席弗雷德·阿门特先生发来修改意见，创建团队在南京大学刘成教授协助下，继续补充资料、图片，完成整改。

—— On December 25, 2020, Mr. J Fred Arment, director of International Cities of Peace, sent the feedback. With the assistance of Professor Liu Cheng from Nanjing University, the team revised the report with added information and photos.

——2021 年 1 月 6 日，创建团队向国际和平城市协会再次提交 84 页的申请报告。

——On January 6, 2021, the team again submitted the 84-page application report to the International Cities of Peace.

——2021 年 1 月 16 日，国际和平城市协会主席弗雷德·阿门特先生发来邮件，祝贺潍坊成为国际和平城市，并决定于 2 月 3 日向全球正式发布公告。

——On January 16, 2021, Director Fred Arment congratulated Weifang on becoming an International City of Peace. The official announcement was made on February 3 by the International Cities of Peace Association.

图 7 中共潍坊市委书记田庆盈同志陪同中共山东省委书记刘家义同志视察乐道院潍县集中营博物馆
Picture 7 Liu Jiayi, Secretary of the CPC Shandong Provincial Party Committee, accompanied by Tian Qingying, Secretary of CPC Weifang Municipal Party Committee, visited the Courtyard of the Happy Way·Weihsien Concentration Camp Museum

图 8 中共潍坊市委副书记、市长刘运同志陪同文化和旅游部副部长、国家文物局局长李群同志视察乐道院潍县集中营博物馆

Picture8 Mr. Li Qun, Deputy Director of the Ministry of Culture and Tourism of China and Director of National Cultural Heritage Administration, accompanied by Mr. Liu Yun, Deputy Secretary of the CPC Weifang Municipal Committee and Mayor of Weifang, visited the Courtyard of the Happy Way·Weihsien Concentration Camp Museum

第二节 潍坊市举行荣获“国际和平城市”庆祝活动

4.2 Celebration of Weifang becoming an “International City of Peace”

2021 年 2 月 3 日，国际和平城市协会主席弗雷德・阿门特（J. Frederick Arment）先生向全球宣布新一期国际和平城市名单，潍坊市荣登榜单，成为继南京之后中国新的国际和平城市。

On February 3, 2021, Mr. J. Frederick Arment, President of the non-profit organization International Cities of Peace, announced a new list of peace cities to the world. Weifang joined other participating cities across the globe to be named an International City of Peace, making it the second city in China to participate, after Nanjing.

上午 10 时，伴随着悠扬的钟声，上千只洁白的和平鸽在乐道院潍县集中营博物馆上空凌空飞翔。100 多名潍坊各界市民代表汇聚在和平・友谊纪念广场，庄严诵读“潍坊国际和平城市宣言”，热烈庆祝潍坊国际和平城市申办成功。

At 10 o’clock in the morning, as a peal of bells rang out, thousands of white doves flew in the sky over the Weihsien Courtyard of the Happy Way and Concentration Camp Museum. More than a hundred Weifang citizens representing all walks of life gathered at the Peace Friendship Memorial Square, and read the “Weifang International City of Peace Declaration” to celebrate this wonderful achievement.

庆祝活动过程中，志愿者宣读了国际和平城市协会主席弗雷德·阿门特先生的贺信、海外潍县集中营专题网站“Weihsien-Paintings”（画说潍县）管理者利奥波特·潘德的祝福信，以及南京国际和平城市联合申报人、南京大学联合国教科文组织和平学教席、和平学研究所所长刘成教授贺信。中共潍坊市委常委、宣传部部长初宝杰同志做了讲话。初宝杰同志和市人民医院原院长、乐道院潍县集中营博物馆顾问夏宝枢同志，共同为“和平·友谊”纪念碑揭牌。

During the celebration, volunteers read letters of congratulation from Mr Frederick Arment, the president of International Cities of Peace, Leopold Pander, the webmaster of "Weihsien Paintings"—a Weihsien Concentration Camp themed website, and Professor Liu Cheng, a member of the Nanjing International City of Peace bid committee, holder of UNESCO Chair on Peace Studies in Nanjing University, and director of Peace Studies Institute. Chu Baojie, member of the CPC Weifang Municipal Party Committee Standing Committee and Minister of Weifang Publicity Department, made a speech. Together, Chu Baojie and Xia Baoshu, former president of Weifang People's Hospital and consultant of Weihsien Courtyard and Concentration Camp Museum, unveiled the monument of "Peace · Friendship."

图 9 中共潍坊市委常委、宣传部部长初宝杰同志在庆祝活动上讲话
Picture 9 Chu Baojie, member of the CPC Weifang Municipal Party Committee Standing Committee, and Minister of Weifang Publicity Department, making a speech

图 10 潍坊市副市长马清民同志主持庆祝活动
Picture 10 Ma Qingmin, Vice Mayor of Weifang, presiding the celebration event

图 11 初宝杰部长和夏宝枢先生为“和平 · 友谊”纪念碑揭牌
Picture 11 Chu Baojie and Xia Baoshu unveiling the monument of “Peace · Friendship”

图 12 志愿者代表诵读“潍坊国际和平城市宣言”

Picture 12 Representatives of Weifang citizens reading the “Weifang International City of Peace Declaration”

图 13 活动现场放飞和平鸽

Picture 13 Peace doves were released at the event

和平是一种理念，和平是尊重，是理解，是安定，是繁荣，是人们可以享有高质量的生活。和平的种子只有播撒在广大民众的心间，才能孕育出无数祈愿和平的希望和守护的力量。善作善成，久久为功，和平城市建设只有起点、没有终点。下一步潍坊市将充分利用“国际和平城市”这一平台，发挥其桥梁纽带作用，向全世界展示中国和平文化、介绍和平故事、发出和平愿景，传递中国人民爱好和平、积极践行和平理念的心声！

Peace is an idea; peace is respect, understanding, stability and prosperity; peace means people could enjoy a higher quality of life. Only after the vision of peace is firmly rooted in the hearts of all the people can we enjoy the hope for peace and have the strength to protect peace. Roma was not built in one day. The establishment of a City of Peace is only a starting point, not the ending one. Weifang will use “International City of Peace” as a platform, a bridge to extend China’s peace culture, peace stories and peace vision to the world, and pass on the Chinese people’s peace-loving and peace-making aspirations.

第三节　潍坊成功创建国际和平城市的意义

4.3 The Significance of Weifang becoming an International City of Peace

第二次世界大战是迄今为止人类历史上规模空前、伤亡最惨重、造成破坏最大的全球性战争。潍坊作为二战期间亚洲最大的外国侨民集中营所在地，承载着世界反法西斯战争共同的伤痛记忆，对于拓宽公共外交空间具有不可替代的地位和重要作用。成功创建为国际和平城市为潍坊提供了对外交往新平台，可以让世界更好地认识潍坊、了解潍坊，提升潍坊的国际影响力，加快推进现代化高品质城市建设。

The Second World War was the largest and the most destructive global war with the most injuries and deaths in human history. Weifang, as the place of largest concentration camp for foreign residents in Asia during WWII, bears the painful memories of the war, playing an irreplaceable role in expanding the space of public diplomacy. The successful establishment of an International City of Peace provides Weifang with a new platform for international communications, which help the world understand Weifang better, enhance the city’s international influence, and accelerate the construction of a modern high-quality city.

政治意义。习近平总书记提出的构建人类命运共同体理念，就是潍坊开展国际和平城市创建的“根”与“魂”。积极稳妥地创建国际和平城市，有利于全面贯彻落实习近平新时代中国特色社会主义思想，坚持传播中国和平之声，把国际关注、中国方案和潍坊实践有机结合起来，不仅可以让全世界爱好和平的人民了解中华民族热爱、追求和平的悠久传统，更可以向全世界展现中国城市在共建世界和平目标中做出的努力，彰显中国力量，展示中国形象。

Political significance: the concept of building a community with a shared future for mankind is the foundation of Weifang to build an International City of Peace. The establishment of an International City of Peace spreads China’s peaceful voice to the world, which is part of the implementation of the thoughts on socialism with Chinese characteristics for a new era. Building the International City of Peace combines the international attention, China’s approaches and Weifang’s practice in the matter of peace. It makes the peace-loving people around the world better understand the long tradition of Chinese nation’s love and pursuit of peace; it also shows the efforts made by the China’s cities to build world peace, demonstrating the power and image of a peace-loving China.

经济意义。国际和平城市为潍坊打造了一张新的具有较高国际知名度的名片，不仅可以让潍坊通过积极融入世界和平城市网络体系，举行国际性和平文化论坛、和平学术会议等系列活动，为国际城市间经贸合作、招商引资搭建起新桥梁，还可以把潍坊国际风筝会、中日韩产业博览会、鲁台经贸洽谈会等纳入其中，搭建起国际经贸合作的新平台。同时，和平城市的成功创建，将进一步整合、挖掘乐道院·潍县集中营旧址、坊茨小镇、大英烟厂旧址等特色城市历史文遗产资源，尤其是对众多和平元素的萃取、锻造，可为打造以“和平合作、开放包容”为主题的特色旅游路线，推动潍坊文化旅游事业的发展，开辟新道路，注入新血液。

Economic significance: the honorable title International City of Peace improved Weifang's reputation in the world. Joining the International Cities of Peace, organizing peace culture forums, and arranging academic meetings help Weifang to set up new bridges for international economic and trade cooperation and attract international companies and organizations to do investment in Weifang. It also combines the Weifang International Kite Festival, China-Japan-Korea Industrial Expo, Shandong-Taiwan Economic and Trade Fair to create an international economic and trade cooperation platform. At the same time, the building of a peace city will further integrate the city's historical heritage resources such as the former site of the Weihsien Courtyard of the Happy Way and Concentration Camp, Fangtze German and Japanese Building Group, the old site of British Tobacco Company. It will also help to refine the city's peace culture. We will design a peace and cooperation themed tourism route which help to bring new forces to the development of tourism industry in Weifang.

文化意义。和平城市的创建，不仅可为潍坊世界风筝都、中国画都、中国金石之都的文化传承、传播开辟新窗口，提供新载体，同时和平文化的萃取、提炼、重塑、宣传，将进一步丰富城市文化内涵，打造城市独特文化，培育、满足市民文化需求。另外，通过充分融入国际和平城市体系，可有效推进潍坊对外文化交流合作，依托“铭记历史、珍爱和平、开创未来——纪念反法西斯战争胜利”全球巡展、“风筝展”等积极走出去，承担和平文化使者的历史使命，将潍坊以东夷文化及大舜为代表的历史文化，以王尽美为代表的红色文化，以风筝为代表的民俗文化，以沂山为代表自然文化，以乐道院·潍县集中营为代表的和平文化等更好地宣传，为发掘潍坊、宣传潍坊、讴歌潍坊开辟新路径，为弘扬中华优秀文化贡献磅礴力量。

Cultural significance: as the World's Kite Capital, China's Painting, and Ancient Inscription, Capital, establishing of Weifang as a City of Peace can open new windows for the cultural development of the city. In the meantime, implementing, refining and promoting peace culture will further enrich the city's cultural connotation, bring more unique elements to the local culture, and enhance the culture of the local citizens. In addition, joining the International Cities of Peace can effectively promote Weifang's cultural exchanges and cooperation with the rest of the world. "Remembering History, Cherishing Peace and Creating Future — Commemorating the Victory of WWII" world exhibition tour and "Kite Exhibition" will help Weifang to introduce its culture to the outside world. In this way, it will take the historical mission of being a peace culture envoy, spreading Weifang's historic culture, revolutionary history, folk culture represented in kites, natural culture exhibited in Yishan mountain, and peace culture expressed by the Courtyard and concentration camp. We will open up a new path to make people better understand Weifang, and carry forward the fineness and richness of Chinese culture.

社会意义。和平城市的创建，尤其是和平理念的广泛宣传、弘扬，和平场馆设施的建设、使用，和平教育活动的深入开展、普及等，将以和为贵、和谐为美，尊重理解、宽容包含，爱护和平、守护和平的理念，不断内化于心，外显于形，成为广大市民共同遵循的原则和尊崇的社会风尚，为市民和睦相处、和谐共治的和谐社会构建提供强大助力。

Social significance: we will widely spread the concept of peace, carry forward the construction and holding peace exhibitions, and enhance peace education activities. We hope that harmony, respect, understanding, tolerance, and peace maintenance will become the principles and virtues of the general public, providing a strong force for a harmonious society.

为进一步擦亮、用好潍坊“国际和平城市”这一名片，充分发挥其作为桥梁、纽带、平台的作用，潍坊市将从和平资源保护利用、和平教育研究、和平建设合作、和平传播等方面继续深耕细作，实现多维度和平项目创建，全面提升城市发展，推动国内、国际和平建设。

In order to better use “International City of Peace” as a bridge and platform, Weifang will strengthen its peace resource conservation and utilization, peace education and research, and peace cooperation. It will also promote peace culture, implement peace construction projects, improve the city’s development, and promote peaceful projects in China as well as the rest of the world.

图 14 国际和平城市协会对潍坊进行宣传的网页
Picture 14 The webpage about Weifang on International Cities of Peace

风雨乐道院，百年沧桑史

The Courtyard of the Happy Way: A Century of Cultural Exchange, Educational Development and Resilience

我们今天回顾乐道院的百年风雨沧桑历程，会发现传教士们为传教而带来的西方科学文化，无时无刻不在影响着潍坊的发展，潍坊的历史在兼收并蓄中得到了进步和升华；潍县集中营的痛苦记忆，充分印证了构建人类命运共同体思想是实现世界和平发展的根本之策。

Today, when we look back on one hundred years' history of the Courtyard of the Happy Way, we notice that the Western sciences brought by the Western missionaries have had a huge impact on the development process of Weifang. Being exposed to different cultures for more than one hundred years has helped the people of Weifang to embrace and appreciate people who are different from them. This has consequently led to developing a community that excel in enhancing varying conditions. The painful memory of Weihsien Concentration Camp has proved that building a diverse community with shared values is fundamental for achieving sustainable, lasting world peace and development.

远去了蹉跎岁月，熄灭了硝烟战火，历尽了苦难坎坷，而今的潍县乐道院虽陈迹斑驳、格局不再，却历久而弥新，必将永载史册。

Having been experienced ups and downs, the Courtyard of the Happy Way in Weihsien is far away from warfare now. Although its old structure has changed, it is and will be everlasting and forever recorded in history.

潍县乐道院暨西方侨民集中营旧址，将立足潍坊， 面向世界，以其永不磨灭的历史记忆、跨越时空的精神力量昭示世人：只有铭记历史，珍爱和平，推动不同种族、不同文明之间的交流互鉴，才能促进人类共同进步，实现和平与发展的永恒主题。

The history and spirit of the Courtyard will always demonstrate the fact that only by remembering the past, and promotion of mutual understanding and cultural exchange with foreign countries and civilizations can we promote common progress of mankind and realize a sustainable, lasting peace and development.

后记

Epilogue

2019年5月，潍县乐道院暨西方侨民集中营旧址整建制划归潍坊市博物馆管理，市博物馆随即组织专门人员，邀请有关专家，聘请专门机构对乐道院潍县集中营博物馆展陈工作进行策划制作，同步推进乐道院历史建筑群的修缮和保护工作。2019年下半年，潍县乐道院暨西方侨民集中营旧址被国务院核定公布为全国重点文物保护单位、被中共中央宣传部命名为全国爱国主义教育示范基地。

In May of 2019, Weifang Museum was appointed to be in charge of the old site of the Weihsien Courtyard of the Happy Way and Concentration Camp. The museum invited professionals and experts to do the planning, renovation and preservation of the Courtyard. By the end of 2019, the Courtyard of the Happy Way – the former site of the Weihsien Concentration Camp – was declared a National Protected Cultural Heritage Site by the State Council. It was also selected as the National Demonstration Base of Patriotic Education by the Publicity Department of the CPC Central Committee.

《乐道沧桑》为《潍坊历史文化图鉴大系》第一辑第一分卷，中共潍坊市委宣传部对编纂工作非常重视，组织有关专家学者和市博物馆相关专业的精干人员对乐道院暨潍县侨民集中营创建发展历史资料进行整理研究，历史图片收集和内容解读。潍坊市博物馆馆长吉树春同志高度重视《乐道沧桑》的编纂工作，亲自拟定编纂思路、组织编纂人员开展工作，确保了编纂工作的紧张有序进行。

The Courtyard of the Happy Way — Over One Hundred Years of History is from the first volume of Weifang History and Culture Series. Designated by the Weifang Publicity Department, experts and the Weifang Museum's professionals prepared and edited the

Courtyard's historical stories and pictures. Ji Shuchun, the Curator of Weifang Museum, praised this compilation work; he designed and supervised the edition process.

《乐道沧桑》以时间先后为主线，共分为四个板块：即 1942 年之前的乐道院、成为西方侨民集中营的乐道院、乐道院的红色记忆、新时代的乐道院，对乐道院的教育、医疗和传教布道等活动，潍县集中营的设立、关押人员、侨民生活和抗争、潍县人民对侨民的救助、集中营解放，我党早期在乐道院的革命活动等，都进行了图文并茂的介绍，以资社会各界对潍县乐道院的发展历程、对潍县西方侨民集中营有一个更全面、直观的了解，启迪人民群众对习总书记倡导的“构建人类命运共同体”的设想、“文明因交流而多彩，文明因互鉴而丰富”论断的深刻认知。

Organized chronologically, the book covers four time periods, the Courtyard of the Hapy Way before 1942, the time when it was converted into a concentration camp, the period when the revolutionary uprisings were initiated in the Courtyard, and, finally, the Courtyard of the Happy Way in the New Era. The book provides lively depictions and illustrations of the Courtyard's history, including educational development, medical service and missionary work. It also revisits the history of the Weihsien Concentration Camp which revolves around the life and struggles of the imprisoned Western residents, the support and assistance offered by the local people, the liberation of the camp, and the earliest signs of the CPC's revolutionary activities at the Courtyard. The book presents a more comprehensive and straightforward understanding of the development of the Courtyard and the Weihsien Concentration Camp. It also bestows the public with a more profound knowledge of President Xi's vision of a community with shared future for mankind and his declaration that “Exchanges and mutual learning are what make civilizations flourish”.

由于乐道院横跨 130 多年的历史，许多图片、资料缺失，建筑仅存 7 处，加之编纂工作时间仓促，缺点错误和疏漏之处在所难免，敬请社会各界指正，以利我们必要时予以修正和作今后借鉴。

Due to the long span of more than 130 years of history, missing photos, undiscovered materials and the limited time for compilation, mistakes and defects are inevitable. Any corrections and suggestion will be appreciated.

编 者

2020 年 8 月

The Editor

August of 2020

参考书目

references

潍坊市外事与侨务办公室编：《潍县集中营》，中国文史出版社，2017 年。

山东省潍县私立广文中学编：《山东潍县广文中学五十周年纪念特刊》特刊，1933 年。

贺乐德著：《旧中国的新震动：山东潍县传教生涯》，美国纽约 Hodder & Stoughton 出版社，1913 年。

《潍坊市人民院志》编纂委员会编：《潍坊市人民医院院志》，齐鲁书社，1991 年。

【英】狄兰著，崔书田编译：《中国逃亡记》，山东人民出版社，2015 年。

潍坊市外侨办、市对外友好协会编：《放飞和平》山东文艺出版社，2005 年。

【英】李提摩太著，李宪堂、侯林莉译：《亲历晚清四十五年》，江苏人民出版社，2018 年。

邓华著：《乐道院兴衰史》，团结出版社，2013 年。

王冰、夏宝枢编著：《乐道院医院往事纪实》，2020 年。

韩同文编著：《广文校谱》，1993 年。

走近圣贤丛书

走近韩非子

丛书总主编 舒大刚

黄也平 著

◎ 在先秦诸子之中，韩非无疑是一个思想和精神的“另类”。作为法家的代表人物，他集前人的“法、术、势”政治思想之大成，为后世的帝王统治术做出了重大贡献。其犀利的思想，来源于他对人性的深刻洞察。他由“人性恶”出发，搭建起了自己的法家思想大厦，对我们今人认识现代社会和理解复杂的社会关系，又颇多启迪。

山东城市出版传媒集团·济南出版社

ISBN 978-7-5488-4082-4

9 787548 840824 >

定价：37.00元

山东城市出版传媒集团·济南出版社